PRAISE FOR
THE TROUBLE WITH WHITE WOMEN

"Kyla Schuller turns her razor-sharp focus and intimate understanding of the intersection of race and gender to some of the giant figures of white feminism—and their contemporaries who challenged them from the get-go. From Frances Harper and Elizabeth Cady Stanton to Pauli Murray and Betty Friedan, Schuller reminds us that even from its beginnings, white feminism has seen significant and sustained challenges from Black, Indigenous, and other women of color. In highlighting this counterhistory, Schuller digs not only into the professional output of these historical figures but into their personal lives, deftly demonstrating how the two interact. With her characteristic originality and insight, Schuller offers a gripping contribution to the growing mainstream critical literature on white feminism, and in the process delivers a master class not only on how the personal is indeed political but on how the specific is universal."

—Ruby Hamad, author of *White Tears/Brown Scars*

"Kyla Schuller has always impressed me as a brilliant human being and outstanding scholar, but *The Trouble with White Women* overshoots even my greatest expectations. Kyla reveals the facts—what we need to know as well as what we fear—but she also shows a way out. As a brown Muslim woman living in America, I never tire of context for the mess we're in, and Kyla tells the stories of so many women we've heard too much of and those we've been straining to hear—all of their tales surprise and in fact inspire. This is a great model for how to make a takedown a work of great art, how devotion to the truth can cut into a dominant narrative not just like a knife but with the hard wiring of real love. When I read this book, I feel like America just maybe has a future after all."

—Porochista Khakpour, author of *Brown Album*

"In *The Trouble with White Women: A Counterhistory of Feminism*, Schuller offers an indispensable gift and a profoundly illuminating resource. The systemic inequality of our world relies, too often, on myths of our own making. In these pages, Schuller dismantles injustice with an urgent and critical lens, offering a new dialogue and a way forward. Schuller is an expert at articulating the malignant disjunctions and hypocrisies of our culture with stunning craft, style, insight, and narrative suspense. Schuller is one of the most essential writers and scholars of our time."

—T Kira Madden, author of *Long Live the Tribe of Fatherless Girls*

"Clarifying, challenging, exquisitely researched and argued, *The Trouble with White Women* will give you so much to sit with and to revisit—it prepares us to do the hard, essential labor of dismantling white feminism."

—Anne Helen Petersen, author of *Can't Even*

THE
TROUBLE
WITH
WHITE
WOMEN

THE TROUBLE WITH WHITE WOMEN

A COUNTERHISTORY OF FEMINISM

KYLA SCHULLER

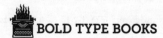 BOLD TYPE BOOKS

New York

Bold Type Books
116 East 16th Street, 8th Floor, New York, NY 10003
www.boldtypebooks.org
@BoldTypeBooks

Printed in the United States of America

First Edition: October 2021

Published by Bold Type Books, an imprint of Perseus Books, LLC, a subsidiary of Hachette Book Group, Inc. Bold Type Books is a co-publishing venture of the Type Media Center and Perseus Books.

The Hachette Speakers Bureau provides a wide range of authors for speaking events. To find out more, go to www.hachettespeakersbureau.com or call (866) 376-6591.

The publisher is not responsible for websites (or their content) that are not owned by the publisher.

Print book interior design by Amy Quinn

Library of Congress Cataloging-in-Publication Data
Names: Schuller, Kyla, 1977– author.
Title: The trouble with white women : a counterhistory of feminism / Kyla Schuller.
Description: First edition. | New York : Bold Type Books, [2021] | Includes bibliographical references.
Identifiers: LCCN 2021008089 | ISBN 9781645036890 (hardcover) | ISBN 9781645036883 (ebook)
Subjects: LCSH: Feminism—Moral and ethical aspects—United States—History. | Women, White—Civil rights—United States—History. | Minority women—Civil rights—United States—History. | Minority women activists—United States—History. | Racism—United States—History.
Classification: LCC HQ1426 .S35 2021 | DDC 305.420973—dc23
LC record available at https://lccn.loc.gov/2021008089

ISBNs: 978-1-64503-689-0 (hardcover), 978-1-64503-688-3 (ebook)

LSC-C

Printing 1, 2021

To my parents

All flourishing is mutual.

—Robin Wall Kimmerer,

Braiding Sweetgrass

CONTENTS

FOREWORD

ONE OF THE BIGGEST CHALLENGES I HAVE FACED AS A BLACK FEMINIST TEACHER AND WRITER has been convincing Black women that feminism is relevant to their lives. Black women's resistance to feminist politics and ideas has never been about a resistance to gender equality. We live with the intimate and structural consequences of patriarchy every day. The biggest stumbling block in Black women's journey to fly the flag of feminism has been white women. Somewhere a white woman is talking about how we all need to be united "as women," regardless of race or creed. And somewhere a Black woman is giving that white woman a side eye.

Given the perennial challenge white women pose to cross-racial feminist solidarity, the clearer we get about the nature of that threat, the better equipped we will be to address the problem. Kyla Schuller's *The Trouble with White Women* faces the challenge head-on with aplomb, erudition, and excellent storytelling. Schuller makes clear precisely what the problem is: "The trouble with white feminist politics is not what it fails to address and whom it leaves out. The trouble with white feminism is what it does and whom it suppresses." It's not that white women can't do good in the world or be useful allies in feminist world-making. The problem, rather, is white feminism and its gravely limited conception of how to address the injustices that all women face.

This book is a deeply erudite and much needed historically grounded treatment of a phenomenon that mostly makes for wars among feminists on social media. It represents the signature approaches that Kyla Schuller is known for—a rich textual analysis covered with both a broad and deep understanding of the archive.

Schuller traces the genesis of white feminism across several generations beginning with the shameless invocations of racism that marked Elizabeth Cady Stanton's fight for suffrage. Though I am a student of this history, I was still floored at just how strident Stanton was in her willingness to throw Black men under the bus, trafficking in the most racist stereotypes of her day, in order to procure the vote for white women. Schuller goes on to demonstrate the changing same of white feminist politics among figures like Margaret Sanger, Betty Friedan, and Sheryl Sandberg. Admirably, Schuller manages to resist the kind of liberal self-flagellation that is a hallmark of an unhelpful white guilt, and desiccates white women's tears, refusing the safety, comfort, and space-taking that so often follow them.

One of our nation's top gender studies scholars and, quite frankly, one of my favorite scholars to read period, Schuller pairs each white woman thinker under examination here with a generational peer who is Black or Indigenous, or Latinx, or trans. In doing so, she reminds us that cisgender white women did not invent feminism, and that white feminism as a project has been premised in large part on a refusal to engage the work of Black, Indigenous, and trans women who call into question the end goals, not to mention the organizing tactics, of white feminists. It's not that we haven't been there; it's that white women have refused to listen.

For the Black women who need white women to admit it, this book will do that. For white women who continually ask me *how to get better*, I say, begin here.

We can no longer afford a fractured feminist movement. All of the things women won for themselves a generation ago have come under pressing attack in these first two decades of the new millennium, and all of us are having to gird ourselves for battle again. It goes without saying that we will be stronger together, but part of the argument of this book is that white feminism is a feminist politics we can and should leave behind. In its place, white women can come together with other groups of women and embrace their visions of an intersectional, trans- and Indigenous inclusive future.

Anyone who knows me or has read me knows that I don't count very many white women among my friend groups, for precisely the reasons that this book so deftly analyzes. But I have called Kyla my friend for nearly a decade now. She produced this work because she lives her commitment to a feminism not grounded in white women's racism or civilizing imperatives. She is an ally for Black women and women of color colleagues both publicly and privately in ways that make a difference. Anyone can write a scholarly tome analyzing these issues, but living these politics is the thing that matters most. Kyla practices what she preaches in her teaching, her writing, and her relationships. Rich and rigorous in both method and content, this book is one I will return to again and again.

Brittney Cooper

INTRODUCTION

FEMINIST FAULT LINES

The history of American feminism has been primarily a narrative about the heroic deeds of white women.

—Beverly Guy-Sheftall, *Words of Fire*

INFAMOUSLY, HALF OF ALL WHITE WOMEN VOTED FOR DONALD TRUMP IN 2016 AND 2020— yet despite the repetition of these notorious statistics almost to the point of incantation, we're still missing the full scale of the problem. We know that twice, one out of two white women supported the most misogynist, white supremacist US president in a century. This is widely recognized as a crisis for racial justice. But it is also a hidden crisis for feminism. A lurking threat remains obscured, even as professional and social media obsess about these voters' attitudes toward gender equality. Surely, commentators declare, Trump-supporting women must not be feminists. After all, the candidate bragged about sexual assault. And, they continue, liberals generally support women's rights while conservatives oppose them. Republican white women, the standard line of thinking goes, chose their whiteness and their class status over their gender, unwittingly sacrificing themselves.

But the problem is not that so many white women apparently lack any kind of feminist consciousness. The trouble we've been overlooking is that a large number of white women Trump supporters *are* feminists.

Feminism and hard-line conservativism have become compatible. Today, nearly half of all women who vote Republican—specifically, 42 percent—describe themselves as feminists. These women, mostly white, support a party that has become an explicit platform for the white supremacist far right. Some go so far as to claim that the Trump administration supported gender equality. "My father is a feminist," Ivanka Trump announced while campaigning in 2016; once installed in the White House, she fashioned herself a feminist leader, launching a women's career advice book, a women's empowerment agenda, and a campaign for paid family leave and affordable childcare.[1] Scholar Jessie Daniels has even found that online white supremacist communities like Stormfront host vibrant discussions among women who support equal pay for women, access to abortions for people of color, and sometimes gay rights.[2]

As a movement for social justice, feminism now seems to stand for nothing at all—as likely to be motivated by racist self-interest as by a desire to minimize suffering and fight for equality.

How did we get here? How did feminism come to be such a meaningless position, as easily proclaimed by #MeToo campaigners as by avowed white supremacists?

This book reveals that feminism has long been fractured by an internal battle fought along the lines of racism, capitalism, and empire. The struggle over what it means to be a feminist, and what kind of world feminists want to build, may seem new. But there's never been just one feminism, just one singular and solitary politics of women's rights and equality. Dating back to the early days of the woman's suffrage campaign, there've always been at least two prominent factions within feminism wrestling over what gender equality looks like and to whom it applies. These movements work at times in coalition, and at many other times in opposition. The differences among the various groups who gather under the feminist umbrella are often ignored, buried under the reductive idea that feminism simply means endorsing equality between the sexes. But recognizing the distinctions among forms of feminism has never had higher stakes than it does today.

As surprising as feminist Trump voters may seem, they were nearly a foregone conclusion. For nearly two hundred years, a large and vibrant tradition of white women has framed sex equality to mean gaining access to the positions historically reserved for white middle-class and wealthy men. The goal, for these feminists, is to empower women to assume positions of influence within a fundamentally unequal system. Many of these feminists even argue, explicitly or implicitly, that their whiteness authorizes their rights. They weave feminism, racism, and wealth accumulation together as necessary partners, a phenomenon that has a tidy name: white feminism.

Of the factions within feminism, white feminism has been the loudest, has claimed the most attention, and has motivated many of the histories written about the struggles for women's rights. White feminism thus declares itself the one and only game in town. In part due to this posturing, white feminism attracts people of all sexes, races, sexualities, and class backgrounds, though straight, white, middle-class women have been its primary architects. Naming this individualist, status quo–driven paradigm "white feminism" refuses its claimed universality and identifies who benefits the most from its approach.

For feminism to continue to have any meaning as a social justice movement, we must out-organize white feminism. Happily, today many are calling out its dangers. The concept of white feminism has moved from the pages of legal and feminist academic journals, where it was first named by Black and Indigenous feminist theorists in the 1980s and 1990s, to homemade videos posted to YouTube and hand-drawn cardboard signs marched down Broadway.[3] But in this exciting broad pushback against white feminism, we nonetheless frequently underestimate its true destructiveness. Even its critics regularly minimize its power and pervasiveness. Just as we miss the feminist Trump voter, we miss the larger problem of white feminism.

Journalists, writers, and now dictionaries typically describe white feminism as an approach to women's rights that prioritizes the needs and concerns of white women and neglects the struggles of women of color.[4] According to this dominant formulation, the problems with white feminism stem from its centering of middle-class, white, cis women and its exclusion of everyone else. Its shortcomings lie in what it fails to do and whom it fails to see.

From this standpoint, the remedy to white feminism appears to be a strong dose of liberals' favorite elixirs: awareness, diversity, equity, and inclusion. If white feminism enlarges its vision to include women of color, poor women, and trans women, this line of thinking implies, then it will no longer be white feminism. But this understanding of white feminism misses, and even risks reproducing, the nature and extent of its harm. Expanding white feminism's tent will not transform the materials of which it is made.

The trouble with white feminist politics is not what it fails to address and whom it leaves out. The trouble with white feminism is what it does and whom it suppresses.

White feminism is an active form of harm, not simply a by-product of self-absorption. Gender equality, for contemporary white feminists, means advancing individual women up the corporate ladder; protecting reproductive freedom, which it defines solely as the ability to prevent and terminate pregnancy; and heightening prison sentences for rapists and abusers. These objectives discount entirely the gross disparities of capitalism, the barriers to pregnancy and healthy child-raising that poor women face, and the violence perpetrated by cops, courts, and prisons. White feminist objectives work to liberate privileged women while keeping other structures of injustice intact.

Attempting to redress white feminism through awareness and inclusion will not solve the problem of the feminist Trump voter or the feminist Stormfront member. Instead, it will only further obscure and entrench the race and class hierarchy at the core of this approach to women's equality. "White American women along with their counterparts across the former British Empire have always been heavily invested in maintaining white power structures," writes journalist and scholar Ruby Hamad. "They often did this by not merely neglecting, but actively throwing other women under the proverbial bus." White feminism needs to be demolished, not renovated to look up-to-date. Black lesbian poet Audre Lorde put it succinctly decades ago: "The master's tools will never dismantle the master's house."[5]

Since the days of the suffrage movement, white feminism has posed such trouble because of the specific ideology it advances, one that has been remarkably consistent over time. First, white feminist politics promotes the theory that women should fight for the full political and economic advantages that wealthy white men enjoy within capitalist empire. Second, it approaches the lives of Black and Indigenous people, other people of color, and the poor as raw resources that can fuel women's rise in status. Finally, white feminism promises that women's full participation in white-dominated society and politics will not only improve their own social position; thanks to their supposedly innate superior morality, their leadership will redeem society itself. The harm in this approach to feminism results from its tunnel vision, its belief that progress moves along the axis of gender alone. This single-axis approach legitimates victory for women through whatever means it deems necessary. White feminism becomes success for some at the expense of others.

If inclusion and awareness might only expand white feminism's violence instead of ending it, then what is the alternative? Fortunately, within the past, another major trajectory of women's rights kindled that burns bright up into the present: the counterhistory of feminism.

There's long been a forceful alternative to white feminism that provides an entirely different analysis and set of political strategies, promising success for women *with* success for others. While it has been sidelined, it is nonetheless strong. While on the margins, it is nonetheless coherent. Intersectional feminism pushes back against white feminism and advances new horizons of justice. It is both a theory and a movement emphasizing that the fight for gender justice must be approached in tandem with the fights for racial, economic, sexual, and disability justice, and ought to be led by those most affected by these systems of exploitation working in coalition with everyone else. Intersectional feminism not only represents antiracist feminism—it nurtures a radically distinct vision of society. Too often, mainstream accounts position intersectional feminism to be an innovation of feminism's third wave, which began in the late 1980s and 1990s. Yet the counterhistory of feminism is as old as the history of feminism.

White feminism, legal scholar Kimberlé Crenshaw wrote in 1989, comprises women who are "individually seeking to protect [their] source of privilege within the hierarchy." Instead, she proposed an intersectional feminist praxis to "collectively challeng[e] the hierarchy." While Crenshaw coined the term "intersectionality" in this same essay and sociologist Patricia Hill Collins further elucidated the concept starting in 1990, the radical Black feminist practice of contesting power in its multiple forms had developed much earlier.[6] Since the mid-nineteenth century, Black feminists have pushed back against white feminism and developed intersectional feminist theory to identify how white supremacy, misogyny, and capitalism converge. Fighting only the barrier of sex as white women do, they have argued repeatedly, actually reinforces the overarching structures of exploitation that so unfairly distribute the basic chances of life and death. Black feminists such as Angela Davis, bell hooks, Paula Giddings, and Beverly Guy-Sheftall further elaborated the history and theory of intersectionality, and a wider coalition of Black, Indigenous, Latinx, and some white women and men have built the framework into a movement.

But their work has often been obscured in favor of a popular narrative that sees the feminist past to be a white past. White feminists have even attempted to steal, weaken, and bury their work. Dominant accounts figure women like Elizabeth Cady Stanton, Margaret Sanger, and Betty Friedan as feminism's chief innovators and portray intersectionality as the new kid on the block, an upstart livening up the party during the more enlightened present. These white leaders all appear in this book. But so do the leaders of another feminist past, including writer and activist Frances E. W. Harper, who in the wake of the abolition of slavery insisted that the campaign for women's suffrage must be an ally of Black male suffrage; Yankton Sioux author and organizer Zitkala-Ša, who protested off-reservation boarding schools like the one she attended as a child and built a coalition of tribes across the country to fight the loss of their children and lands; and Black trans lawyer Pauli Murray, who fought legalized segregation on the basis of race and extended her campaign to sex-based segregation.

The consequences of not knowing the counterhistory of feminism are stark. White feminism succeeds in positioning itself as feminism, full stop. Among conservatives, feminism seems to be a ready partner of pro-capitalist, pro-white platforms. Among liberals, white feminists lay claim to the work of Black, Indigenous, and other feminists of color and now often tout their intersectional approach. Today, intersectionality as a theory and movement risks being co-opted and degraded into a buzzword. But in their rendering, intersectionality becomes merely an account of the multiplicity of identity—the acknowledgment that we all have a race, gender, class, *and* sexuality. This account does do some important work: it demolishes the mythical singular category of moral, virtuous Woman that white feminism historically enshrined, insisting instead that multiple dimensions of power shape our life chances. But at the same time, this appropriated version of intersectionality reproduces white feminist politics into the future. In this "inclusive" version of white feminism, white women may no longer be the harbingers of morality—it throws that burden onto token women of color. Those women and nonbinary people with the most marginalized identities become white feminism's most valuable assets. Intersectionality, especially as promoted within institutions like corporations and universities, attempts to capture the magic of marginalized "intersectional people" and harness them to their cause.

But the value of intersectionality emanates not only from the identities it acknowledges and whom it includes. The value of intersectionality also arises from what it does and what it confronts.

A *person* cannot be intersectional—only a *politics* can be intersectional. The experiences of marginalized people expose the true workings of power in all its forms. Identity forms a key piece of intersectionality, but it provides the lens, not the target. In the words of my colleague Brittney Cooper, intersectionality "was never meant to be an account of identity; it was meant to be an account of how structures of power interact."[7]

To abolish white feminism and build a world in which all can flourish, we need to fully grasp the history, contours, and consequences of these distinct forms of feminism. Resisting white feminism's attempts to bury or co-opt intersectionality, emptying it of its true force, requires listening to the Black feminists who have developed its theory and the coalition of feminists who have developed its politics.

～ ～

The Trouble with White Women brings feminism's counterhistory to life through narrating nearly two hundred years of debates, tensions, and even treacheries between white feminists and the intersectional feminists who fought back. It captures the politics and the emotions of the struggle over the true meanings of feminist justice in the aftermath of the Civil War in the North and South, on the western plains in the waning years of Indigenous sovereignty, in early twentieth-century New York tenements, in the civil rights movement, within 1970s lesbian separatist collectives, and in twenty-first-century corporate boardrooms. The conflicts unearthed here give us the context we need today to distinguish between the distinct forms of feminism, to not be swayed or fooled by a feminism that is "white supremacy in heels," in the words of activist and author Rachel Cargle.[8] My focus is on the movement for sex equality in the United States, though this analysis has resonance across empires founded on enslavement, Indigenous removal, and patriarchy.

Feminists of all stripes fight systemic inequality that concentrates money and authority in the hands of men. The logic of sexism is deeply entrenched within economic and social life, and some of feminists' most dramatic gains were won only relatively recently. "No Ladies" signs were posted in the windows of business-district restaurants through the late 1960s; married women in the United States and United Kingdom were only permitted to open checking accounts and credit cards in their own names in the 1970s; and the last Ivy League institution to go coed opened its doors to female undergraduates in the early 1980s. Yet from the nineteenth century to the present, white feminists have broken through appalling barriers for themselves by reinforcing the barriers faced by others.

To be sure, gaining access to the key institutions of society wasn't an easy fight for white women. When Stanton and Harper first faced off over the best direction for the antislavery, feminist movement to take, not even white women could speak in public, own property if married, or, in almost all cases, obtain an advanced education. Despite these formidable structural obstacles, white women fought with verve and vision. Stanton not only became a public speaker—she matured into a sophisticated and quick-witted rhetorician. When a front-row heckler interrupted a conversation following a suffrage speech she delivered in Nebraska to challenge her that his homebound wife had accomplished the most important work of all—delivering and raising eight sons—Stanton merely paused, looked him up and down, and pronounced, "I have met few men in my life worth repeating eight times."[9] Stanton wanted women in politics, not in the parlor. Yet hers, like the white feminist movement she launched, was a fight for access to the status quo powered by the fantasy that white women's participation would improve civilization itself.

Across the decades, white feminists' overwhelming insistence that sex oppression is the most prominent and widespread form of oppression ironically enshrines the identity of Woman as the sine qua non of feminism while minimizing the force of sexism itself. White feminist politics produces the fantasy of a common, even uniform, identity of Woman, a morally upright creature whose full participation in the capitalist, white supremacist status quo will allegedly absolve it of its sins. The individual obscures the structure.

Under white feminism, the goal of gender justice shrinks to defending women's qualities and identities. The agenda today becomes empowering individual women to own their voice, refuse to be mansplained to, and embrace their right to equality with men. These are fine practices on their own, but they do not convey the devastating nature of sexism, nor do they offer realistic methods of demolishing it. In fact, fetishizing the identity of Woman as the basis of feminist politics actually makes it more difficult to recognize sexism as a structure of exploitation and extraction. For sexism is not merely the silencing, interrupting, and overlooking of women. Sexism is the use of the male/female binary as an instrument to monopolize social, political, and economic power—and those assigned female at birth are not its only victims.

Consistently, white feminism wins more rights and opportunities for white women *through* further dispossessing the most marginalized. It seeks to install women at the helm of the systems that have brought the planet to the brink of ecological collapse and to declare the battle won, cleansed by their tears. White feminism has supported the denial of suffrage to men of color, the eradication of Native ties to land and community, eugenics, homophobia, transphobia, and neoliberal capitalism. Today, it comprises the delusions that Girl Power will solve inequality, that if the investment bank Lehman Brothers were instead Lehman Sisters we would have a better kind of capitalism, and that putting a woman in the White House will necessarily create a more moral empire.[10] While seemingly ignoring non-middle-class white women, white feminism actually raids more marginalized groups in order to shore up its own political power. White feminism is theft disguised as liberation.

Yet while white feminists attempt to win their rights and opportunities through fighting for inclusion within fundamentally unequal systems, those benefits are largely mythical, even for women as wealthy as Sheryl Sandberg. Sexism is so fully interwoven within structures of domination that the single-axis fight to support women is itself a delusion: patriarchy threads through all forms of inequality. Eradicating sexism requires unravelling the entire system.

Meanwhile, over and over again, intersectional feminists expose sexism to be a powerful structure of systemic inequality and attempt to untangle its deep threads with other forms of domination, while also building new practices of care, coalition, faith, and solidarity that don't rely on women's mythical purity. "I do not believe that white women are dew-drops just exhaled from the skies," Frances E. W. Harper declared from the stage while sitting next to Stanton just after the Civil War.[11] Hers was a campaign for a new vision of justice, not for the fantasy of a redemptive female identity. Devoted to mutual aid, she rallied formerly enslaved women and men throughout the South to secure land while rejecting the idea that wealth confers worth. Harper, like many other intersectional feminists into the present, also drew from a politics that goes far beyond access to rights and material advantages, expanding into a spiritual cosmology of justice whose final aim is harmony, not the seizure of power. For many intersectional feminists, power is something to be nurtured and shared. It far exceeds the realm of the human, extending into the universe. Rather than a battle over resources, intersectional feminism articulates a planetary vision in which all have access to what they need to thrive in mind, body, and spirit.

The Trouble with White Women reveals the counterhistory of feminism across seven key episodes. Each chapter takes readers inside the debate between an intersectional feminist activist and a white feminist activist as they wrestle over the best approach to women's rights. By listening directly to debates between the two main factions of feminism, we can gain a new understanding of the fight for women's suffrage, for women's access to the professions, for birth control, for lesbian feminism, for trans rights, and for women's national leadership roles. We see that white feminists weren't just products of their time—they chose to promote competitive, resource-hoarding ideologies, even as their contemporaries made different decisions. The struggles between suffrage campaigners Stanton and Harper, authors Harriet Beecher Stowe and Harriet Jacobs, Native rights reformers Alice Fletcher and Zitkala-Ša, birth control activists Margaret Sanger and Dr. Dorothy Ferebee, civil rights leaders Betty Friedan and Pauli Murray, anti-trans feminist Janice Raymond and trans theorist Sandy Stone, and Facebook COO Sheryl Sandberg and Representative Alexandria Ocasio-Cortez reveal when and where they made choices that either reinforced the politics of disposability or interrupted a system that declares some lives raw resources ripe for extraction.

These stories are so crucial to understand because they are not simple narratives of heroes and villains. My goal is not to outline for readers who should be summarily tossed in the dustbin of history, never to be mentioned or praised again. No person can have pure or perfect politics, nor should anyone be expected to. Furthermore, feminism, like all social movements, is a site of ongoing struggle, not static agreement, a tension that is necessary for hashing out its vision. Instead, I have tried to capture the figures in their complexity—many are both inspiring and infuriating. In the voices, insights, contradictions, and shortcomings of each of these leaders, key lessons ring out for our ongoing reckoning with these two distinct strands of feminism today. Feminism is about the long-term collective. Its measure of success is what we articulate together—and maybe even accomplish—not our private virtue. Positions and campaigns, victories and losses register over the time of generations.

I bring the conflict and tension between these two forms of feminism down to the human level to uncover how systemic change happens. Seemingly impermeable structures of oppression are reinforced or destroyed through groups of people making deliberate decisions over and over again to defend their own interests or to fight for the commons. Understanding how feminists have made those decisions can help us navigate similar dilemmas as we face them today as individuals and as collectives. This book uncovers the active harm of white feminist politics and the centuries of struggle for a world in which all can flourish, in the hope it will give readers the tools to help carry this fight into the future.

We need to know the counterhistory of feminism because the past is not merely a prologue—it lingers on within the present. History is never safely lodged in anterior time. Instead, past, present, and future materialize simultaneously. The violence revealed here, including Stanton's campaign for whites-only suffrage, Stowe's urging that Black adults were like children who needed raising by white women, Sanger's belief that 25 percent of the world's people were unworthy of bearing children, and Raymond's insistence that trans women rape feminist spaces by their mere existence, is ongoing. These outrages live on as flesh, as hauntings, as institutional structures, as autonomic responses, and as discourse—surfacing in outraged Beckys who call the cops and feminists who voted for Trump. But so, too, do Jacobs's invention of Black women's autobiography to articulate her own subjectivity, Zitkala-Ša's defense of Indigenous children's right to remain among their tribes, and Dr. Ferebee's insistence that poor Black women need birth control alongside a wide range of healthcare access for them and their children all persist, animating what feminist justice can look like today.

We engage with these legacies wittingly and unwittingly. Whether white women will interrogate their long-standing cozy relationship with the racist status quo and their self-interested notion of women's rights remains an open question. The Trump feminist poses a danger, but so, too, do liberals who think white feminism simply needs to become inclusive. But out-organizing white feminism will be difficult if white women don't grapple with the history of racist feminism and don't appreciate the distinct vision of justice intersectional feminists articulate.

"The history of white women who are unable to hear Black women's words, or to maintain dialogue with us, is long and discouraging," wrote Audre Lorde.[12] As a white woman scholar, I offer this portrait of the struggles within feminism in the spirit of solidarity and coalition with intersectional feminists. Yet professing solidarity has its limits. This book is an attempt to listen and learn—but I also acknowledge that these approaches are not enough. Solidarity and social change manifest through the daily practice of fundamentally redistributing power and resources, not through the balms of awareness and attention.

Today, white feminism is attempting to reform itself—when it needs to be abolished. Inclusive white feminist politics threatens to absorb and nullify the power of intersectional world-building. Making white feminism inclusive only results in longer tentacles wrapped around more necks. But the intersectional feminist movement is not only ongoing. It is building strength. Abolition refers to the practice of eradicating systemic racial injustice—as well as building more sustainable, life-giving structures in its place. Intersectional feminism represents a praxis of care and coalition as old as white feminism, an abolitionist practice that both dismantles systems and invents solidarities anew. Far from a celebration of identity and diversity, it is a full-throated confrontation with power *from* the vantage of the most marginalized. This is the counterhistory of feminism. Two movements remain in ongoing struggle, yet only one fights for the continued breath of the many.

PART I
CIVILIZING

CHAPTER ONE

WOMAN'S RIGHTS ARE WHITE RIGHTS?

Elizabeth Cady Stanton and Frances E. W. Harper

White supremacy will be strengthened, not weakened, by woman suffrage.
—Carrie Chapman Catt, *Woman Suffrage by Constitutional Amendment*

THE SENECA FALLS CONVENTION OF 1848, ONE OF THE FIRST PUBLIC EVENTS DEVOTED TO women's rights held anywhere in the world, had an inauspicious beginning. When organizer Elizabeth Cady Stanton told her husband, a talented abolitionist speaker, of her plan to demand voting rights for women, he was "thunderstruck." "You will turn the proceedings into a farce," he protested, vowing that he would refuse to even "enter the chapel during the session."[1] Henry Brewster Stanton accordingly booked a lecture thirty miles away and fled town to avoid any association with his wife's cause. The day of the event, Elizabeth Cady Stanton and her co-organizers arrived at the red-bricked Wesleyan Methodist Chapel in Seneca Falls for the 10 a.m. opening session—only to find its doors locked and a large crowd of western New York reformers milling about outside. Yet a window had been left open to the late July heat, and Stanton's young nephew was lifted up to its sill so that he could crawl through. Stanton began the proceedings by giving her third-ever public speech, an occasion all the more momentous given that women were generally forbidden from speaking in public.[2] She was barely audible. But the "Declaration of Sentiments," the organizers' woman's rights manifesto modeled after the Declaration of Independence, stirred lively discussion and broad agreement after she read it a second time.

Stanton presented eleven resolutions. Ten garnered unanimous approval by sixty-eight women and thirty-two men willing to sign on, though they made radical demands for legal and social change: that married women be legally permitted to own property; "that the same amount of virtue, delicacy, and refinement of behavior that is required of woman . . . also be required of man"; and for men and women to gain equal access to artisanal work, the professions, and business. An eleventh resolution, however, met with severe reproach: that it was women's "duty" to fight for the right to vote. Co-organizers including famed Quaker abolitionist Lucretia Mott balked that woman suffrage was outlandish, even "ridiculous." Her objection, however, did not arise from conservativism; it stemmed instead from debates about the utility of voting that were rocking the abolitionist movement at the time. Mott and many others in attendance were part of a faction led by William Lloyd Garrison that abstained from electoral politics on the grounds that it was a moral duty to disobey the laws and procedures of a government that permitted slavery. The opposing faction, which insisted electoral politics was the way to abolish enslavement, was led by none other than Stanton's husband.[3] Yet his position that expanding the suffrage would bring about justice did not extend to women's rights.

Only one man spoke in favor of Elizabeth Cady Stanton's resolution for woman's suffrage that day. The abolitionist firebrand Frederick Douglass, who was also the only African American member of the three-hundred-person audience, arose from his seat. In his resonant voice issuing forth from his six-foot frame, he declared that he would not fight for voting rights for himself without also fighting for voting rights for women. To bar women from the ballot, as he saw it, entailed "the maiming and repudiation of one-half of the moral and intellectual power" of the globe.[4] Douglass's rousing speech stirred up the crowd, already sweating in the ninety-degree heat. Thanks to his intervention, the resolution passed by a narrow margin.

Stanton, with characteristic grandiosity, later claimed that the Seneca Falls Convention commenced "the most momentous reform that had yet been launched on the world." What is now considered to be the convention's signature achievement, the call for woman's suffrage, succeeded only because Douglass staked Black voting rights and women's voting rights as necessary partners. He had not always been so sympathetic to the cause. Douglass praised his fellow abolitionist Stanton for having earlier refuted point by point his initial arguments against women's suffrage, transforming him into a "woman's-rights man."[5] The motto of his *North Star* newspaper, launched seven months before the convention, proclaimed, "Right is of no sex—Truth is of no color." At Seneca Falls, Douglass backed his new ideals with concrete action. His solidarity work helped set the course of modern feminism, a movement Stanton and her close friend Susan B. Anthony are widely credited with creating and then sustaining until their deaths at the turn of the twentieth century.

Yet when the Civil War ended nearly two decades later, and Black men were enfranchised while women of any race were not, Elizabeth Cady Stanton retreated from the cause of racial equality and anchored white women's rights in the logic of white supremacy. She fought bitterly against the proposed Fifteenth Amendment, the third and final amendment of the Reconstruction era. The amendment aimed to prevent states from denying anyone the right to vote on the basis of "race, color or previous condition of servitude." Sex was not included, however, and the amendment would not extend voting rights to women of any race, a stipulation that enraged Stanton.

In May 1869, she presided over the meeting of the American Equal Rights Association (AERA), an organization founded by Douglass, Mott, Stanton, and Anthony among others to fight for universal suffrage regardless of "race, color, or sex." As chair, Stanton had the honor of delivering the opening speech from the podium of the grand, new Steinway Hall in New York City, a three-tiered concert and lecture auditorium attached to the piano emporium's showrooms. By now she was an expert orator. Full of fury, she seized the opportunity to unleash her favorite argument against the pending amendment, which had been approved by Congress and was awaiting ratification by the states: that womanhood was a state of imperiled whiteness, threatened by depraved Black and immigrant men who were soon to have more legal rights than the ladies who presided over the nation's finest homes.

"Remember, the Fifteenth Amendment takes in a larger population than the 2,000,000 black men on the Southern plantation," Stanton thundered. "It takes in all the foreigners daily landing in our eastern cities, [and] the Chinese crowding our western shores. . . . Think of Patrick and Sambo and Hans and Yung Tung, who do not know the difference between a monarchy and a republic, who cannot read the Declaration of Independence or Webster's spelling book, making laws for Lucretia Mott . . . [or] Susan B. Anthony." Congressmen who were about to expand suffrage to men alone would "make their wives and mothers the political inferiors of unlettered and unwashed ditch-diggers, boot-blacks, butchers, and barbers, fresh from the slave plantations of the South and the effete civilizations of the old world." What terrors lay in the nation's future, she asked, when "clowns make laws for queens?" Stanton's bag of racist tricks was deep. She even pulled out the mythical specter of the Black male rapist, claiming that to "the ignorant African . . . woman is simply the being of man's lust," such that Black men's voting rights "must culminate in tearful outrages on womanhood."[6] Voting rights would also make Black men themselves more vulnerable to exploitation, she asserted preposterously; the Fifteenth Amendment should thus be rejected in hopes of a future amendment that expanded the franchise to women *and* men.

As he had twenty-one years prior, Douglass stood up from the congregation to speak. While he first honored Stanton's decades of work for abolition and their long personal friendship, he bristled at her increasingly frequent use of the derogatory term "Sambo," her blatantly racist objections to enfranchising Black men, and her central claim: that bourgeois white women were most in need of the protection of the ballot.

"With us, the matter is a question of life and death," Douglass countered. "When women, because they are women, are hunted down through the cities of New York and New Orleans; when they are dragged from their houses and hung upon lamp-posts; when their children are torn from their arms, and their brains dashed out upon the pavement; when they are objects of insult and outrage at every turn; when they are in danger of having their homes burnt down over their heads; when their children are not allowed to enter schools; then they will have an urgency to obtain the ballot equal to our own."[7]

During Reconstruction, when white abolitionists needed to expand their horizons beyond the existence of slavery and recognize the pervasive violence of antiblackness, many instead remained invested in racism. For Stanton, white supremacy became her choice strategy for advancing woman's suffrage. When it became clear that her goal of universal enfranchisement for all women and the formerly enslaved was not a legislative reality, she deliberately put the two groups in conflict with each other. She advanced a false choice: voting rights for Black men *or* for (white) women. Stanton might have opted for solidarity, electing to support the Fifteenth Amendment to ensure formerly enslaved men became full citizens and forming coalitions with abolitionists to fight for women's suffrage in the future. But instead, she opted to frame universal male suffrage as menacing white women's dignity and purity.

Douglass became one of her most eloquent critics, provoked to defending the primacy of Black male voting rights over enfranchising women as the KKK unleashed its reign of terror and anti-Black violence proliferated across the country. The alliances comprising the AERA had been torn asunder, and the organization dissolved immediately after the meeting in Steinway Hall. That evening, Stanton and Anthony founded a new organization, called the National Woman Suffrage Association, to oppose the Fifteenth Amendment because it did not extend voting rights to women. Their position was firm. "I'd sooner cut off my right hand than ask for the ballot for the Black man and not for woman," Susan B. Anthony earlier declared.[8]

The nation's leading feminists had become outright antagonists of Black suffrage when the legislation excluded them. Stanton's unabashed racism threatened to turn the nascent movement for women's rights into a white supremacist campaign to advance the position of white women at all costs.

~ ~

Elizabeth Cady Stanton, in other words, invented white feminism. She began this project in Seneca Falls in 1848 and cemented its platform at Steinway Hall in 1869. For her, women's rights meant that white women would gain access to the rights and privileges of elite white men. She framed white civilization as imperiled *until* it made room for white women's leadership, which she figured as more moral, just, and ultimately profitable than men's leadership. Yet this vision of reform was starkly individualist, imagining people as isolated units in continual competition. While seemingly in common cause with abolition, for example, Stanton approached enslavement primarily as an analogy for white women's own suffering. Black men with voting rights became a threat, rather than potential allies.

During the first five decades of women's rights, Elizabeth Cady Stanton was one of the most famous women in the United States. She possessed the wealth and the self-confidence to ensure that her intellectual influence on the movement was widely known and her legacy endured, two feats assisted by the tireless organizing work of her compatriot, Susan B. Anthony. While Stanton was largely forgotten during the first three-quarters of the twentieth century, the rise of feminist history in the 1960s and 1970s restored her self-proclaimed position as the intellectual leader of the campaign for women's rights.

Another tradition of feminism began, however, during the same years that Stanton stumped for white women's rights. On the second day of the May 1869 AERA conference at Steinway Hall, Stanton reiterated, to applause, "I do not believe in allowing ignorant Negroes and ignorant and debased Chinamen to make laws for me to obey."[9] Frances Ellen Watkins Harper, a leading Black author, feminist-abolitionist lecturer, and founding AERA member, intervened immediately.

"When it is a question of race, I let the lesser question of sex go," Harper counseled. "But the white women all go for sex, letting race occupy a minor position."

Harper called out how the logic of Woman worked for white feminists: they imagined a group bound only by the oppressions of sex. They pushed race to the side as a "minor" issue. White women's emphasis on sex was implicitly a position that reinforced whiteness, for it elevated the concerns of womanhood—an identity that white scientific, political, and cultural elites at the time thought only bourgeois white families had achieved—above all other dynamics of power. Harper pushed back against Stanton's increasingly bald racism, using a prior speaker's emphasis on the needs of working women as her counterpoint.

"I like the idea of fighting for working women. But will 'working women' be broad enough to take colored women?" interrogated Harper.

Susan B. Anthony and others agreed enthusiastically—of course their concern for working women extended to Black women. But Harper continued: "When I was at Boston, there were sixty women who rose up and left work because one colored woman went to gain a livelihood in their midst."[10]

Harper's anecdote shattered the myth echoing throughout the auditorium: that women were naturally bonded together against a common oppressor—men. Harper made it plain that she and the white women gathered there did not have the same concerns or priorities, despite their shared status as women. Harper would make this point repeatedly over her long activist career: white women could be allies—but they could also be trouble. White women's commitment to the preeminence of sex, and thus of whiteness, meant that sometimes white women were the greatest danger Black women faced. While many white women romanticized their moral purity and alleged isolation from the world of business and politics, they nonetheless gained tremendous advantage from slavery and colonialism. White women enslavers in the South were thus often deeply personally and financially invested in their human property, as historian Stephanie Jones-Rogers has shown.[11] Harper's example of white women's racism came from Boston; it could just as easily have come from Stanton's presidential perch right inside Steinway Hall.

In the bitter debates about the Fifteenth Amendment unfolding in 1869, activists were forced to pick sides: support the present legislation enfranchising only Black men, or hold out for a long-shot simultaneous Sixteenth Amendment that would enfranchise all women. Harper chose her battle.

"If the nation could only handle one question, I would not have the black women put a single straw in the way if only the race of men could get what they wanted," Harper concluded, affirming her support for the Fifteenth Amendment.[12] The room broke out in applause.

Harper's intervention into what is now called "the great schism" in women's rights, when the AERA broke into two competing factions, was one of the first key moments in the development of intersectional feminism. That Harper would be pivotal in the rise of intersectionality politics is no surprise: she was one of the first Black feminist theorists.[13] A prolific author of poetry and fiction, as well as a tireless lecturer on the speaking circuit, Harper was the most widely read Black poet in the nineteenth-century United States. Her intersectional feminism was not merely a reaction to white feminism's implicit and explicit commitment to white supremacy. She also articulated a new kind of political subject and new sources of knowledge. Her deeply spiritual approach to liberation envisioned a world governed by morality, instead of competition and profit. Whereas Stanton portrayed women's rights as a lever for advancing white civilization and drew sensational analogies between slavery and the condition of white womanhood to dramatize her cause, Harper's intersectional feminism advocated for alliances and contact between enslaved and free people, feminists and antiracists, and spiritual belief and secular politics.

～ ～

Stanton and Harper were two of the most politically active women in the United States during the second half of the nineteenth century, though Harper was much less known. The conditions motivating each woman to become involved in politics dramatize the different ways class, race, and sex shaped their personal lives as well as the distinct feminist strategies they developed. In one important respect, however, the two had overlapping experiences: each was fortunate enough to receive, and fight for, the highest quality educations then available to white girls and Black girls, respectively.

Stanton's access to education came by virtue of growing up in the largest house in Johnstown, New York. Born in 1815, she liked to say, to one of the "blue-blooded first families" of New York descended from Puritans, Stanton boasted of "several generations of vigorous, enterprising ancestors behind [her]." Her father served a term in the US Congress and became a state Supreme Court justice, while her mother was descended from a Revolutionary War hero. Yet Stanton was a constant disappointment to her father. Her mother had borne eleven children, but five died in childhood. Only one son, Eleazar, survived to adulthood; this son alone thus bore all the weight of maintaining the ancestral line's wealth and prominence. But when he was twenty, Eleazar took seriously ill, and he came home from college to die.[14] Though Stanton was only eleven at the time, she could see her father's devastation. She recalled finding him sitting vigil in the parlor next to his son's casket, looking as white as the cloth that draped the coffin, mirrors, and paintings: "I climbed upon his knee, when he mechanically put his arm around me . . . we both sat in silence, he thinking of the wreck of all his hopes in the loss of a dear son. . . . At length he heaved a deep sigh and said: 'Oh, my daughter, I wish you were a boy!' Throwing my arms about his neck, I replied: 'I will try to be all my brother was.'"

The next morning, she sought the services of her neighbor, the family's pastor, asking him for help learning two skills that had been denied to her on account of sex: reading ancient Greek and riding horseback. He opened his library and stables to the precocious child and provided regular lessons. Before long, Stanton added Latin and mathematics to her regime at the Johnstown Academy, becoming the only girl in her school to study these subjects. Despite being years younger than many of her classmates, she eventually won second prize in the academy's Greek competition, which was awarded in the form of her own copy of the Greek New Testament. Certain she had won her father's approval at last, Stanton triumphantly ran down the hill to her father's office to display her book. But, she relayed, while he was "evidently pleased," praise was not forthcoming. He only "kissed me on the forehead and exclaimed, with a sigh, 'Ah, you should have been a boy!'" She soon faced a structural disappointment as well: at sixteen, her male classmates all went off to Union College, where Eleazar had attended. There was not a college or university in the country that accepted women. Stanton was able to attend Emma Willard's seminary, however, which Stanton's biographer Lori Ginzberg notes provided the best education in the country then available to girls.[15] Throughout her life, Stanton positioned her conservative father as the foil against whom she developed her budding feminist consciousness, and she positioned herself as the inheritor of the family's blue-blooded potential: a potential she used to dismantle her father's sex-divided world.

Frances Ellen Watkins Harper, born in 1825, also received a high-quality education through a mixture of luck, pluck, and tragedy. Harper's parents were free, though they lived in the slave state of Maryland. But as among other early nineteenth-century families, death was widespread; both her parents had died by the time she reached three years old. Her mother's brother William Watkins, and his wife Henrietta, raised Harper as one of their own children. She attended Watkins's Academy for Negro Youth in Baltimore, where she undertook one of the most rigorous courses of study then available to Black children. A shoemaker and preacher by trade, her uncle William Watkins was also a master orator and active anti-imperialist who wrote articles for Garrison's *Liberator* newspaper; his pupils wrote essays almost daily and were trained in elocution, history, geography, mathematics, natural philosophy, Greek, Latin, and music, among other subjects.[16] Watkins's son would go on to work with Frederick Douglass on the *North Star* newspaper.

But Harper's studies ended at thirteen, when she needed to obtain a job in order to support herself. She found work as a domestic servant in the home of a Baltimore book merchant, looking after the children, sewing the family's clothes, and providing other housekeeping services. The merchant was kindly and his wife duly impressed by an article Harper had penned, so they granted Harper full access to their home's library when she could steal away "occasional half-hours of leisure." Harper's situation brings to mind Jane Austen's famously constrained writing conditions, two decades prior and an ocean away: cramped on a parlor table, writing in short bursts of precious uninterrupted time when her family and their many guests would be otherwise occupied.[17] But the differences between Austen and Harper, and Stanton and Harper, are stark. Harper not only lacked a room of her own; her destiny was to clean the rooms of other people.

Yet it was in this library that Harper developed as a reader and writer, entirely by her own direction. She continued writing poetry and prose, and she published her first collection of poetry, *Forest Leaves* (circa 1846), while still in her early twenties. Without this early, formative access to the literature of her day, Harper may never have gone on to publish eleven books, plus three novels serialized in magazines. By 1871, she had sold fifty thousand books, almost entirely to a Black audience—an astonishing number during an era in which only 20 percent of African Americans were literate.[18]

If there are intriguing parallels amid the generally stark divergences in the ways that Stanton and Harper maneuvered themselves into advanced educations, those parallels drift widely apart as each woman became involved in the abolitionist, and then feminist, movements.

Two days after marrying star abolitionist lecturer Henry Brewster Stanton, Stanton and her new husband set off on a three-week voyage to London, where Henry served as a delegate to the first World Anti-Slavery Conference. The June 1840 conference proved pivotal to Stanton's political awakening. It introduced her to a wider circle of abolitionists, including Lucretia Mott, a prominent activist who had founded the well-known Female Anti-Slavery Society in the United States seven years prior, with whom she walked arm in arm throughout London. But ultimately of more consequence, it introduced her to her *own* marginalized status. When the delegates arrived at Freemasons' Hall, the women—both wives like Stanton and official delegates like Mott—were escorted to a "low curtained seat" removed from the main congregation seating, as if they composed the "church choir."

Despite the eloquent objections of William Lloyd Garrison; Charles Remond, arguably the first Black abolitionist public speaker; and a few others—who backed up their words by walking out in protest with the women—a vote was held to determine the status of women's participation in the convention. As a result, women delegates were denied the right to vote and to speak. At issue was less hypocrisy than strategy: the winning side, which included Stanton's husband, maintained an overly narrow approach in which they objected to any political stance that might threaten or dilute their single-prong focus on abolishing slavery in the Americas. They consequently decided to sidestep the volatile issue of women speaking in public. Stanton wryly noted that she and the women delegates, relegated to their position on the sidelines, "modestly listened to the French, British, and American Solons [a Greek statesman] for twelve of the longest days in June." The conference began to crystallize her own priorities. She later claimed that her time in London spurred her to the realization that "to me there was no question so important as the emancipation of women from the dogmas of the past."[19]

Two and a half million people were enslaved in the United States in 1840, and at the conference—as within the abolitionist community that formed her lively social circle back home—Stanton would have heard graphic tales of whippings, murder, and children stolen at the hand of slave owners. Yet what she felt most keenly was her own degradation. On the one hand, her reaction is understandable. Nothing pricks the skin as deeply as one's own experience, particularly exclusion and humiliation, and there is a deep injustice in men fighting for the fundamental rights of others while silencing the very women in their midst. Free white women in the North and South lacked many of the most basic individual rights: the right to own property after marriage,[20] including any wages they earned and money they inherited; the right to have guardianship over their own children after separation; and the right to initiate divorce. If abolitionists weren't going to push back against the rightlessness of women, who would?

On the other hand, a hierarchy of priority structured Stanton's approach to abolition and women's rights throughout her career. Stanton faced a choice: she could align the budding women's movement with enslaved people, or she could call in the powers of whiteness to elevate her own community. For decades, Stanton chose the latter. The priority she placed on "white women's rights" severely compromised her commitment to Black rights.[21] The moral outrage of enslavement, to Stanton, was ultimately most useful as a dramatic analogy that threw into relief her *own* lack of rights. In her perspective, she was legally barred from the rights her whiteness merited and unfairly shared the status of a slave. She thereby began the white feminist political tradition that wins rights and liberties for middle-class white women by further marginalizing others.

"The world waits the coming of some new element, some purifying power, some spirit of mercy and love," she instructed, and this elevating spirit was the force of civilized womanhood.[22] Stanton positioned women's lack of access to rights as a gross injustice that threatened the progress of civilization. Denied the full privileges of citizenship that belonged to them by virtue of their whiteness, she argued, white women were robbed of their moral powers to refine and elevate society. But the United States could reach civilization's full potential, Stanton argued, if women were granted rights and influence.

Just six years after the Seneca Falls Convention, Stanton gave her first major speech, addressing the New York state legislature on the legal status of women. Susan B. Anthony had worked for months to earn the Valentine's Day hearing, coordinating sixty women who gathered ten thousand signatures on a petition; Stanton, for her part, felt more nervous in advance of the speech than any other she gave.[23] Stanton spoke to the legislators as a peer in heritage and merit, who was outrageously legally "classed with idiots, lunatics, and negroes." In addition to being barred from the rights to vote and to trial by a jury of peers, white women, once married, lost all legal standing. "The wife who inherits no property holds about the same legal position that does the slave of the Southern plantation. She can own nothing, sell nothing." Women didn't even have the right to determine their own children's futures, she explained. Husbands could bind sons out to abusive masters, or send daughters into prostitution, but wives had no legal authority to intervene. Once more, she grounded women's claims to rights in whiteness. Anthony had twenty thousand copies of Stanton's speech printed, and she delivered one to the desk of each New York state legislator.

The legal inequalities married white women faced were monumental. But Stanton dramatized her situation as one of not only political standing but also of being robbed of the rights and prerogatives of whiteness and thrust into a community of slaves. The inability to own property was not, of course, the same as *being* property, a condition that white middle-class wives were wholly spared. But as a rhetorical move, dramatizing the fall of Woman to the status of Slave was extremely useful to Stanton. The two halves of her analogy were meant to strike horror in her listeners' hearts: that white women, who deserved "the full recognition of all our rights as . . . persons; native, free-born citizens; property-holders, [and] tax-payers," conditions they shared with white men yet were denied, were unjustly treated as slaves. Meanwhile, an undivulged source informed her sense that another social structure was possible: the matriarchal culture of the Haudenosaunee (Iroquois) in whose territory her family had settled.[24]

An analogy like the one Stanton articulated over and over again between "woman" and "Negroes" refuses to acknowledge any shared systems of oppression. Instead, it walls each side off into distinct partitions: one in which, in the words of a key Black feminist anthology from the 1980s, "all the women are white, and all the Blacks are men."[25] Analogy renders the political status of enslaved women invisible and negligible.

To be clear, Elizabeth Cady Stanton was no mere dilettante in the abolition movement. She was immersed in antislavery activity for decades and supported militant tactics such as John Brown's 1859 attempt to begin an armed uprising of enslaved people by raiding the federal arsenal at Harpers Ferry. During the Civil War, she and Susan B. Anthony halted their now annual women's rights convention in order to devote their energies entirely to supporting Black emancipation. Intent on contributing more to the war cause than women's typical, but necessary, tasks of "nursing the sick and wounded, knitting socks, scraping lint, and making jellies," they intervened directly in the legislative process. Anthony and Stanton organized thousands of women and men into the Women's National Loyal League, which became the country's first national political organization led by women, and aimed to gather one million signatures in favor of a constitutional amendment ending slavery. Petitions, Stanton explained, are "seemingly so inefficient," but were the only means through which people denied the vote could add their voice to the political process. Their petition circulated throughout the North and was "signed on fence posts, plows, the anvil, the shoemaker's bench—by women of fashion and those in the industries, alike in the parlor and kitchen."[26] While the nearly four hundred thousand names the organization delivered on hefty scrolls to Senator Charles Sumner fell substantially short of their goal, Stanton and Anthony's petition drive was nonetheless the largest the country had yet seen in its history. It is credited with helping smooth the way to the adoption of the Thirteenth Amendment abolishing slavery in 1865.

Yet in the words of Lori Ginzberg, Stanton "did not seriously stretch her thinking, sacrifice wealth or comfort, or evince a strong or urgent concern for those who were actually enslaved." Stanton, Ginzberg writes, "had always been clear about what she wanted the Civil War to accomplish: the emancipation of the slaves, she was sure, would pave the way for emancipating women as well." This is all the more striking given that slavery, for Stanton, wasn't only an abstract political cause. It was also an intimate reality in her own childhood home. Although slavery was officially abolished in New York in 1799, it remained legal to own slaves there until 1827 under the state's Gradual Emancipation act. Three people were enslaved within Stanton's own Johnstown house. Nonetheless, Stanton painted the principle domestic injustice of her childhood to be her father's refusal to recognize her own intellectual value and potential. Her autobiography refers to her family's servants, Abraham, Peter, and Jacob, as her closest childhood friends—natural companions, despite their adulthood, to her juvenile adventures.[27] She does not disclose that these men were enslaved by her father.

This choice to center her own degradation and remain silent about her position among a slaveholding family exemplifies Stanton's white feminism. White feminism is a political position, not an identity. The trouble with Stanton is not that she grew up in a blue-blooded slaveholding house and married a man also descended from Mayflower stock so, therefore, her politics are suspect. Privilege doesn't necessarily result in myopic self-interest, just as marginalization doesn't directly lead to a more ethical or radical politics. Instead, her white feminist politics resulted from the choices she made to exploit enslavement as a sensational analogy to dramatize her own condition.

Stanton nonetheless considered herself a devoted friend of the slave who made valiant sacrifices to the cause of abolition. And when slavery was abolished at last in 1865, she would come to expect payback for the services she had rendered.

In her mid-twenties, Harper left Baltimore to take up a teaching job in Ohio, and then in Little York, Pennsylvania, less than twenty miles north of the Maryland border. Fifty-three students crammed into her one Pennsylvania classroom, and she found teaching quite tiring. Meanwhile, the growing anti-blackness of the 1850s devastated her. As for other abolitionists, the passage of the Fugitive Slave Act in 1850 was a tremendous blow for Harper. The act expanded the reach of slavery across the continent. A person escaping slavery could be captured in any state of the union and remanded back to a person who claimed to own her. The act also fined local authorities $1,000 if they failed to arrest anyone a white Southerner testified under oath was their property, and it fined and imprisoned for six months anyone who aided a person fleeing bondage.[28] These terms also made it relatively easy to capture freeborn children and adults living in free states and send them into slavery. Effectively, slavery had become a national institution.

While in Little York, Harper met many people escaping north, now all the way to Canada, via the Underground Railroad's network of secret routes and safe houses, and the danger of their plight aroused Harper's care and concern. "These poor fugitives are a property that can walk," she wrote to a friend. "Just to think that from the rainbow-crowned Niagara to the swollen waters of the Mexican Gulf, from the restless murmur of the Atlantic to the ceaseless roar of the Pacific, the poor, half-starved, flying fugitive has no resting place for the sole of his foot!"[29]

Within three years, slavery's burgeoning legal standing rendered Harper a potential fugitive. A new Maryland law, enacted in 1853, prohibited any free, Northern person of color from entering Maryland via the border it shared with Pennsylvania. Punishment for crossing the border was extreme: imprisonment and remand into slavery. Harper was suddenly in exile. Though freeborn, of free parents, if she returned home to Baltimore, she could be enslaved. Yet it was someone else's suffering that galvanized her into action. A free Black man, unaware of the statute, traveled south to Maryland, where he was captured and sold into slavery in Georgia. He escaped, hiding behind the wheelhouse of a boat churning north. But he was caught and enslaved once more; he died soon after. The man's plight, which was well known to Philadelphia abolitionists, struck Harper to the bone. "Upon that grave I pledged myself to the Anti-Slavery cause," she wrote a friend. She left teaching to join the movement.[30]

Harper traveled to Philadelphia and Boston, where she became active in the Underground Railroad and began to give public lectures. Her uncle's elocution training paid off: she soon was giving lectures most nights of the week, to crowds that could reach six hundred. Within a month, the State Anti-Slavery Society of Maine hired Harper, on her twenty-ninth birthday, to become a professional lecturer. The position was akin to the one that had propelled Henry Brewster Stanton's early career. In the span of a mere six weeks during her first season on the speaking circuit, she delivered thirty-three lectures in twenty-one towns. The work energized her—"my life reminds me of a beautiful dream," she wrote to her friend William Still, a writer, historian, and conductor in the Underground Railroad. Harper's lecture tours raised significant funding for the Railroad, which she regularly sent to Still along with a portion of her own speaking fees. She sometimes scolded him to be forthcoming about the organization's financial situation, assuring him that she was in a position to support its basic operating expenses.[31]

While clearly successful, Harper had to tread a fine line as a Black woman lecturer speaking on topics such as "On the Elevation and Education of Our People." It was only in abolitionist societies and in women's rights meetings that women were granted the right to address the public. And white crowds, which formed the majority of her audiences up North, were not at all accustomed to listening to a Black woman speaker. "My voice is not wanting in strength, as I am aware of, to reach pretty well over the house," she wrote to Still, acknowledging her justified pride at holding forth to large crowds for lectures that lasted two hours.[32] Yet this very strength could be a liability in a time and place that generally reserved the status of *Woman* for whites alone. Harper spoke before crowds in the North, and later throughout the South, that were predisposed to see her as a novelty and as the member of a suffering race, but not simultaneously as belonging to the allegedly delicate sex of women.

From her podium and her pen, Harper pressed forward in beginning intersectional feminism, a feminism that seeks to demolish the status of civilized whiteness rather than to gain access to its privileges. She took pains to show that Black women were women, but she did so by validating their experience as mothers rather than their civilized refinement. The same year Harper began lecturing professionally, she published *Poems on Miscellaneous Subjects* (1854);

this collection of work on slavery, Christianity, and the plight of women became her best-selling book and went into twenty printings. Perhaps its most famous poem, "The Slave Mother," begins by emphasizing the seeming animal strangeness of an enslaved woman. It addresses the reader directly, as if demanding a response: "Heard you that shriek? It rose so wildly in the air." But by the end of the poem the feral cry becomes proof of her status as a human woman: the very trait that seemingly disqualified her from the ranks of civilized personhood proves the depth of her human feeling. For the woman unleashes her cry when her boy is torn "from her circling arms" on the slave block. "No marvel, then, these bitter shrieks Disturb the listening air: She is a mother, and her heart Is breaking in despair."[33] Harper humanizes the enslaved mother by showing her gnashing pain.

Other poems in the collection, as with her short story "The Two Offers" (1859), the first short story published by a Black woman in the United States, tell tales of women abandoned and mistreated by profligate men and subject to double standards that punish the women for their former partners' behavior. Intriguingly, these tales often do not identify their characters by race. Their lack of specificity draws alliances, rather than analogies, between women Black and white.

Harper's intersectional feminist politics stressed one key theme: fighting for an entirely new society based on broad social justice. This society would be distinguished by a more equal distribution of resources, including land; solidarity among the movements for women's rights, racial justice, and working people, for "we are all bound up together in one great bundle of humanity"; and a body politic guided by Christian faith instead of the money-centric, secular structure of power that was rapidly replacing God with capital.[34]

Stanton addressed white male legislators as a proud Saxon daughter of the American Revolution who deserved full access to the state's authority. Harper, however, wrote to Black audiences about the ethical and political failings of white civilization and their power to resist its sway. She pushed back against the idea that Black access to wealth alone would bring about justice, that "the richer we are the nearer we are to social and political equality." Money, but also "intelligence, and talent," she argued to Black readers, may be the prized qualities at the heart of the nation's corrupt power structure, but they would not bring about justice.[35] The status quo was sustained by the surplus wealth of the Southern plantations and thus was against the interests of Black people everywhere. Harper's vision of justice was one of interdependence, in which the needs of the poor, the enslaved, and women would all be met.

Harper didn't want Black people to prove themselves worthy of white civilization, gaining access to the runaway profits of capitalism and the ranks of government: she wanted the entire bloodstained structure to crumble and a new system to rise in its place. "It is no honor to shake hands politically with men who whip women and steal babies," she quipped. Stirring poems reminded her readers of their individual power as consumers to choose not to become cogs in the machinery of bondage by boycotting clothing made from cotton that enslaved people had picked. "This fabric is too light to bear / The weight of bondsmen's tears / I shall not in its texture trace / The agony of years," she wrote of free labor cotton, which freed the customer of wrapping themselves in the very anguish of the cotton fields.[36]

Harper made her national debut on the women's rights stage in early May 1866 at the New York meeting of the National Women's Rights Convention, with Stanton presiding as president. Now in its eleventh year, Stanton and Anthony's organization was reconvening after their five-year break during the Civil War. It was a contentious gathering, for this congregation of abolitionists and women's rights campaigners faced a thorny dilemma: the proposed Fourteenth Amendment, which would guarantee citizenship rights to those born or naturalized in the United States as well as equal protection before the law, would also introduce the word "male" into the Constitution for the very first time. The amendment would restrict voting rights solely and exclusively to "male citizens." Women's voting rights were not only ignored—they were thwarted.

Held under the stone arches of the Church of the Puritans near Union Square in New York City, the convention became the scene of the first battle that pitted women's rights against Black men's rights. This war presaged the rupture of the women's movement three short years later. Stanton and Anthony opposed ratification of the Fourteenth Amendment, arguing that it would be a blow to their goal for suffrage "without distinction of race, color or sex." Stanton also made firm that while abolitionists such as Wendell Phillips and Lucretia Mott argued it was "the hour of the Negro," she believed wholeheartedly "that woman's hour has come."[37] White women had sacrificed to win the abolition of slavery, in her mind, and now deserved the antislavery movement's full support for suffrage regardless of sex or no suffrage at all. The Fourteenth Amendment codifying voting rights for men was a threat she predicted would set women's rights back by a hundred years.

In the midst of this tense meeting, Frances Harper addressed Stanton, Anthony, Mott, and Phillips for the first time. "I feel I am something of a novice upon this platform," she began once she had climbed up to the church altar the convention used as its stage. While Harper was new to women's rights meetings, by this point she was a significant public intellectual with twelve years of experience as a lecturer. She also read prominent political theorists including Alexis de Tocqueville and John Stuart Mill and kept up with the magazines and weeklies of the day.[38] On this firm grounding, she didn't hold back from issuing forth an incisive critique of white feminism.

Beginning with a statement of solidarity, she explained that before her husband Fenton Harper died after only four short years of marriage, she felt herself more aligned with the cause of her race rather than with woman's rights. Her lecturing and writing career had slowed while she was married and established herself as a "farmer's wife" in Ohio, looking after Fenton's three children, giving birth to a child of their own, and making butter she sold at the Columbus market. But all this changed upon Fenton's death, when she felt acutely the legal deprivation of married women who were denied all claims to their widow's property. She narrated, "My husband died in debt; and before he had been in his grave three months, the administrator had swept the very milk crocks and wash tubs from my hands. . . . They left me one thing, and that was a looking glass!" Robbed of her means of making a living, Harper related that, for the first time, she felt "keenly" that she deserved "these rights, in common with other women" for which the convention fought.

Harper legally shared the position widowed wives across the country faced: stripped of any claim to the fruits of their own wages and the property they shared with their husbands. She was legally worthy of laying claim to just one item: a mirror to satisfy her social obligation to be pleasantly attractive to others. "Justice is not fulfilled so long as woman is unequal before the law," she pronounced. Harper also recognized, however, numerous aspects of social status that extended beyond legal rights, something Stanton, who learned from and also worshipped her father's legal acumen, was reluctant to acknowledge. White women, Harper explained, may lack legal status, but they wielded plenty of authority and were among those who "trample on the weakest and feeblest" of society.[39] Granting white women political power, she emphasized, would not necessarily elevate civilization into reaching its loftiest heights. White women's morality was often compromised by their racism.

"I do not believe that giving the woman the ballot is immediately going to cure all the ills of life. I do not believe that white women are dew-drops just exhaled from the skies. I think that like men, they may be divided into three classes: the good, the bad, and the indifferent. The good would vote according to their convictions and principles; the bad, as dictated by prejudice or malice."[40] The vote, she implied, would weaponize racist white women just as it would grant political authority to antiracist women.

"You white women speak here of rights," Harper continued. "I speak of wrongs." Her experience "as a colored woman" shattered the myth that woman's rights would bring equality to all women. She emphasized that the violence done to Black women and men, such as being thrust from streetcars, was often supported and perpetrated by white women, as well as men.[41]

From the platform, Stanton had argued that the ballot would enable white women to propel the nation into a higher level of civilization. Harper objected that it was white women themselves who would be improved through the right of suffrage. "Talk of giving women the ballot box? Go on. It is a normal school. And the white women of this country need it. . . . I tell you that if there is any class of people who need to be lifted out of their airy nothings and selfishness, it is the white women of America."[42]

Roused to action, Susan B. Anthony responded to Harper's speech by presenting a new resolution she and Lucretia Mott had been working up: the launch of a new organization, the American Equal Rights Association, that would "demand universal suffrage." Harper became a founding member of the AERA that evening, along with Anthony, Stanton, Douglass, Mott, and others.

Yet three years later in New York's Steinway Hall, the AERA and the women's rights movement would tear asunder as Stanton railed against "Sambo's" acquiring the right to vote before she did. And when Stanton and Anthony spent years in the 1880s compiling their six-volume *History of Woman Suffrage*, which included transcriptions of most major meetings such as the pivotal 1866 convention, they left out Harper's speech. If Harper's name is unfamiliar to you today, the singular authority Stanton and Anthony wielded over the "official" account of the suffrage battle is a significant reason why.

~ ~

After the Civil War, Harper took to the dirt roads of the Reconstruction South on a lecture tour to spread the message of "Literacy, Land, and Liberation." Whereas Stanton was increasingly turning to racism to clinch her argument for white women's rights, Harper further developed her intersectional feminist analysis in conversation with Black and white people across the region. For three years, she traveled among plantations, towns, and cities throughout South Carolina, Georgia, Alabama, and Tennessee. Speaking to formerly enslaved people and to former enslavers alike in schools, churches, and state buildings, she sometimes lectured twice a day, passing the nights at the homes of freedpeople. Harper told friends of the tremendous "brain-power" she found in Black schools and homes as well as the exposed "Southern shells" in which she passed miserable winter nights, cabins in which the windows lacked glass and the gaps in the walls were big enough to plumb her finger right through. She often didn't charge for her lectures, especially when the price of cotton was low, and never to the all-women groups she convened. Speaking to women particularly excited her. "Now is the time for our women to begin to try and lift up their heads and plant the roots of progress under the hearthstone," she wrote to Still, celebrating Black women's potential role in improving the conditions of Black life in Reconstruction.[43]

Even the travel itself could present an opportunity to spread her message about the necessity for legal equality and for Black people to acquire education, land, and moral righteousness. On one train ride in South Carolina, a group of passengers clustered around Harper as she spoke, including a former slave dealer. Despite traveling alone, she engaged him directly and they had "rather an exciting time," she later wrote to a friend. A subsequent line of her letter provides a glimpse of the potential danger she faced: "There's less murdering," she noted hopefully of the progress she saw in the state as Reconstruction was under way, though plantation owners still regularly stole the wages of their sharecroppers for years at a time. Among the insults Harper received while lecturing were accusations that she was a man and that she was

Author photograph of Frances E. W. Harper from her
1898 poetry collection.
(Courtesy of Prints and Photographs Division, Library of
Congress)

a white person performing in blackface. Her response was to laugh at the ab-
surdity of a world unwilling to acknowledge eloquence and wisdom when it
took Black female form, reflecting instead on the "very fine meetings" she held
for mixed-race audiences. Now and again her audiences included Confederate soldiers and officers, to whom she delivered the "gospel truth" about the
abuses of slavery and delighted in her good fortune, the next day, at finding
herself alive.[44]

Yet Harper also endorsed nineteenth-century civilization rhetoric, however. Throughout her six-decade career, Harper argued passionately that civilization and respectability were not the exclusive purview of whiteness and
that Black people were capable of joining the ranks of the civilized. Civilizing
was a pervasive framework for reformers in the era, a common worldview that
saw property accumulation, Christian faith, genteel and properly feminine or
masculine manners, sexual monogamy, and a rigorously maintained divide
between the public world of the nation and the private world of the domestic to be the necessary elements of progress. A civilizing agenda is inherently
conservative, elevating hierarchy, self-discipline, and wealth acquisition to

be the meaning of life. She preached self-control and self-regulation as tools for elevating the race, something that aligned her with the rising Black bourgeoisie rather than with the sharecroppers she traveled among. Harper was forthright, however, that the civilizing project she desired was not only about individuals learning moral uprightness, "the value of a home life," and other aspects of bourgeois personhood that propertied white reformers stressed.[45] In Harper's view, civilizing also entailed structural changes at the collective level. For her, as for many other Black reformers, civilizing was a means of racial uplift they could bring to the masses.

"Get land, every one that can, and as fast as you can," she instructed a sizable crowd at an 1871 lecture at the African Methodist Episcopal Zion Church in Mobile, Alabama. Within the large, gaslit church festooned with wreaths and flowers, her famously crystal clear voice rang out with stark edicts: "A landless people must be dependent upon the landed people," she warned. During this period, whites continued to monopolize land ownership. According to the 1870 census, the rate of homeownership for Black people was only 8 percent, compared to nearly 60 percent for whites. Harper argued that if poor Black families did not have their own means of economic support in the form of cultivatable land, they would forever be powerless. Though she was invested in the civilizing project, she wasn't interested in mere window-dressing: she knew Black people had to seize land and property if there was any hope of shifting the lethal monopolization of power in the hands of whites. Many held a similar view, and by 1900, formerly enslaved people and their children acquired fifteen million acres of land.[46]

Within the elegant setting of this Black-run church, she did not refrain from challenging the boundaries of decorum in order to fight misogyny. For Black women, even more so than for other women, the most dangerous place of all could be their own homes. She was circumspect about how she brought up male violence against women, a topic she nonetheless regularly broached. "Why," she voiced with surprise, "I have actually heard since I have been South that sometimes colored husbands positively beat their wives! I do not mean to insinuate for a moment that such things can possibly happen in Mobile. The very appearance of this congregation forbids it; but I did hear of one terrible husband defending himself for the unmanly practice with 'Well, I have got to whip her or leave her.'"[47] The quip is typical of her use of civilizing rhetoric—on the surface, she reassuringly equates genteel appearance with ethical behavior, while just below lurks her radical challenge to power.

⌐ ⌐

Meanwhile, Reconstruction unleashed the full force of Stanton's racism into the mainstream women's rights movement. Part of her fury was a logical outcome of her own method of analogy, which saw Black people as fundamentally distinct from, but structurally equivalent to, white women. This individualist, competitive notion of rights envisioned each group to occupy distinct halves of a weighted scale, a scale that had been level as long as neither group had voting rights. But she believed the Fifteenth Amendment would tip the scale wholly over to the side of African American men, leaving white women dangling midair. At the first anniversary of the American Equal Rights Association, held in May 1867 at the Church of the Puritans, Stanton made clear that her goal of universal suffrage prioritized tipping the scales in favor of white women. "With the black man we have no new elements in government," she informed her audience of fellow abolitionists and women's rights campaigners, "but with the education and elevation of woman we have a power that is to galvanize the Saxon race into a higher and nobler life, and thus, by the law of attraction, to lift all races to a more even platform."[48] White women were the true force of civilization, she insisted, and thus they must assume power over Black men.

Later that year, Stanton's vision of suffrage rights as a competition fully materialized when she and Susan B. Anthony joined forces with a notorious white supremacist. Kansas was the stage for this conflagration, which was holding two state referenda in the 1867 election: one for Black male suffrage, the other for women's suffrage. The AERA was in full support of both, and Stanton and Anthony were among the campaigners who traveled throughout the state for three months. But other prominent abolitionists, including Wendell Phillips, opposed the referendum enfranchising women on the grounds it would weaken the chances of Black male suffrage to earn enough votes—an echo of the cautious, one-issue-at-a-time approach to electoral politics Stanton's own husband had taken decades prior. Desperate for more funds and support for the woman's suffrage referendum, Anthony and Stanton teamed up with a shipping magnate and blatant racist by the name of George Francis Train. Train paid the bills as the three of them traveled through Kansas together on a joint lecture tour. Train supported women's suffrage on the grounds that elevating the social position of white women would strengthen white supremacy; his motto was "Woman first and negro last." This partnership made apparent that while Stanton and Anthony technically supported the Black male suffrage campaign, it was white women's right to vote they were after. Frances Harper and Frederick Douglass were deeply troubled, refusing invitations to join the campaign in Kansas. But Stanton defended their union with Train. "A gentleman in dress and manner, neither smoking, chewing, drinking, nor gormandizing," she insisted, Train was civilized and thus valuable to their cause.[49]

After the Kansas election, in which both referenda failed to win enough support to become law, Stanton and Anthony doubled down on their relationship with Train. Using Train's funds as well as Anthony's life savings of $10,000, in January 1868 they launched a weekly newspaper, the *Revolution*, headquartered in New York City. The newspaper, which became a broadside for white women's rights and issues, frequently included a letter to readers from Train. Stanton and Anthony courted *Uncle Tom's Cabin* author Harriet Beecher Stowe as editor, sure her fame would propel them into success. Stowe declined, however, on account of the militancy of the name. "There could not be a better name than *Revolution*," retorted Stanton. Stowe also objected to the newspaper's association with Train; contra Stanton, her family found him "coarse"—in a word, uncivilized. "The establishing of woman on her rightful throne is the greatest revolution the world has ever known or ever will know."[50]

Unfortunately, the revolution Stanton and Anthony sought was for white women to gain political equality with white men in order to further elevate whiteness. "Women faced the hostility everywhere of black men themselves," she declared on the very first page of the very first issue. From the pages of the weekly, Stanton continued her attack on "outside barbarians," "the unfortunate and degraded black race," and "the effete civilizations of the old world," who she saw as having been unfairly elevated above "the refined and intelligent women of the land." In these constructions, women of color and immigrant women disappear. Stanton was not merely ignoring their political predicament; she was actively dispossessing more marginalized groups in pursuit of rights and liberties for white women. Another article made Stanton's

Elizabeth Cady Stanton,
seated, and Susan B. An-
thony, standing. (Courtesy of
Prints and Photographs Division, Library of Congress)

case plain: she celebrated the founding of what she called a "White Woman's
Suffrage Association" in New York City.[51]

By the time of the infamous fourth annual meeting of the AERA at Steinway Hall in 1869, tensions were running high. Stanton railed against "Patrick"
and "Sambo" lording over her, Douglass evocatively called up the epidemic of
lynching and murder beginning to terrorize the Reconstruction South, and
Harper called out white women for consistently choosing sex over race. The
AERA dissolved at the convention's close—the alliance with white feminists
had become untenable. Stanton and Anthony formed the National Woman's Suffrage Association, an all-female group that opposed the ratification
of the Fifteenth Amendment because it was not accompanied by a Sixteenth
Amendment granting women the right to the ballot. But theirs wasn't the only
new organization. Harper, Lucy Stone, and a handful of other women and
men also united together, forming the American Woman Suffrage Association
to support the males-only clause of the Fifteenth Amendment as a necessary

first step and keep their eyes on the goal of voting rights for women. Despite vociferous efforts, which included further petitions, packing courts, aligning with racist Democrats, and even running for Congress herself, Stanton's efforts to oppose Black suffrage in favor of universal suffrage were largely ineffectual at the legislative level. Instead, she succeeded at alienating many of their former allies.[52] The women's rights movement would remain split in half for the next two decades.

Harper and Stanton each remained active in national political leadership until the late 1890s, and they met multiple times at national women's rights conventions. But across those decades, each was immersed in their own work and communities that drew into stark relief their differences in politics and methods.

Stanton drilled down on the rights of the individual as the path to women's liberation. While she was the mother of seven children and one-half of the nineteenth century's most famous female friendship, by the end of her life she had an increasingly individualist, alienated view of human life that saw each person to be entirely alone. "Each soul must depend wholly on itself," she imparted in 1892 during her final speech as leader of the women's rights movement, and "lives alone forever. . . . Our inner being which we call ourself, no eye nor touch of man or angel has ever pierced." Stanton considered this speech, "The Solitude of Self," her greatest piece of writing, and while her fellow suffragettes in the audience were largely appalled, twentieth- and twenty-first-century authors from Vivian Gornick to feminist historians have praised the prescience of her atheistic vision that embraced the materialist logic of the individuated and isolated psyche decades before many of her contemporaries did. The solitude of each individual, Stanton argued, was also the condition of women's "birthright to self-sovereignty."[53]

"Solitude of Self" represented the culmination of Stanton's lifelong work developing a white feminism that sees people as isolated units in competition with one another. The speech also foreshadows the white feminism that was to develop in the late twentieth century: she articulates a cold, combative vision of women fighting their way up the capitalist ladder, freeing themselves from the primitive tasks of sitting at "the loom and the spinning wheel" and ascending into their right to "fill the editor's and professor's chair, and plead at the bar of justice, walk the wards of the hospital, and speak from the pulpit and the platform."[54] In this individualist vision, middle-class women lean into the professional ranks of capitalism, and white civilization improves as a result. Meanwhile, the women who continue to operate the loom and the wheel, and who are tied to the factory floor, become anachronisms skulking in the shadows.

A few years later, Stanton published her monumental attack on Christianity's suppression of women, *The Woman's Bible*, a controversial yet best-selling book that further outraged her movement contemporaries and charmed feminist readers a century later. Yet Stanton was not alone in death. When she was buried in 1902, above her casket was mounted a picture of her life's companion—not her husband, who had died fifteen years prior—but Susan B. Anthony.[55]

～ ～

For Stanton, progress was dependent upon liberating the secular individual. But for Harper, faith, contact, and interdependence underwrite the conditions of liberation, a liberation imagined at the scale of the collective instead of at the isolated unit of the self-sovereign psyche.

After Reconstruction, Harper worked to improve the conditions of Black women. She published four novels including the well-regarded *Iola Leroy* (1892) and dozens more poems and short stories, gave a host of prominent speeches throughout the Northeast at temperance societies and women's rights conventions, and, when she and Harriet Tubman were in their seventies, cofounded the National Association of Colored Women with Ida B. Wells and others to fight for suffrage and against Jim Crow. Harper held the office of vice president of the organization for the last fifteen years of her life. Across these platforms, she advocated for Christian faith, moral righteousness, abstinence from drink, and the "enlightenment" of women, praising individuals who identified proudly with Blackness and devoted themselves to spreading education, faith, and morality among the race.[56]

Yet Harper refused the white feminist logic that women, by their virtuous nature, would exert a moral force on society. "I am not sure that women are naturally so much better than men that they will clear the stream by the virtue of their womanhood; it is not through sex but through character that the best influence of women upon the life of the nation must be exerted," Harper advised from the women's stage at Chicago's World's Columbian Exposition in 1893.[57]

This stress on character and moralizing expressed through the overwrought style of nineteenth-century prose did not win Harper fans in the twentieth century. W. E. B. Du Bois offered the lukewarm eulogy at her death in 1911 that "she was not a great writer, but she wrote much worth reading";[58] some critics during the revival of African American literature in the 1980s and 1990s argued that she was so eager to encourage Black respectability that her fiction and poetry courted trite sentimentalism and repressed sexuality altogether.[59] Harper's line in her novel *Iola Leroy* applauding a character for "wearing sobriety as a crown and righteousness as the girdle of her loins" is the kind of passage that has earned her a reputation as the most prudish and saccharine, and thus least modern, of nineteenth-century Black women writers.[60]

Yet evoking loins wrapped in the fabric of righteousness is a strange way to repress sexuality. While Harper was later portrayed as overly prim and conventional, her writing about race politics envisioned something new altogether. She imagined a kind of solidarity and spirituality that wasn't afraid of bodies. Civilizing the race, for Harper, is partly the result of physical touch and close intimacy with humankind and with God. Rather than scales of justice weighing the rights of one analogous group against the rights of another, the key metaphors of her writing are bodies that surge with life for one another and hands that fold together in prayer across class lines. Far from repression, what emerges instead is a vision of contact between people—in sensual and erotic form—as a prized method of solidarity work.[61] Hers is an embodied feminism where flesh and spirit unite to bring forth a new world, an agenda that has become pivotal to twenty-first-century Black feminism.

Civilized respectability, however, wields its own hierarchies. It is relentlessly ethnocentric, colonial, and capitalist. "I do not believe in unrestricted and universal suffrage for either men or women," she told her audience at the Columbian Exposition. "I do not believe that the most ignorant and brutal man is better prepared to add value to the strength and durability of the government than the most cultured, upright, and intelligent woman." The words sound remarkably like Stanton's. Yet even though Harper worked within the deeply flawed civilization paradigm, she also reworked its criteria to articulate ethics and solidarity, rather than the supremacy of race and sex. The "drunk-ard" and "lynchers" whose hands are "red with blood" were her examples of brutal men who should be barred from the vote—not uneducated Black men or immigrants from China and Ireland.[62]

Meanwhile, by the 1890s, Stanton was similarly affected by claims that en-franchising women would double the amount of ignorance among the elec-torate, and she advocated drawing "some dignity and sacredness around the ballot box." Once more, the apparatus of the state was her god. Her proposal was characteristically extreme: a constitutional amendment for educated suf-frage, which restricted voting rights to US-born men and women who "read and write the English language intelligently."[63]

By the time the Nineteenth Amendment granted the ballot to women, but particularly white women, in 1920, both Stanton and Harper had passed away. Anthony's protégé Carrie Chapman Catt led the final, successful stages of the campaign for women's suffrage, in part by mimicking what abolition-ists including Stanton's husband had done fifty years prior: excluding any is-sue but one, in this case the ballot, from their platform. Stanton's atheism had caused particular embarrassment and anxiety to Catt and to the movement in the 1890s—they found her attacks on Christianity damaging to their public standing. Stanton had preached a revolution of white women's place in soci-ety, but Catt and her compatriots focused on the ballot alone. Nonetheless, in many ways, Catt was firmly part of Stanton's legacy. One of her tactics to gain national approval for women's suffrage was openly recruiting white suprem-acist women's groups in the South. "White supremacy will be strengthened, not weakened, by woman suffrage," she infamously proclaimed.[64]

Other white feminists would have a different agenda, however, than court-ing white nationalists. A competing strategy was to insist that white women's moral purity and faculty of sympathy rendered them rescuers of the formerly enslaved. As long as the civilizing paradigm remained firmly in place, people deemed to fall outside of the norms of genteel white respectability would face ongoing threats from vicious enemies and sympathetic saviors alike, often in the name of feminism. But fortunately, there has never been just one approach to women's rights.

CHAPTER TWO

WHITE SYMPATHY VERSUS BLACK SELF-DETERMINATION

Harriet Beecher Stowe and Harriet Jacobs

Mrs. Stowe has *invented* the Negro novel.

—George Eliot

IN JUNE 1835, HARRIET JACOBS DECIDED IT WAS TIME TO RISK EVERYTHING TO PROTECT HER children from enslavement. Jacobs, then twenty-two years old, was enslaved by Dr. James Norcom and his family in the coastal town of Edenton, North Carolina. Though her two young children were legally Norcom property, they lived with her emancipated grandmother, Molly Horniblow. Jacobs and Horniblow were laying careful plans to secure the children's freedom. But one June evening Jacobs learned that Joseph, age six, and Louisa, age two, were to arrive the following day at Dr. Norcom's plantation to be "broken in." She knew what that meant: once her children were trained to be valuable property, the Norcoms would never consent to selling them to her friends and family who would set them free. Her children faced a lifetime of plantation slavery.[1]

At half past midnight, Jacobs snuck down two flights of the Norcoms' creaking stairs and stole through a window into the rain. She walked six miles into town, arriving at the house of a friend who sequestered her for the next week. The following morning, Dr. Norcom unleashed considerable force to

track down the woman he considered his commodity; the sheriff, slave pa-
trols, and later the courts and press were all in pursuit of Jacobs. They stopped
all port traffic in the North Carolina town, rendering her further movement
impossible. A white woman, who with her husband enslaved multiple people, nonetheless offered Jacobs a place of refuge in a small, unused storeroom
above her bedroom. The woman was friendly with Jacobs's grandmother, a
respected baker in town, and wished to help her family. Jacobs remained shut
up in the room for nearly two months, keeping her body quiet and motionless,
while being supported by the enslaved cook Betty. Meanwhile, Dr. Norcom
continued in hot pursuit, searching premises throughout town and jailing Jacobs's children, brother, and aunt in an attempt to extort information leading
to her whereabouts. To escape detection during these searches, Betty hid Jacobs under the flooring of the outdoor kitchen. Lying supine in this damp,
shallow space, she had just enough room to shield her eyes from cascading
dirt as Betty walked to and fro inches above her head. As unimaginable as
Jacobs's cramped retreat might be, it presaged years of sacrifice yet to come.

By August, with repeated searches and jailings, ramped up surveillance
of Jacobs's friends and family, and a suspicious enslaved housemaid who one
morning tried every one of the household's keys attempting to unlock the storeroom, Jacobs's community knew they had to make a sudden move. That night,
her friend Peter brought her a set of sailor's clothes and they walked in disguise
to the wharf. Jacobs spent a humid night and the next day hidden in the Great
Dismal Swamp, surrounded by large snakes she beat off with a stick while thick
clouds of mosquitoes descended upon her flesh. The steamy quagmire was all
the more terrifying to Jacobs given that she was still recovering from a venom-
ous snakebite incurred during the first week of her escape and she had no idea
where she might go next. That night, much to her surprise, Peter told Jacobs she
was to be hidden at her grandmother's house.

"But every nook and cranny is known to Dr. Norcom," Jacobs worried. She
couldn't envision where in the house would possibly be safe.

"Wait and see," Peter advised as he walked alongside the ersatz sailor
through the darkened streets. "A place has been created for you. But you must
make the most of this walk, for you may not have another very soon."[2]

With apprehension, Jacobs noted the sad tone seeping through her friend's
reassuring words.

They arrived at a small uninsulated shed attached to the side of her grand-mother's house. While she had been hiding in the swamp, her uncle Mark Ramsey had built a trapdoor, concealed from below, accessing a small attic crawl space beneath the shed's thin, sloped roof.[3] It was the perfect hiding spot, one Jacobs herself hadn't even considered, because it all but defied the basic requirements for human life. Seven feet long by nine feet wide, and reaching only three feet high at the slope's peak, the space was roughly the size of four coffins laid side by side.

Into this pitch-black cavity, Jacobs climbed. Finding a mattress in the center, she learned through touch, not sight, that she lacked the clearing to roll from one side to the other: when she turned, her shoulders crashed into the roof's downward slope. This living grave, as Jacobs came to call it, initially admitted no air or light. But a few weeks into her confinement, as she was crawling about for exercise, her head struck something protruding from the wall. It was a loophole, a small hand tool for drilling holes, left intentionally or not by her uncle when he constructed the trapdoor. Late at night, she bore small holes facing King Street until she had a one-by-one-inch aperture onto the world outside. Here she hunched, reading the Bible, watching her children and sewing their clothes, and observing Dr. Norcom and others walking down the street. Yet despite this narrow opening, the air remained so close that not even North Carolina's mosquitoes deigned to enter.

The suffocating heat of summer turned into the frost of winter, and still Jacobs had yet to rise to standing. Through illness, frostbite, unconsciousness, and the assault of the elements, Jacobs remained in the attic year after year. By the time her friends were able to secure her safe passage north out of Eden-ton's harbor it was June 1842. She had spent seven years in the living grave.[4]

Seven years hidden in a crawl space so small Dr. Norcom never suspected she was hidden a mere block from his house in town. Jacobs wryly called the crawl space her "loophole of retreat": an ambiguity that creates a means of escape.[5]

Once north, Jacobs joined her brother John Jacobs, who had also freed himself, in the western New York abolitionist movement. The pair frequented the Anti-Slavery Office and Reading Room, which had opened the previous year above the offices of Frederick Douglass's North Star newspaper in Roch-ester, about fifty miles west of Seneca Falls. Jacobs was eventually appointed

agent of the Reading Room, and on Thursdays, she joined a circle of abolitionist women "to sew, knit, read, and talk for the cause."[6] While the reading room
venture didn't last two years, Jacobs's desire to participate in the movement
continued unabated, especially after the Fugitive Slave Law in 1850 left her
and others vulnerable to capture in the streets of her now home, New York
City. The North was no longer a refuge.

Jacobs decided that sharing her story was the most significant contribution
to dislodging slavery's increasing stranglehold on the country that she could
make. Many whites, North and South, persisted in believing that slavery was
a civilizing institution that provided care and protection for people too primitive to provide for themselves. Her narrative would illuminate the suffering
that enslaved women endured—for they were used as breeders to create more
human "property"—and the extraordinary lengths they went to in order to
escape bondage.

Yet to tell the truth in service of the cause would open her up to scorn and
shame. Dr. Norcom began sexually abusing Jacobs when she was fifteen. She
had managed to avoid his ultimate design: installing her in the isolated house
he had built just for the purpose of sequestering her four miles away from
the watchful eyes of his jealous wife and Jacobs's protective grandmother.
But her safety came at great personal cost. Jacobs thwarted his attempts to
make her his full-time concubine, nearly a decade prior to her retreat into the
crawl space, through a "deliberate calculation."[7] To avoid being shut away for
Norcom's pleasure and profit, she became the mistress of a prominent white
man in town, Samuel Tredwell Sawyer, and he fathered her two children.

Jacobs needed a writer who understood the delicacy of her task. She wanted
simultaneously to expose the sexual abuses enslaved girls and women suffered
while also forming alliances with white women in the North. This would be
a tricky maneuver, for these readers would initially be more likely to judge,
rather than empathize with, her choice to strike up an extramarital relationship with Sawyer in order to avoid her enslaver's grasp. Jacobs had been reading and writing since childhood, thanks to one of the Norcom daughters, but
she didn't feel up to the task of composing her own narrative for print. In the
early 1850s, no Black woman in the United States had yet published a short
story, novel, or autobiography; Frances Harper's short story "The Two Offers"
wouldn't appear until the end of the decade.

In New York, Jacobs worked as a nanny for Cornelia Grinnell Willis and Nathaniel Parker Willis. Nathaniel was the most prominent magazine writer of the era and, as founder of the magazine now known as *Town & Country*, was well connected to the literary world. When Cornelia suggested that Harriet Beecher Stowe could be entrusted with bringing Jacobs's story to the public, Jacobs thought they had identified an ally. Stowe had published the blockbuster *Uncle Tom's Cabin* the prior year. The antislavery novel had already sold three hundred thousand copies; over the course of the nineteenth century, only the Bible sold better. Stowe elicited tears of sympathy for the slave, and white women of the North sobbed in chorus, turning against the institution of slavery. Many commentators would later declare that the novel—and white women's tears—led to the Civil War, thus flushing the sin of slavery from the nation. And, despite Stowe's position as a white woman writer coming from a prominent New England reform family, *Uncle Tom's Cabin* didn't shy away from confronting white men's sexual abuse of enslaved women.

Jacobs asked her close friend Amy Post, a prominent white Quaker activist who had attended the Seneca Falls Convention five years earlier, to approach Stowe about writing Jacobs's narrative. Stowe's response would change the course of Jacobs's life and of American women's writing. Once more, Harriet Jacobs took decisive action. But this time, it would be to take control of her own story.

~ ~

Harriet Beecher Stowe was the most popular writer and best-known abolitionist in the nineteenth-century United States. Through decades of deft storytelling in the sentimental vein, she translated the traditional domain of white women's authority—the home and the heart—into a method of political power. Whereas Elizabeth Cady Stanton and Susan B. Anthony were best known for approaching women's rights and abolition via the apparatuses of the state, such as petitions, elections, and amendments, Stowe and other sentimental writers fought for social change through appealing directly to readers' emotions, hoping to inspire a change of feeling.

Public opinion widely afforded white men of the emerging middle class the faculties of reason and rationality that authorized them to monopolize business and politics. At the same time, it simultaneously restricted white women to the role of "angel of the house." Their alleged purity and delicacy of feeling would guard the family from the morbid calculations and dangerous self-interest of government and the marketplace. Nation- and empire-building was bloody work, and commentators regularly smoothed the contradictions of civilization by assigning white women the task of absorbing and softening its violence. This gave white women an important, though largely obscured, public position. When white women first gained roles outside the home in the United States and the British empire, it was on account of white feminist advocates who stressed their role as civilizers who would spread refined feeling, the arts of bourgeois domesticity, and Protestant-capitalist self-discipline. Stowe and her sister, the white feminist writer Catharine Beecher, were among the most prominent figures who grabbed ahold of white women's assigned roles as domestic angels and stabilizers of civilization, expanding them into a platform for influence that reached far beyond the house and into the nation.

In best-selling housekeeping manuals, novels, and short stories, Stowe and Beecher argued that women had a special purview of their own: the emotional realm. In their vision, women's capacity for sympathy was not primarily of private, interior significance. Instead, their delicacy of feeling was their *public* value, and it formed the foundation of true civilization. Civilization, as one of Stowe's fictional characters attests, meant a nation that was "noble, simple, pure, and religious; and women can do more towards this even than men, for women are the real architects of society."[8] Deeply felt tears enabled middle-class white women to cast their housecleaning and sewing aside and emerge into the public sphere—as the civilizers of the nation.

If women were the real architects of civilization, then tears and the sentimental fiction and poetry that elicited them were their building blocks. Stowe argued that sympathy with the travails of the less fortunate ought to guide all public and private decisions—and this emotional identification depended upon reading about the brutality they experienced. Yet readers' outpouring of tearful sympathy wasn't primarily intended to improve the condition of the oppressed. Instead, commentators widely touted that learning of others' suffering cultivated the character and moral authority of the person who did the crying. As a genre, sentimental writing like Stowe's displays the anguish of the marginalized to build the character and influence of the more privileged. "Sentimentality," James Baldwin memorably wrote of *Uncle Tom's Cabin*, traffics in "the ostentatious parading of excessive and spurious emotion," disguising the "catalogue of violence" lurking at its core: Black pain, splayed across the page, becomes a mere foil for white (women's) power.[9]

The public value accorded to white women's tears today flows forth from these earliest days of white feminism. Luvvie Ajayi, Brittney Cooper, Robin DiAngelo, and others have explained how white women weaponize their tears, using their overwhelmed reaction when they are called out for their racism to center *themselves* as the true victims of racism.[10] When white women are confronted with the possibility they can be perpetrators, and not only victims, of oppressive actions and they burst out crying, antiracist work grinds to a halt. A white woman sobs, and the room falls to her feet. These tears seemingly perform a self-baptism. They cleanse the sufferer of any past wrongs and invest her with a martyred authority flowing from the realm of allegedly indisputable truth: her own hurt feelings.

Some of the sanctifying innocence widely afforded to white women when they cry can be traced back to an original wellspring: the inkpot of Harriet Beecher Stowe.

～ ～

In 1850, slavery was expanding, rather than retreating, in the United States. Stowe, like Jacobs, was compelled into action by the Fugitive Slave Law. In the spring of 1850, Harriet Beecher Stowe's husband Calvin was appointed professor of theology at Bowdoin College in Maine. As the couple traveled east from Cincinnati to their new home, they stopped for a week with each of Stowe's siblings. At the Boston house of her abolitionist brother Edward Beecher and his wife Isabella, she was immersed in talk of the pending law, which would make harboring a self-emancipated person a serious crime and effectively turn every police squad in the country into a slave patrol. Edward and Isabella were outraged that the North would no longer provide refuge for the formerly enslaved. Stowe, for her part, remained silent, absorbing the conversations. When the Fugitive Slave Law was passed in September as part of the Missouri Compromise of 1850, Isabella reached out to her sister-in-law to goad her into action.

"Hattie," Isabella wrote, "if I could use a pen as you can, I would write something that would make this whole nation feel what an accursed thing slavery is."[11] The forty-year-old Stowe was a prominent writer who had been publishing essays and short stories in national periodicals for a decade.

Isabella's letter became Stowe's charge. A personal tragedy also spurred her to act. Her sixth child had succumbed to cholera just before their move, and she felt that the pain of watching her child die gave her new insight into how enslaved mothers feel when their children are sold away from them. Through her talents with the pen, Stowe would "make this whole nation feel" the evils of slavery as she now did—though she had to wait until her seventh child was old enough to let her sleep. A year later, the infant was out of her bed, Stowe's capacity to write returned, and she dashed off a note to her editor at the *National Era* magazine: "Now that the time is come when even a woman or a child who can speak a word for freedom and humanity is bound to speak. . . . I hope every woman who can write will not be silent."[12]

Harriet Beecher Stowe. (Courtesy of the State Archive of Florida)

But what kind of revolution would be inspired by white women's feelings? Would the focus on their feelings about Black lives render white women the true heroes of abolition? Turning to sentimentalism to rouse public opinion against slavery risked rendering the enslaved mere objects of sympathy, a passive cast of characters absorbing abuse while white readers enjoyed the cathartic, and ultimately self-serving, spilling of tears.

~ ~

Harriet Beecher Stowe was born to a famous, and at times infamous, family of reformers. She proposed a clear method for joining them in the abolitionist movement: sketch a story that would portray slavery "in the most lifelike and graphic manner possible."[13] Fiction carefully drawn, she knew, could pry open the heart. Nonetheless, she faced a significant obstacle in rendering slavery palpable on the page. Stowe had never been to the plantation South. Though she lived in Cincinnati for nearly twenty years, located just across the Ohio River from Kentucky, she had boarded a boat across the river's mile-long span only once, seventeen years earlier. And she had never traveled farther south, a not uncommon situation for middle-class white women in particular, given the horse-drawn carriages and crater-filled dirt roads that congealed into mud that characterized the transportation system of the nineteenth-century United States. Given her lack of firsthand experience, how could she create vivid scenes of places and characters entirely foreign to her?

Stowe, however, was confident in her command of the material. "I have had ample opportunities for studying" the "negro character," she informed her editor. Stowe's biographer Joan D. Hedrick reveals who served as the novelist's primary specimens: her servants. Hedrick surmises that Stowe's position of power over the only formerly enslaved people whom she knew personally "radically compromised her perceptions."[14] The result in *Uncle Tom's Cabin* is a mixture all too common among white abolitionists—a fierce antislavery argument propped up by racist portrayals of African Americans as naïve, highly impressionable dependents in desperate need of white women's guiding hand.

Stowe extracted significant amounts of material from her cook, "poor Eliza Buck," who had formerly been enslaved in Virginia and Kentucky, and on a Louisiana plantation. Buck conjured "scenes" for Stowe of both agency and utter dispossession. She told of brutal plantation whippings and the serious injuries that resulted, injuries that she would sneak out after nightfall to tend. She also told Stowe of the children she bore, fathered by her Kentucky master, which may well have shocked the writer and certainly inspired her pity. "You know, Mrs. Stowe, slave women cannot help themselves," Buck retorted.[15]

If Stowe's sense of propriety was shaken, she learned nonetheless that sexual abuse was an intrinsic part of enslavement for women. The global slave trade, which captured individuals in Africa and imported them to Europe and the Americas, had ceased in 1808. Yet its end had ratcheted up Southern planters' demands on enslaved women's bodies in the United States, for the only way slavery could persist was by keeping women pregnant. However discreetly Stowe's novel approached the topic, *Uncle Tom's Cabin* became one of the first texts to whisper about the rape of enslaved women directly into the ears of readers lounging comfortably in Northern homes—an aspect of the novel that most likely encouraged Harriet Jacobs's trust.

Stowe's goal for *Uncle Tom's Cabin* was to show "the *best side*" of slavery "and something *faintly approaching the worst*," perhaps aiming to turn readers against the institution while seemingly giving it a fair shake. But hinting at the worst was necessary to her goal to elicit rivers of tears. To approximate slavery's most outrageous abuses, she dispatched her main character, the eponymous Uncle Tom, to a Louisiana cotton plantation. This setting was entirely beyond her ken. Stowe could easily gather the perspective of enslavers: their accounts spilled out from newspapers, journals, and books across the expanding nation. But her blockbuster-in-progress, which aimed to animate the slave's plight in vivid detail, depended on knowledge that was much harder to obtain and, therefore, all the more important to broadcast. "Stowe's access to information was as important as her ability to cast details in an imaginative frame," her biographer Hedrick emphasizes.[16] Wishing to gain further the viewpoint of the enslaved, Stowe approached Frederick Douglass, a man she had never met.

"In the course of my story, the scene will fall upon a cotton plantation. I am very desirous, therefore, to gain information from one who has been an actual labourer on one," Stowe wrote to Douglass. "Such a person as Henry Bibb, if in the country, might give me just the kind of information I desire." The prior year, Bibb had self-published a popular account of his life on a Kentucky plantation and his dramatic escape from slavery. She enclosed a list of questions for Bibb with the "request that he will at earliest convenience answer them." Stowe held nothing back in making her demand. Her need for details seemingly entitled her to request specific information from two of the country's best-known self-emancipated slaves, as if she were ordering from a menu. Her letter to Douglass concluded with an imperious attempt to persuade him that two of his deeply held convictions were wrong. She insisted that Christian churches were *not* generally proslavery and that colonization schemes to send Black Americans to Africa were highly advisable.[17]

Bibb, for his part, was already in Canada founding the nation's first Black newspaper. Douglass, as far as we know, never replied. Eliza Buck, the occasional person escaping enslavement on the Underground Railroad who posted at Stowe's house, Stowe's brother Charles who had traveled to Louisiana, and a few published firsthand accounts of slavery remained her primary sources of the plantation South.

Today, *Uncle Tom's Cabin* has become synonymous with the misfortune of its protagonist Uncle Tom, though the meaning of the now epithet—a cringing, subservient Black man eagerly falling to his knees at a white man's bidding—arises from hundreds of stage adaptations of the tale, not from Stowe's novel. The book conveys the suffering of the enslaved and articulates a method for lifting slaves out of the status of property. True to its sentimental agenda, however, the most significant figures are not enslaved characters like Uncle Tom. The principal actors are the white women who alternately enslave them and help set them free.

White people, and white women especially, *Uncle Tom's Cabin* seeks to impress on the reader, have the power to mold the character of Black people. History and biology have combined to elevate whites into the position of parents while Blacks remain vulnerable youth, as if mostly blank, still-malleable slates waiting for further inscription. Uncle Tom, for example, is described as possessing "the soft, impressible nature of his kindly race, ever yearning toward the simple and childlike." For Stowe, Anglo-Saxons have by contrast accumulated racial vigor on account of being "born of ages of cultivation, command, education, physical and moral eminence" under civilization. It is thus the duty of white women, as she sees it, to impress new influences into Black souls and flesh.[18]

Stowe does portray enslaved characters whose agency ripples off the page, if outlandishly so: to escape the Kentucky slave catchers pursuing her young son, Eliza Harris clutches him to her chest and leaps from one shuddering ice chunk to another across the Ohio River's mile-wide span. Nonetheless, the novel's thrust pushes toward one central source of agency: the white woman in the parlor. "There is all the difference in the world in the servants of Southern establishments," Stowe's narrator opines, "according to the character and capacity of the mistresses who have brought them up." Eliza, for her part, had been enslaved by the quasi-abolitionist Mrs. Shelby, who took it upon herself "to do [her] duty to these poor, simple, dependent creatures" by civilizing them.[19] Eliza's leaps of faith are simultaneously repercussions of discipline.

The novel's paradigmatic white woman is not a woman at all, but a child. When enslaved by an extravagantly wealthy family in New Orleans, Tom forms an unshakeable bond with the master's daughter, the five- or six-year-old Eva St. Clare. Though slavery's wrongs seep into her malleable body, weakening her constitution, she welcomes the opportunity to sacrifice herself for the enslaved. "I *would die* for them, Tom, if I could," Eva confides. She soon does just that—but not before gathering the enslaved around her deathbed to impart her final wish: "You must not live idle, careless, thoughtless lives. You must be Christians."[20] In her life and death, Eva stamps herself on Tom's impressible nature. By the novel's close, Uncle Tom is beaten to death on the Louisiana cotton plantation because he refuses to whip a fellow slave; Eva's sacrifice has become his charge. If Eva has been born in Christ's image, Tom is molded in Eva's own.

Uncle Tom's Cabin exalts white women's sympathy as the most powerful civilizing force. Lest the reader miss this message, Stowe places an abolitionist aunt from Vermont in the St. Clare household. Miss Ophelia insists that it is the environment of slavery, not the innate nature of Black people, that conditions the enslaved to deceit, immorality, and debasement. To test Ophelia's theory, Eva's father purchases a naughty young orphan named Topsy to serve as the "fresh-caught specimen" of Ophelia's new "experiment": Could a white woman elevate even the "blackest," most "animalized" and "degraded" slave child? But Miss Ophelia's horror at slavery is matched only by her revulsion to Black people, and she can't bring herself even to touch Topsy. Topsy, for her part, continues nicking ribbons, swinging from bedposts, and cutting up Ophelia's bonnet trimmings to make coats for her dolls. Eva, however, showers Topsy with af-fection and religious instruction. After Eva's death, Ophelia learns the secret of Eva's sway over Topsy: "honest tears," shed in pity. When Ophelia finally breaks down and sobs, "from that hour, she acquired an influence over the mind of the destitute child that she never lost."[21] Ophelia cries, and Topsy transforms.

Sentimental novels "always traffic in cliché, the reproduction of a person as a thing, and thus indulge in the confirmation of the marginal subject's em-bodiment of *inhumanity* on the way to providing the privileged with heroic occasions of recognition, rescue, and inclusion," literary critic Lauren Berlant writes, building on James Baldwin's classic takedown of *Uncle Tom's Cabin*.[22] The real significance of white girls' and white women's tears, Stowe's novel suggests, is their clout: a conduit of discipline, a determinative power, an up-per hand. Sentimental sympathy is a tear-stained cloak for authority.

When the Fugitive Slave Act passed in September 1850, Harriet Jacobs had lived in the North for eight years. But she was still forced to run from the Norcom family, who continued to pursue her. The act's passage only inten-sified their aim to capture. She learned to dread summer, when "snakes and slaveholders make their appearance." Jacobs rarely left the Willises' Fourth Street house and every night she scanned the newspapers' coverage of vis-itors arrived in New York for familiar names; twice she fled to Boston. The first escape was motivated by a warning she received from North Carolina that Dr. Norcom was soon to resume his search for Jacobs and her children. Unbeknownst to her, given the difficulties her contacts faced posting her a letter, he had died months prior. His death only escalated Jacobs's danger, however, for Norcom's son, James Norcom Jr., had driven the family into debt. Norcom's daughter and her husband Daniel Messmore, desperate for funds, continued the pursuit.[23]

Early one February morning in 1852, one month before three printing presses would begin churning twenty-four hours a day to keep up with the instantaneous demand for *Uncle Tom's Cabin*, Jacobs realized her nanny duties the prior night had distracted her from examining the *Evening Express*. She rushed into the parlor and grabbed the daily just as a servant boy was about to crumple it up for the morning's fire. The words gripped her heart like a tightening fist: Daniel Messmore had arrived in New York and was posted at what she deemed a "third-rate hotel."[24] She feared especially for her daughter Louisa, now nineteen and visiting Jacobs in the city; to evade slave catchers emboldened by the Fugitive Slave Law, her son Joseph had joined her brother John in the gold mines of California. Jacobs escaped to Boston once more, again with Cornelia Willis's assistance. Willis wrote to Jacobs that she would like to purchase her freedom from Messmore to end his "persecution." Just as in the South, for Jacobs to be free in New York, she would have to be sold.

Jacobs was grateful but wounded. To give the Norcom family money, after all she had suffered, would transform her "triumph" into defeat.

"Being sold from one owner to another seems too much like slavery," Jacobs replied to Willis. "I prefer to go to my brother in California."

Eager to assist her friend and employee, Cornelia approached Messmore anyway and negotiated the sale of Jacobs, and the relinquishment of any claims on her children, for the bargain price of $300. Jacobs was stung, disgusted that she was "*sold*," like property, "in the free city of New York!" But she also breathed easier upon being able to board the train back to the city with her face uncovered and her gaze forthright.[25]

No longer hunted, Jacobs could think about contributing to the abolition movement by sharing her story. Her friend Amy Post had been encouraging Jacobs to tell her tale for years, but Jacobs was "mortified" to imagine revealing her sexual persecution and her affair with Sawyer. "If it was the life of a heroine with no degradation," she confided in Post—one of only two people in the North whom she had told the circumstances of her children's origin— she would be happy to share.[26] Two years of prayer to overcome her own "pride" so that she may "save another from my fate" softened her to the idea. Cornelia suggested to Jacobs that Stowe could be entrusted with bringing the story of her life and escape to the public. At the close of 1852, Jacobs asked Post to make the approach.

"I should like to be with her a month," Jacobs proposed along with ideas for the structure of the text, and in return "I could give her some fine sketches for her pen on slavery."[27] Post wrote to Stowe, delicately broaching the details of Jacobs's life—including her self-entombment and her affair with Sawyer—to communicate the urgency of the tale and their hope Stowe could take on the sensitive project.

The return mail was silent.

A month later, Jacobs read a notice in the newspaper that Stowe was soon to sail for Great Britain to meet with abolitionists. Realizing her opportunity to work with Stowe, and thus her chance "to be useful" to the cause, was slipping away, she thought of another tactic to gain the author's ear. Her daughter Louisa, who had recently finished boarding school, could accompany Stowe on her speaking tour, at Jacobs's expense. She "would be a very good representative of a Southern Slave" for British audiences to meet, Jacobs argued, and could assist Stowe's abolition work while gaining experience on the abolitionist lecture circuit. At the same time, Louisa would build a relationship with Stowe that might enable a future partnership with Jacobs herself. Jacobs, unlike Stowe, had traveled to England before, while working as Nathaniel's nanny after the death of his first wife, and she was also eager for Louisa to similarly experience the temporary reprieve from the racism saturating American life. Cornelia Willis agreed that Jacobs's plan was sound and she, too, wrote to Stowe.[28]

This time, Stowe replied, and her letter lit a fire inside Jacobs.[29]

It would be "much care" to take along Louisa, Stowe wrote, especially since she was traveling at the invitation of the Anti-Slavery Society of Glasgow—a perhaps reasonable objection. But what incensed Jacobs was Stowe's immediate follow-up. Louisa would "be subject to much petting and patronizing" by the English when they learned of her history as a slave, Stowe condescended. Louisa would no doubt find the attention "pleasing," to which Stowe was "very much opposed . . . with this class of people."[30] Stowe, it seems, trusted only white abolitionists like herself with receiving the esteem and acclaim of British antislavery activists.

Stowe pushed further. She saw Jacobs as a source of material for her new book, a factual follow-up to her blockbuster novel. *A Key to Uncle Tom's Cabin* was conceived to fend off proslavery accusations that she materialized the abuses of slavery solely from the mist of her imagination. Because Stowe had created a character who hid in a Louisiana attic on the way to self-emancipation, Jacobs's seven-year confinement represented a potential jackpot. She could now proffer Jacobs's story, after the fact, as the alleged basis of her plot. Stowe had been eager to extract stories from Bibb for her own use; her method now remained the same.

Desirous to authenticate these details of Jacobs's life in order to publish her story in *A Key*, Stowe had not replied directly to Jacobs. Instead, she wrote to Jacobs's employer, Cornelia Willis. In the envelope, she tucked in Amy Post's letter divulging the sensitive details about the origin of Jacobs's children, requesting Willis corroborate its contents so that she could use Jacobs's story as the basis of her own. She sought Willis's verification, rather than Jacobs's permission.

Jacobs felt the hot flush of shame when Willis, outraged, showed her Stowe's breach of confidence. Willis had been kind enough to never ask Jacobs about Louisa and Joseph's father, understanding that it was a wound she preferred to tend by herself. When Stowe included Post's letter, she revealed details Willis hadn't known. No one had anticipated that Stowe would circumvent Jacobs's authority and puncture her privacy.[31]

Jacobs now had no desire to give her narrative over to Stowe and resolved her intention to tell "the history of my life entirely by itself." Cornelia wrote to Stowe, begging her to leave the material out of *A Key to Uncle Tom's Cabin* and sharing Jacobs's offer that "if she wanted some facts for her book," Jacobs "would be most happy to share some." Stowe didn't reply, so Cornelia wrote again. Jacobs then penned two letters to Stowe.

No reply ever came, and Stowe sailed for Liverpool.[32]

⌒ ⌒

In England and Scotland, Stowe was received as a star and savior. She met her first adoring crowd, quite by surprise, at the Liverpool wharf where they disembarked. Stowe had nurtured interest in Great Britain from the initial publication of her novel, having sent a copy and friendly letter to many of the nations' dukes, lords, and other noblemen and to distinguished writers like Charles Dickens. *Uncle Tom's Cabin*, now one year old, was well on its way to becoming the first international bestseller. Forty different editions issued from London alone, while ten different theatrical productions of the novel were on the city's stages. One publisher estimated over 1.5 million copies already circulated throughout Great Britain and its colonized territories.[33]

Harriet Beecher Stowe adopted her new public role with a mixture of humility and authority. The abolitionist movement had been churning for decades without her participation; suddenly now the white public saw her as its leader. She understood herself to be taking on the burden of getting elbow-deep in the horrors of slavery in order to fight its existence. Her letters during the time she was compiling *A Key to Uncle Tom's Cabin* reveal the emotional toll of a daily labor that required immersing herself in the graphic details of whippings, kidnappings, and torture. The majority of white authors chose to avert their eyes altogether from an industry built on cruelty. While Stowe's position cannot be compared to experiencing the lash firsthand, her dedication to writing about slavery had tremendous effect in rallying white audiences to oppose the institution.

Yet Stowe was also encouraged by a sense of her own responsibility and ownership over the cause, a position she authorized on the grounds that as a woman and mother who had lost a child to early death, she could best sympathize with the sufferings of slave women. Defenders of slavery argued that Black Americans lacked the same capacity of feeling that whites did. White women abolitionists like Stowe countered that all women, enslaved and not, shared a commonality of feeling.

"I wrote what I did because as a woman, as a mother I was oppressed and broken-hearted," Stowe explained to a prominent British judge a few weeks before she rebuffed Jacobs. "It is no merit," she continued, "that I *must* speak for the oppressed—who cannot speak for themselves."[34] But this was precisely the bind: white women who insisted that they knew exactly how enslaved women felt also felt entitled to assume authority over them, even when Black men like Douglass, Bibb, Jacobs's brother John Jacobs, and numerous others wrote and spoke for themselves.

Meanwhile, *Uncle Tom's Cabin* began raking in profits for its author and its publisher. Within the first three months of its release, Stowe earned a record-breaking $10,000 in royalties, more than $300,000 in today's terms. Stowe and her professor husband had barely been making ends meet, a situation that prevented her from accepting her publisher's first proposal: splitting the expense of production and the ensuing profit fifty-fifty. If they had been able to afford to take on this risk, she may well have found herself in a position somewhat similar to the one Louisa May Alcott would negotiate sixteen years later for *Little Women*: full copyright and an ensuing fortune that supported her family for generations. Stowe's publisher, however, went to considerable expense marketing the book and soliciting theatrical interest, doubtlessly contributing to its massive sales, and her 10 percent royalties piled up.[35]

Stowe's UK trip presented another windfall. She received no royalties from international sales since copyright law did not yet cross borders, but in response British supporters organized a "penny offering" campaign encouraging each reader to donate one pence to the author. These voluntary contributions amounted to nearly $20,000. Hundreds of pounds were also presented to Stowe to distribute to the antislavery cause, particularly the Underground Railroad. While the penny offering was explicitly intended for Stowe's own use, some grumbled nonetheless about Stowe's reluctance to fund the actual practice of antislavery reform.[36]

This reticence was a consequence of her strategy to appeal to the heart and stay out of the dirty business of politics, particularly the conflict roiling between different branches of the antislavery movement. As would soon be true of the campaign for women's suffrage, the abolitionist movement comprised multiple conflicting approaches. These factions included the Garrisonians, who fought for immediate abolition and, since the 1840 London antislavery conference Stanton had witnessed from the balcony, supported women's involvement; a second organization founded in 1840 by Lewis Tappan who fought to keep women out of abolition; and a conservative wing who supported incremental emancipation and compensating enslavers for their financial losses. Amid these debates that generated the energy and momentum of the movement, Stowe adopted a position of lucrative neutrality that did not go unnoticed. Stowe was "quite willing to get all she can out of us, but means to be very careful how she mixes up herself with the Old org[anizations]," commented one Garrisonian activist. Of Stowe's $20,000 penny offering purse, she later accounted for spending a little over $6,000 to support antislavery, including funding tracts, initiating a petition campaign, and aiding fugitives. The bulk of the funds, she promised, would go toward constructing "a large & elegant building" for Miss Miner's, an all-Black school in Washington, DC, whose patronage she urged.[37] Yet no building ever came.

While it was one thing to be an antislavery writer, and another thing altogether to be part of the antislavery social movement, Stowe inspired abolitionists of all stripes—an influence she no doubt calculated to maintain. And in some ways, Hedrick notes, her neutrality was of use to activists, for she divorced antislavery sentiment from the messy, but necessary, battles of movement politics, framing it instead as a straightforward matter of the civilized heart. Such a tactic may not have produced legions of activists. Nonetheless, her novel has often been deemed one of the single most important factors in shifting white opinion in the North and in the United Kingdom against slavery, especially among the women she most sought to reach. Feminists applauded the public role she helped create for women's feelings, leading Stanton and Anthony to approach her about serving as editor of the *Revolution*. In the South, booksellers often banned the book, sometimes after intimidating threats from anti-abolition activists and authors. Within the movement, Stowe's novel earned high praise from radicals and incrementalists alike for rallying new supporters of the cause. Frederick Douglass, a Garrisonian, enthused that "nothing could have better suited the moral and humane requirements of the hour. Its effect was amazing, instantaneous, and universal." Stowe's son made a rather grander claim, one that still regularly finds its way into print today despite its apocryphal status: that upon meeting the five-foot-tall Stowe, President Abraham Lincoln allegedly exclaimed, "So you're the little lady who started the big war!"[38]

But not all abolitionists were delighted. Martin Delany, a radical Garrisonian physician, novelist, and Black nationalist, expressed horror at Douglass's support. Stowe, he objected, sought to displace African Americans by sending them to Africa, didn't support Black teachers of Black children, and was attracting all the "pecuniary advantages" of antislavery writing, "thereby depriving" Black authors of opportunity. "No enterprise, institution, or anything else," he concluded, "should be commenced *for us*, or our general benefit, without *first consulting us*." Douglass countered Delany with the biting logic of a seasoned organizer. "Where will he find '*us*' to consult with?" he beseeched. "Through what organization, or what channel could such consulting be carried on? . . . *How many*, in this case, constitute '*us*'?"[39]

As the months went on, Stowe's US royalties continued to amass. Within eighteen months of publication, Stowe earned $60,000. Requests for support likewise piled up, especially from her own family. Douglass sought her patronage for an industrial school for Black men he hoped to found. Though she had earlier approached him for advice about how to fund antislavery, she spilled out her frustration at his request for Black freedpeople: "If they want one [a school] why don't they *have* one—many men among the colored people are richer than I am—& better able to help such an object—Will they *ever* learn to walk?"[40]

At times, Stowe resented her responsibility to the antislavery movement, but at others she assumed the mantle of its white-appointed leader with pride. A highlight of her 1853 trip to England was a lunch reception at Stafford House, the London mansion of the philanthropists the Duke and Duchess of Sutherland and an internationally famous center of reform. Inspired by Stowe's novel, the duchess had helped coordinate a petition appealing to American white women to oppose slavery on the same sentimental grounds that Stowe had articulated in *Uncle Tom's Cabin*: slavery violated the sanctity of marriage, removed children from parents, and prevented slaves from obtaining Christian educations. The signatures of the 560,000 British women who endorsed the "Stafford House Address" were delivered as a personal gift to Stowe in twenty-six leather-bound volumes. This was a triumph for the author and evidence of her prominence within a key strain of feminism: white women's moral authority.

At the mansion, Stowe was presented to lords and ladies, marquises and marchionesses, and poets and archbishops under the glow of a skylight forty feet aloft illuminating the gilt interior of the most lavish grand hall and double staircase in Europe. The duchess awarded the author with a valuable token to mark her personal appreciation for Stowe's efforts: a heavy gold chain-link bracelet shaped in the form of slave shackles. "We trust it is a memorial of a chain that is soon to be broken," the bracelet proclaimed, and other links were inscribed with the 1807 date of the vote to abolish the global slave trade and the 1833 abolition of slavery in British territory. Following the Emancipation Proclamation, Stowe had the 1863 date of US abolition inscribed on her golden slave-shackle bracelet.[41]

As news of Stowe's trip appeared in the American press, Jacobs was needled by Stowe's presumed ownership over the cause. "Think dear Amy that a visit to Stafford House would spoil me as Mrs. Stowe thinks petting is more than my race can bear," she wrote to her confidante. "Well what a pity we poor blacks can't have the firmness and stability of character that you white people have."[42] Stowe, she continued, was rather *herself* letting the success of *Uncle Tom's Cabin* get to her head.

While Harriet Beecher Stowe was being feted in England, Harriet Jacobs began to write in New York. The Willises had built a home on the Hudson River in order for Nathaniel Parker Willis to write and recover his failing health. Cornelia was pregnant once more, so it was left to Jacobs and the other four servants to pack up the Fourth Street house for their move upstate. Immersed in old newspapers, a public letter in the *New York Tribune* addressed to the Duchess of Sutherland and the ladies of England and authored by "Mrs. Ex-President Tyler" caught Jacobs's eye. The former first lady Julia B. Tyler declaimed the "Stafford House Address," defending slavery as a benevolent institution, alleging slave families were seldom separated, and telling British women to back off their high horse. "Leave it to the women of the South to alleviate the sufferings of their dependents while you take care of your own," she scolded, referencing Britain's widespread pauperism.[43]

Jacobs was incensed. That night, she picked up a pen to write something for the public eye for the first time. White women were holding a transatlantic debate about slavery, and she resolved to add her voice and experience, despite her lack of formal education. "Poor as [my account] may be, I had rather give it from my own hand, than have it said that I employed others to do it for me," she wrote to the *New York Tribune*'s editor. Mrs. Tyler was wrong to assert that slaves are rarely sold, Jacobs insisted. In a tone both circumspect and blistering, she wondered aloud at white women like Tyler who defended a system that depended on sexual vice. "Would you not think that Southern Women had cause to despise that Slavery which forces them to bear so much deception practiced by their *husbands*?" she inquired. "A slaveholder seldom takes a white mistress, for she is an expensive commodity, not submissive as he would like." She concluded her lengthy letter by endorsing the veracity of Stowe's portrayal of slavery's cruelties, adding, "But in *Uncle Tom's Cabin* she has not told the half. Would that I had one spark from her store house of genius and talent I would tell you of my own sufferings." Writing until the morning, she signed her letter "A Fugitive Slave," sent it off to the *Tribune*, and boarded an early boat up the Hudson.[44]

That summer, while working sun-up to sundown tending the five Willis children, including caring for the newborn and sewing them all dolls, Jacobs found a spark. With Amy's encouragement, she began to write her own narrative, by candlelight, after the children had gone to bed. She wrote in secret. Jacobs never trusted Nathaniel Parker Willis, who defended slavery. She didn't tell Cornelia of her project either, a decision Jacobs's biographer Jean Fagan Yellin attributes to her desire to maintain ownership over her text. "Mrs. Willis had bought her freedom," Yellin writes, "but Jacobs alone would tell her story."[45]

Nathaniel, a dandy famous for his extravagant style, had commissioned the architect Calvert Vaux, who the following decade would codesign Central Park, to create the eighteen-room house they called Idlewild. He intended the gabled estate to be a writers' retreat for himself and his famous friends, including Edgar Allan Poe and Henry Wadsworth Longfellow. Yet the most significant text ever written at Idlewild was penned by the nanny, up in the servants' quarters, by the cover of night.

Jacobs wrote her narrative to invite solidarity with free Black Northerners and to kindle abolitionist fervor among Northern women by revealing that "slavery is terrible for men; but it is far more terrible for women." In *Incidents in the Life of a Slave Girl*, Jacobs invited alliance with white women while refusing the analogy they insisted upon that equated white women's experiences with the condition of enslavement. Employing the nineteenth-century style of direct address, she summoned intimacy in one breath while foreclosing the possibility of extractive sympathy in the next. "O reader, can you imagine my joy? No, you cannot, unless you have been a slave mother," she wrote of her Northern reunion with Louisa.[46]

Over the course of two hundred pages, Jacobs achieved a remarkable feat: she portrayed her life to be both structured by a brutal political and economic system that depended on her body's sexual capacity *and* punctuated by negotiations in which she found, against the odds, loopholes of retreat. She named her narrator Linda Brent, a pseudonym that enabled her to conceal her own identity as well as create a new speaking voice. When introducing Brent's parentage on the very first page, Jacobs discreetly broached the topic of enslavers' rape by noting that her grandmother Molly was fathered by a South Carolina planter. In this way, white men's assault of Black women's bodies figures literally as the precondition of her own tale and of her own body. Over and over, she illustrates that the institution of slavery was wrung out of the bruised, bleeding, and leaking bodies of Black women, often with white women's tacit or explicit endorsement. Her account is not of individual bad actors, but of a structure saturated with misery.

Yet Jacobs stopped far short of providing what some readers likely most craved: the prurient details of sentimental torture porn. In the wake of Stowe's novel, the abused, degraded slave woman was becoming a marketable figure of slavery's cruelties. White taste for Black women's pain too easily turned the enslaved into "erotic objects of sympathy," in literary critic Marianne Noble's apt summation. Sigmund Freud, sixty years later, would note how often his patients turned to the slave-beating scenes of *Uncle Tom's Cabin* for masturbation material.[47] Where her white readers would have anticipated finding a desirable object of suffering, Jacobs instead presented them with a Black woman's speaking subjectivity.

Jacobs approached her affair with Samuel Tredwell Sawyer, which violated the respectability politics her grandmother had instilled within her and that

Harriet Jacobs in 1894.

Harriet Jacobs. (Courtesy of Photographs and Prints Division, Schomburg Center for Research in Black Culture, New York Public Library)

her audience would demand of any woman worth their tears, with a mixture of forthrightness and mortification. "I will not try to screen myself behind the plea of compulsion from a master," she advised. "I knew what I did and I did it with deliberate calculation. But, O, ye happy women, whose purity has been sheltered from childhood, who have been free to choose the objects of your affection, whose homes are protected by law, do not judge the poor desolate slave girl too severely!" She closed the lengthy passage with once more asserting her capacity as a reasoning subject in full control of her actions: "Still, in looking back, calmly, on the events of my life, I feel that the slave woman ought not to be judged by the same standard as others."[48]

Throughout her narrative, Jacobs wove an account of Linda Brent as a reasoning subject with agency and feeling together with an appeal to white women readers for their sympathy. The result is akin to the feedback sandwich known to teachers everywhere: package criticism within reassuring praise. Passage by passage, her narrator insists upon her full humanity as a person capable of reason and feeling, a survivor of an abusive system looking for solidarity. While white women readers warmed up easily to Black figures portrayed as subordinates, as "sweet, loving, defenseless, if sometimes naughty children" in Angela Davis's description of the enslaved characters in *Uncle Tom's Cabin*, Jacobs confronts her readers with her own agency and strategic appeals for their compassion. She turned sentimental writing into a vehicle for her own self-determination rather than a genre producing cathartic specimens of the suffering slave that ultimately stimulate the privileged reader.[49]

Morality, Jacobs insisted, does not transcend material conditions; it is enabled by them. Yet her narrator's voice remains somewhat unconvinced by her own claims. Her shame at violating the standards of Christian monogamy bleeds through her writing. Whether this shame is a transparent reflection of Jacobs's own feeling, or a strategic figuration of the trope of the suffering slave her white women readers would have expected of Linda Brent, is difficult to determine. Though she wrote within the sentimental genre, she aimed to elicit empathy and understanding for the position of enslaved women—not to glorify the transformative power of white women's tears. The beating heart of the narrative is Linda Brent's intertwined agency and defeat.

After four years of writing at night between the cries of the Willis babies and lingering pains shooting through her limbs from her seven years entombed, Jacobs completed her manuscript. Her brother John wrote from England, where he was now working as a sailor, inviting her to visit. She knew that American slave narratives were often released first by British publishers before they found backing stateside. In May 1858, she crossed the Atlantic once more, after outfitting herself with letters of introduction from prominent Garrisonian abolitionists in Boston. Her connections did glean her an invitation from the Duchess of Sutherland to a party at Stafford House, but John had already sailed for Constantinople, and she was unable to secure a publisher. Perhaps the sexual content, Yellin speculates, violated the rigid standards of public taste in Victorian England.[50]

Jacobs returned to America, dampened in spirits and in finances. John Brown's attempted raid on Harpers Ferry the following year rekindled her spark, and she approached the Boston publisher Phillips and Sampson. They were interested but only willing to publish her narrative with a preface from a well-known white author, specifically Stowe or Nathaniel Parker Willis. Given the slaveholding guests Willis entertained at Idlewild and the romantic sketches of Southern life he printed in the nation's leading magazines, Jacobs remained convinced that her employer supported slavery, and she wouldn't stoop to asking him.[51] Swallowing her pride, she once more reached out to Stowe.

Once more, Stowe declined to offer any support.

Jacobs approached a second publisher, who offered a contract if she secured a preface from a different white author, the well-known abolitionist novelist and journalist Lydia Maria Child. Fearing Child would behave as Stowe had, Jacobs confided to Amy Post that "I tremble at the thought of approaching another Satellite of so great a magnitude," but am "resolved to make my last effort." Fortunately, while Child was also a sentimental novelist who preferred "Mrs. Stowe to all other writers in the world," she was cut from different cloth than her literary idol. Child accepted the project and offered her editing services to Jacobs, primarily in rearranging the order of sentences, paragraphs, and chapters for continuity and dramatic tension. Remarkably, given Jacobs's utter lack of formal education, Child changed fewer than fifty words of the prose itself. The searing writing of *Incidents in the Life of a Slave Girl* is the work of Jacobs alone.[52]

But the path to publication was not yet smooth. Despite a signed contract, undertaken in Child's name to maintain Jacobs's anonymity, and advertisements announcing the text's impending publication date, the publisher failed to issue Jacobs's book. They had just released the third edition of Walt Whitman's *Leaves of Grass*, an illustrated, 450-page book more lavish than any they had undertaken before, and their coffers were empty. Thayer and Eldridge defaulted on all their contracts and hauled in their sidewalk shingle. Unfortunately, the debut of the Calamus poems, one of the most explicit gay works to be published in the United States for the next half century, had prevented the appearance of the country's first self-authored female slave narrative.[53] Yet again, Jacobs found herself with a book but without a publisher.

With characteristic drive, Jacobs decided to publish and distribute *Incidents* herself. She purchased the stereotyped plates from Thayer and Eldridge, arranged for the book to be printed and bound, and bought a thousand copies of the green-and-gold leather volume. Beginning in the winter of 1861, she toured throughout Boston, New York City, Philadelphia, and Washington, DC, on the Garrisonian abolitionist circuit, selling her book for $1 a copy. The Garrisonian press published warm reviews, though the book didn't gain a broad readership in the United States. A London edition soon followed, however, that received high praise from mainstream English newspapers.[54]

Yet it would take more than a century for Jacobs's book to be recognized as the groundbreaking work it is. As the study of literature consolidated into a profession in university English departments in the twentieth century, scholars insisted that no enslaved woman could have lived such a life or penned such a tale. The text was pure fiction, they declared, invented by the talented Lydia Maria Child. Jacobs's authorship was not forgotten—it was dismissed. Some Black women librarians, however, reportedly refused this new orthodoxy and still cataloged and shelved *Incidents* as Jacobs's work. But it wasn't until feminist scholar Jean Fagan Yellin completed nearly a decade of archival research in the mid-1980s that Jacobs was once more widely recognized to be the author—and publisher!—of her own autobiography.[55]

A few months into Jacobs's book tour, the South Carolina militia bombarded Fort Sumter to force federal retreat from the newly seceded territory, launching the Civil War. Over the next year, tens of thousands of enslaved people fled the homes and plantations of the lately formed Confederacy for the free territory of the North. While Congress had suspended the Fugitive Slave Law among seceded states, refugees from slavery nonetheless faced homelessness, hunger, and severe poverty—many did not even have shoes—as they gathered in the Union-controlled city of Washington, DC, just under a hundred miles from the Confederate capital of Richmond, Virginia.

Jacobs was well on her way to establishing herself as a major abolitionist speaker and writer, a career that likely would have enabled her greatest wish, a home of her own. But as she read of the dangerous conditions those escaping slavery suffered, she felt called instead to solidarity work with her fellow self-emancipators on the streets of DC. She spent the winter of 1862 creating a supply chain of shoes, clothing, and blankets in New York and Philadelphia, and made lengthy trips to DC beginning in early spring.[56] That summer, she worked in the refugee camp, composed mostly of women, children, the elderly, and disabled who couldn't travel as freely nor enlist in the Union Army as younger men could. Conditions were despicable. People often lacked blankets or a change of clothing, and measles, smallpox, and typhoid fever were rampant. Jacobs began each day by counting the dead bodies lying upon the floor; some mornings ten people hadn't made it through the night.

Over the next five years, Jacobs organized with Black women's and white women's groups to improve conditions, gathering supplies, fighting to stop guards from whipping migrants for violating camp rules, and serving as a camp matron in Alexandria, Virginia. Meanwhile, she wrote lengthy letters to the abolitionist press filled with the suffering and self-determination of the self-emancipating; her first communication to William Lloyd Garrison for his *Liberator* ran forty thousand words. At the same time, Jacobs dipped her toes into national feminist organizing. At a fall 1863 meeting in New York, she was unanimously appointed to the executive committee of Stanton and Anthony's Woman's National Loyal League, their organization founded to circulate their mass petition urging emancipation.[57]

Jacobs continued her relief work with refugees and freedmen following Robert E. Lee's surrender in 1865. A common theme emerged throughout her efforts during and after the Civil War, many of which her daughter Louisa joined: they insisted the formerly enslaved could and would lead their own battle for education, wage labor, and family autonomy, and rejected the disciplining hand of whites. But they, too, had to learn to trust Black autonomy.

"These people, born and bred in slavery, had always been so accustomed to look upon the white race as their natural superiors and masters, that we had some doubts whether they could easily throw off the habit," Jacobs wrote to Lydia Maria Child. But Jacobs and Louisa established the Jacobs School for emancipated slaves in Alexandria with the support of freedpeople. The pair were able to block the trustee-appointed white head teacher in favor of Louisa's leadership, and the Jacobses took it as a sign that "even their brief possession of freedom had begun to inspire them with respect for the race." Harriet and Louisa took a similar approach to fundraising, refusing to ask for cash from Northern antislavery societies, and instead requesting surplus rummage sale items, which they then sold, an act closer to mutual aid than to charity. The Jacobses used their positions of influence to teach freedpeople to join, in Jacobs's words, "civilized life."[58]

If some of Jacobs and Louisa's rhetoric echoed the civilizing agenda of Stowe and her cohort of white women, their tactics did not. While assisting refugees in Savannah, Georgia, after the war, Louisa established another Black-led free school, and they both supported the elderly and orphaned while continuing to report back to the North. Louisa, meanwhile, began organizing in the suffrage campaign at the national level. Inspired by Frances E. W. Harper's 1866 speech at the inaugural AERA convention, in which Harper instructed the audience, "You white women speak here of rights. I speak of wrongs," Louisa began touring on the lecture circuit—just as her mother had hoped more than a decade prior when she first reached out to Stowe.[59]

Occasionally, Louisa was joined on the AERA platform by Elizabeth Cady Stanton and Susan B. Anthony, the latter of whom praised Louisa as "good looking" and "everything proper & right in matter and manner—private and public." But Louisa was ultimately more at home providing direct service to fellow former slaves than speaking twice a day with white feminists who painted Black freedmen, not white enslavers, as the true threat to women's rights. By the time the AERA dissolved and Stanton and Anthony formed their white feminist organization in 1869, Louisa had been absent from the women's suffrage movement for two years. Her work, like that of her mother, was among the freedpeople.[60]

While Louisa was on western New York stages alongside Stanton and Anthony, Harriet Beecher Stowe and her husband Calvin packed up their carpets, furniture, and extra china and boarded a ship south to Florida. Together with some friends, they had leased the state's largest cotton plantation, Laurel Grove. The venture took them to the banks of the St. Johns River south of Jacksonville and aimed to provide the Stowe family with income as well as escape: for Stowe, from the Connecticut snowdrifts that accumulated well into April, and for their son Frederick, from the reckless alcoholism plaguing him even before shrapnel pierced his ear on the southern battlefield.[61] It also would enable Stowe to undertake an experiment similar to that of her *Uncle Tom's Cabin* character Miss Ophelia: she herself would attempt to civilize the formerly enslaved.

"My heart is with that poor people whose cause in words I have tried to plead," Stowe explained to her brother Charles, "and who now, ignorant and docile, are just in that formative stage in which whoever seizes has them." Stowe saw that capitalists were keen to exploit the newly emancipated workforce; she, by contrast, intended to wield her beneficent influence and establish "a Christian neighborhood."[62]

Stowe's missionary zeal was part of a larger white feminist movement after the war to save the so-called uncivilized from themselves. In the North, white women raised millions of dollars to support schools and hospitals, while an additional four thousand traveled south to teach newly freedpeople literacy, work habits, and Protestant faith. Much of this work brought desperately needed education to the formerly enslaved. But it emerged from within the civilizing paradigm to spread white women's alleged moral authority and typically came with a host of conditions, such as that the only suitable instructors were white. These Reconstruction projects had echoes across the country. White women reformers established schools, homes, and social welfare organizations to elevate the so-called primitive in places like Mormon settlements in Utah, San Francisco's Chinatown, and Indigenous lands across the West.[63] Yet while white feminist activists were broadly eager to get their hands dirty in civilizing work, few went so far as to take charge of a massive Southern plantation.

Stowe and her friends arrived at the dilapidated planters' house at nightfall, where the women were told to wait on the broad veranda while the men of their party assisted the servants in hauling up the household goods from their boat's landing. Stowe was spooked by the unfamiliar plantation sights around her, especially as the light slipped away, and even more so by the workers returning from the fields. "As one and another passed by," she reported, "they seemed blacker, stranger, and more dismal, than any thing we had ever seen. The women wore men's hats and boots, and had the gait and stride of men."[64] In Stowe's mind, she had not only journeyed south—she had also traveled back to the primitive past, a world in which womanhood had not yet evolved.

At dawn, the February sunshine streaming through the cottage's broken windows reawakened Stowe to her Florida dream. Her view of the plantation's workers was akin to her view of the single-story house, ramshackle after four years of war: relics of the crude past that she would develop into supports for refined white life, for their good as well as her own. She sought to impose order upon house and worker alike. "As the first white ladies upon the ground, Mrs. F—— and myself had the task of organizing this barbaric household," Stowe recalled, "and of bringing it into the forms of civilized life. We commenced with the washing."[65]

Civilizing, as Stowe and her sister Catharine Beecher explained to middle-class readers of their immensely popular housekeeping manuals published before and after the war, required white women to assume "the duties of missionaries" and "supply the place of parents" to an immature, "undeveloped" servant class. Servants were not autonomous people but "raw, untrained" material that "must be *made*, by patience and training," into a household asset. Their maternal language of sympathetic benevolence barely masked the economy of extraction lying beneath, in which they instructed white women to provide servants with comfortable rooms, teach them how to maintain their wardrobes, present them with small gifts of spelling books and other useful items, and, above all, shed sympathetic tears, in order to win their obedience. By subduing their servants—in Stowe's case, the formerly enslaved—with the weapon of sympathy, white women could simultaneously build their own power, authority, and capital. Housewives embraced their message enthusiastically: Stowe and Beecher's jointly authored *New Housekeeper's Manual* was printed over twenty-five times in twenty-five years, making it one of the most important domestic advice books of the era.[66]

Stowe nonetheless felt begrudging respect for one female servant, Minnah, who refused to be disciplined. "Democracy," Stowe opined, "never
assumes a more rampant form than in some of these old negresses" whose
wildness prohibited them from swallowing the insults of their enslavers.
Minnah's back bore the traces of the galling abuse she received in return,
such as being stretched on a log and staked in by her hands and feet while her
enslaver scored her flesh. "For all that, Minnah was neither broken nor hum-
bled: she still asserted her rights as a human being," Stowe noted approv-
ingly. Minnah's resistance extended all the way to Stowe's civilizing agenda.
As the only female worker with some experience in domestic tasks, she was
assigned the role of house servant. But Minnah was often "argumentative,"
and she found housework "disgusting," vastly inferior to working outside.
Soon Minnah had her way: Stowe was forced to admit that the fields suited
her better, and Stowe hired a housekeeper from Jacksonville.[67]

The Civil War had laid the Laurel Grove plantation, along with much of
Florida, to waste. While Laurel Grove once boasted nine thousand acres,
Stowe and partners could afford to plant only two hundred acres of cotton,
from which they nonetheless estimated a sizable $10,000 profit. Nature, how-
ever, had its own designs. When the crop budded and bolled in white, an in-
vasion of army worms chewed through all two hundred acres in two days flat.
Their financial investment had gone to seed. Stowe declared it a victory nonetheless: "Our hands were all duly paid," she wrote to the *Atlantic Monthly*, a
magazine she had helped found, "in many cases with the first money they ever
earned, and it gave them a start in life."[68] All along, Stowe's chosen crop was
the workers themselves.

Foreswearing cotton, that spring Stowe and her husband bought land
across the St. Johns River that included a grove producing seventy-five thousand oranges per year and a house tucked under eighty-foot-tall live oaks festooned with hanging mosses. She and Calvin spent the next eighteen winters
at their Mandarin, Florida, plantation, and they built out the small house
into a gabled cottage encircling a magnificent oak. She lent key support to
building a school and an Episcopalian church for local African Americans,
generally rehabilitating the South in the way she knew how: by raising the
Black worker out of their "barren, confined, undeveloped nature" and into
the service of civilization.[69]

Harriet Beecher Stowe and family on the veranda of their Florida plantation
home. (Courtesy of the State Archive of Florida)

This agenda reflected Stowe's own education since she released *Uncle Tom's
Cabin*, which famously ends with every Black character either dead or having
fled the United States. Her novel found no place for freed African Americans
within the country's borders, a plot detail Black abolitionists like Delany roundly
critiqued. Stowe learned from her mistake and followed up the novel with another, *Dred* (1856), featuring a dark-skinned protagonist who self-emancipates
and encourages broad slave insurrection. Her Florida project was another venture to imagine a national future that had a place for the Black worker.

Yet this is precisely how Stowe conceived of her task: as finding, and assigning, Black workers a place in the transforming capitalist economy of the
South. Their role was as the naturally suited wage laborers of tropical climes.
"Only those black men, with sinews of steel and nerves of wire,—men who
grow stronger and more vigorous under those burning suns that wither the

white men,—are competent to the task" of fieldwork in Florida, she insisted. White men grew "sickly" under the Florida sun, whereas Black workers "ran and shouted and jabbered" in delight. If whites living in Southern heat continued to disdain Black communities, rather than adopt their duty "to educate a docile race who both can and will bear it for them," Stowe warned, they would imperil the fate of Southern capitalism.[70]

Stowe maintained confidence that Northern investment would rehabilitate both the economy and the formerly enslaved people of the South. She sold $1,500 worth of citrus a year packaged in crates with her own label boasting "Oranges from Harriet Beecher Stowe—Mandarin, Fla"; from her stately home she made oil paintings of white blossoms and golden fruits clustered against a blue sky.[71] Her choice crop may have been cultivating the workers, but the products of their labor were hers to reap.

~ ~

One December day six years after the end of the Civil War, the two writers at last met face to face. Jacobs had been working as a clerk at the New England Women's Club in Boston, and in a few months she and Louisa would open a boarding house in Cambridge—their first home in twenty-five years. Stowe, not yet gone south to Florida, came to Cambridge to visit her stepsister, who likely arranged the meeting. Stowe gifted Jacobs with a copy of Uncle Tom's Cabin in which she had written "Mrs. Harriet Jacobs from H.B. Stowe, Christmas, 1871." The honorific "Mrs." may have pleased Jacobs—despite her unmarried status, she had adopted the title during her refugee relief work in Washington and was widely addressed as such by fellow abolitionists. Stowe, in this small gesture, finally acknowledged a measure of Jacobs's self-determination. The volume remained a treasured item in the Jacobs family for the next century.[72]

Meanwhile, at home in Hartford, Connecticut, Stowe had a treasured volume of her own, or rather, twenty-six of them. The half million signatures affirming the Stafford House appeal, all addressed to Stowe, were displayed prominently on oaken shelves.[73] The petition, like the golden slave shackle bracelet she received the same day, reminded Stowe of her place in history: she was a writer who taught white women the power of their sympathy.

CHAPTER THREE

SETTLER MOTHERS AND NATIVE ORPHANS

Alice C. Fletcher and Zitkala-Ša

[By aiding] the Vicious and Dependent classes . . . woman is fast becoming recognized as a human being.

—Anna Garlin Spencer

BEFORE EIGHT-YEAR-OLD ZITKALA-ŠA HEARD ABOUT THE BIG RED APPLES IN THE EAST, she ran free over the prairie and rolling green hills of southeastern South Dakota. Once finished with her morning's work sewing her own beaded designs on buckskin or helping her mother dry fruits or meat for winter, she bounded out into the slopes that ascended behind their canvas wigwam. She and a handful of playmates would dig for sweet roots, regale each other with heroic stories in earnest imitation of the tales their mothers and aunts told over evening campfires, and run through the hills chasing shapeshifting shadows as the wind sent their long black hair flowing like rivers behind them. Safely nestled in the "lap of the prairie" and "alive to the fire within," Zitkala-Ša was sure that her "wild freedom and overflowing spirits" were her "mother's pride."[1] One mid-winter day, however, that freewheeling spirit lured her eight hundred miles away to a boarding school that would transform her bond with her mother, and her tribe, for the rest of her life.

It was February in 1884 when two Quaker missionaries entered the Yankton Indian Reservation village where Zitkala-Ša, then known as Gertrude
Simmons, lived with her mother, Reaches-for-the-Wind. Her father was
gone; a white man, he had abandoned her mother and community soon after she became pregnant. Reaches-for-the-Wind gave her newborn daughter
the surname of her much favored prior husband, who had passed away before Zitkala-Ša was born. She had seen much hardship. The Yankton Dakota
were one of the seven Dakota-, Lakota-, and Nakota-speaking groups comprising the confederated Sioux tribe. Living along the grassy eastern banks
of the muddy, but life-giving, Missouri River, their village had been home
to the tribe for only thirty-five years, after an 1859 treaty stripped them of
rights to 95 percent of their eleven-million-acre Minnesota homeland and
forced them westward.[2] To young Zitkala-Ša, however, the riverbank and
hills were her Eden.

When the two missionaries and their white interpreter approached
Reaches-for-the-Wind's wigwam, young Zitkala-Ša jumped up and down
in impatience, begging her mother to permit them entry. She had heard her
friend Judéwin tell of beautiful lands full of red apple orchards where she was
going to live with the missionaries. Zitkala-Ša had eaten fewer than a dozen
red apples in her life and her desire was piqued. In the wake of the Sioux's
dramatic loss of power, her mother had allowed Zitkala-Ša's older brother to
attend boarding school in hopes he could learn to negotiate the settler society pressing ever closer upon them. This also gave her some familiarity with
the trauma a young child endured when ripped from their community and
housed in an institution.

"Don't believe a word they say!" she cautioned her daughter. "Their words
are sweet, but, my child, their deeds are bitter. You will cry for me, but they
will not even soothe you."

But eventually Reaches-for-the-Wind yielded to her eager child, permitting
the Quaker visitors entry into her wigwam.

"Mother, ask them if little girls may have all the red apples they want, when
they go East," implored Zitkala-Ša.[3]

The interpreter knew just how to answer, and also promised the child a ride
on the iron horse. After a night of pleading and hot tears, Zitkala-Ša outran her
mother's objections with the force of her desire. Though Reaches-for-the-Wind

worried that her daughter was too young, she also wished for Zitkala-Ša to attain an education.

Zitkala-Ša was one of the youngest members of a party of eight children the missionaries removed from the village, taking them eight hundred miles east to White's Manual Labor Institute. The morning of departure, she, Judéwin, and her other friends proudly showed each other their new dresses, belts, and beaded moccasins. From the horse-drawn carriage carrying them toward the train station she watched her mother's figure grow smaller and smaller in the distance. A sense of misgiving flooded her spirit, and the eight-year-old child buried her tears in the soft folds of her best blanket.

White's Manual Labor Institute in Wabash, Indiana, couldn't have been more aptly named. Like other boarding schools established in the early 1880s for Indigenous youth, it was designed to produce assimilated workers. It was also an apparatus of death, for boarding schools' seemingly benevolent intentions to train Indigenous youth simultaneously destroyed tribal communities. Richard Henry Pratt, the founder of the first off-reservation boarding school, agreed in large part with General Philip Sheridan's notorious edict that "the only good Indian is a dead Indian." But Pratt's approach was to grind up the Indian with the machinery of education. Boarding schools would "kill the Indian in him, and save the man," Pratt infamously pronounced.[4] Institutionalizing children for at least three years was intended to break their attachment to their tribes and land.

Off-reservation boarding schools form a notorious episode in the long history of child removal in the United States. This history roared back to life in the summer of 2018, when the Trump administration established child separation policies and built family detention camps on the US-Mexico border that have detained more than three hundred thousand children and separated over a thousand children from their refuge-seeking parents.[5] Whether designed to intimidate and threaten refugee families, as Trump's policies sought to do, or to dispossess tribes of their future by assimilating Native youth into capitalist civilization, as the boarding schools intended, separating children from their parents is widely recognized as a form of trauma and cultural warfare with repercussions that persist for generations.

But less well known is that removing Native children from their families, tribes, and territories simultaneously forms a significant episode in the history and counterhistory of white feminism. The machinery of civilization threatened to pulverize Native youth into mere remnants of the past—and white women would reap many of the profits.

~ ~

In the fall of 1879, while three-year-old Zitkala-Ša was playing with friends in Yankton territory, Alice Cunningham Fletcher, a forty-one-year-old white woman in Brooklyn, found an unexpected new outlet for her feminism. She had been a leader of the burgeoning clubwomen scene in New York for a decade. Enthusiastic about her experience as a member of the first society for career women in the country, Sorosis, she helped expand it into a national organization called the Association for the Advancement of Women (AAW), for which she served as cofounder, secretary, and conference organizer. These clubs shattered decorum, bringing "talented, cultivated and beneficent women" together in public at halls and restaurants without the customary accompaniment of men. Through networking, charity, and educational lectures, clubwomen sought to advance their personal and professional status.[6]

Though many reformers joined Sorosis and AAW, the ultimate goal of these middle-class clubs was respectability, not politics—discussion of suffrage was prohibited. The clubwomen movement soon sprung up in cities across the country, comprising a third, genteel strain of white feminism developing in the wake of Seneca Falls. Its approach was distinct from the strident, political activism of Susan B. Anthony and especially Elizabeth Cady Stanton, who sought to transform laws and social mores. And it differed from the high-handed, emotion-driven patronage of Harriet Beecher Stowe and other sentimentalists who parlayed white women's feelings into sources of authority. Clubwomen, by contrast, drew upon white women's alleged moral authority to carve out a place for themselves in the country's social and professional institutions. Their societies sought access, not civil rights or social transformation. Yet clubwomen's motivations lay not only in self-interested desire to succeed as individuals. They had a collective goal, though a highly limited one: to promote the personal and career success of bourgeois white women. When asked to supply details of her biography for a volume on prominent American women, Fletcher refrained from touting her own accomplishments and replied, "Write me as one who loves her fellow-women."[7]

That winter, Fletcher attended a lecture at Boston's Faneuil Hall that expanded her life's direction. Chief Standing Bear, a leader of the Ponca tribe, was touring the East Coast with the Omaha translator Susette "Bright Eyes" La Flesche and her brother Francis, aiming to gain support for the Poncas' plight. Two years prior, the US government had unilaterally canceled the 1858 treaty that granted the Ponca rights to the northern Nebraska land with which they had lived in dynamic relation for millennia and remanded them south to Arkansas Indian Territory. Standing Bear was advocating for Ponca rights to live in Nebraska, but for much of the white audience, it was his humanity that was up for debate. Fletcher was struck by Susette La Flesche's eloquence, grasping that "the door of language could be unlocked and intelligent relations made possible between the two races."[8]

Within two years, studying—and reforming—Native women and families would become Alice Fletcher's central objective in life. She devoted herself to anthropology, a rapidly developing science that approached the Indigenous as if they held the secrets to the primitive beginnings of humanity. To understand, and revise, "barbarous" traditions and worldviews, she spent months and seasons living among Native tribes in Nebraska, Oklahoma, Ohio, Colorado, Wyoming, Idaho, Wisconsin, and South and North Dakota. Moved to genuine respect for some aspects of Native life and appalled by the treachery of white settlers who surrounded and stole Native lands, Fletcher was moved to join the cause of Indian reform. She became the most prominent white woman activist for Native rights of her era. Yet she positioned Native people as her charges and herself as the benevolent and powerful white mother. "The Indians cling to me like children," she wrote to her mentor from the Nez Perce Reservation in northern Idaho, "and I must and will protect them."[9]

Fletcher shared the civilizing impulse universal to white feminism of her era, though we might call the specific philosophy she and the other clubwomen in Indian reform developed "settler feminism."[10] Their method was severance: severing Indigenous children from their parents and tribes and severing communally held lands into individual property allotments, subjugating Native people to the patriarchal and monogamous norms of settler life. Meanwhile, the more Fletcher dispossessed Native women and tribes of their traditional social roles, the more she broke through norms herself and gained increased political and social power. She became the first woman to be appointed to a research position at Harvard, a full eighty-five years before the institution even admitted female undergraduates. Her prolific output made her the most respected and influential woman scientist of the last quarter of the nineteenth century.

Settler white feminists liberated themselves through assuming authority over the Indigenous. Yet it was far from the only kind of feminism in the West. Zitkala-Ša would become an artist and feminist activist who would unite tribes to push back against theft disguised as benevolence.

⌒ ⌒

When the Civil War came to a close in 1865, the Indian Wars heated up. Across the West, Indigenous tribes fought US soldiers for the next two and a half decades for the right to live among their lands. The confederated Sioux tribes, led by Lakota warriors including Sitting Bull, Red Cloud, and Crazy Horse, executed the most successful resistance ever mounted by Indigenous groups in US history. In 1868, the Lakota Sioux and Cheyenne became the first and only Natives to win a major war against the US government. The Bozeman War resulted in a treaty securing total control of their vast lands and hunting grounds that spread across the Dakotas and reached into present-day Wyoming, Montana, Nebraska, and Colorado.[11] The remarkably recent date of such a major Native victory testifies to the lasting power of the Sioux.

But US officials didn't respect the treaty. When George Armstrong Custer's thousand-person expedition illegally mining Sioux lands struck the gold they were determined to find in the Black Hills in 1874, the tribes' fortunes changed drastically. Settlers prospecting for the valuable mineral, often guided by US troops, flooded the area. Crazy Horse, Sitting Bull, and other Lakota and Cheyenne leaders famously defeated Custer and his Seventh Cavalry at the Battle of the Little Big Horn in 1876, the year Zitkala-Ša was born just to the east among the Yankton Dakota. But the Sioux ultimately lost the Black Hills War and were forced to surrender to US forces by 1877. Sioux lands dwindled to just over 10 percent of their former size as the US Army seized control of everything but central South Dakota. Leaders including Red Cloud and Spotted Tail moved onto Rosebud, Standing Rock, Pine Ridge, and other Dakota reservations to the west and north of the Yanktons', where they were subject to the whims of capricious agents who cut their food rations in half or let the beef, tobacco, and grain spoil entirely.[12] Sitting Bull (Hunkpapa Lakota) had served the Black Hills War as a spiritual adviser after a vision that foresaw their triumph over Custer. Refusing to submit to US control when the war was lost, Sitting Bull and nearly two hundred family members and supporters fled north across the Canadian border to the hills of Saskatchewan to evade capture.

Yet after four years of resistance, the fifty-year-old Sitting Bull and his band of 168 people were forced to travel south and surrender to US forces. The buffalo herds that had sustained their people for millennia had all but disappeared, deliberately slaughtered by determined US and Canadian militaries and private citizens to starve the Plains tribes into death. Only ten to fifteen million buffalo remained in the Great Plains by 1865, down from a precontact population of up to sixty-five million. By the early 1880s, the military had reduced the buffalo population to only a few hundred survivors. Sitting Bull and his band were now held as prisoners of war at Fort Randall, South Dakota, a few miles across the Missouri River from the Yankton village where then five-year-old Zitkala-Ša roamed the hills. An officer counted each person every morning.[13]

In October 1881, two years after she had attended Standing Bear's Boston lecture, Alice Fletcher sat somewhat awkwardly in a tight-waisted, full-skirted dress around a fire in Sitting Bull's tent. Sitting Bull explained to Fletcher that desperate hunger had compelled him to surrender three months prior.

"The old life is gone," Sitting Bull told Fletcher while Buffalo Chip (Omaha) interpreted. "The skill of the hunter is now of no use; nor is the valor of the warrior."[14] The young would have to turn to plowing the prairie and other ways of the settler in order to survive.

As Sitting Bull spoke, his younger wife entered the tipi and threw sticks on the fire before reclining in its glow. Adroitly leaning upon one elbow, she turned her eyes upon Fletcher, no doubt assessing this unusual newcomer. The budding anthropologist looked back, cataloging the woman's bright eyes, good looks, and brass bracelets. Sitting Bull, too, gazed upon his wife, before once more addressing Fletcher.[15]

"You are a woman," he began slowly. "Take pity on my women, for they have no future. The young men can be like the white men, till the soil, supply the food and clothing, they will take the work out of the hands of the women, and the women, to whom we have owed every thing in the past, will be stripped of all which gave them power and position among the people. Give a future to my women!"[16]

Fletcher found herself a guest of Sitting Bull's because she had traveled west to study "the life of Indian women."[17] Earlier that year, Fletcher had approached Susette La Flesche, who arranged for Fletcher to camp with the Omaha in Nebraska for three weeks before traveling northward to the Sioux. To gain permission from the Bureau of Indian Affairs agents to enter the reservations, she secured research sponsorship from the Peabody Museum and the federal Bureau of Ethnology.

"I wish to get at Indian women's life from the inside," she had written to bureau director John Wesley Powell, "and as the segregation of the sexes is marked among barbarous people, I trust that being a woman I may be able to observe and record facts and conditions" inaccessible to male anthropologists.[18] Now she was collecting prime data straight from one of the country's most notorious Native rebels.

Anthropology, as it was understood in the nineteenth century, was the science that investigated the evolution of human society. Anthropologists approached the entire history of human culture as one linear process of development from savagery, to barbarism, to civilization. In this rigid model, only Europeans had arrived at civilized maturity. Racialized people were figured as specimens of arrested development, frozen in earlier life stages of humanity. People of African descent were imagined to be congealed in a savagery from which they would never progress. Natives were consigned to the stage of barbarism, an arrested stage in the evolution of humans; anthropologists approached them as lingering relics of the receding past, not as living members of the present in charge of their own future.

Alice Fletcher made several early innovations in anthropology's methods and application. Her first contribution was to argue that Native societies, because they were the imagined origins of her own, thus held the clue to understanding the oppression of women in civilization. Fletcher would not only promote the further development of professional white women—she intended to pinpoint the origins of their troubles by investigating the Indigenous cultures of the West. This work "preserving the record" of the past, as she put it, would help white women seize a greater role in civilization's boundless future.[19]

White feminism, in other words, had come to the sciences.

⌒　⌒

When she met Sitting Bull, Fletcher was beginning to undertake her first fieldwork. But she was encountering a surprising set of data. The scientific and reform opinion of Fletcher's day was that barbarous groups were sex segregated, meaning that men and women lived largely separate existences characterized by drastic inequality in which men exploited women's labor. Indian societies were imagined to be so far down the evolutionary scale of development that women were drudges, simply menial laborers abused by their idle husbands. Racist images of "squaws" portrayed with papooses strapped to their backs as they stooped over the fields abounded in the popular and scientific press. Sara Kinney, a leader of the Women's National Indian Association (WNAI), a white feminist reform organization founded in 1879, articulated the received wisdom bluntly: "In the native order of society, the home, as we understand it, cannot exist."[20]

Civilized societies, by contrast, were portrayed as having achieved the landmark state of binary sex specialization, a state of complementary opposites in mind, body, and emotion. Sex specialization meant that men managed the public sphere of business and politics and women presided angelically over the private realm of hearth and home, but they formed allegedly equal halves of a partnership. In this fantasy, civilized men freed middle-class white women from the need to labor, as child-rearing and managing the household were misapprehended as free gifts of the heart rather than efforts of the hand.

But Fletcher was realizing that Lakota and Omaha women had freedoms and responsibilities of which white women could only dream. "The Indian woman," Fletcher concluded, "considers herself quite independent. She controls her labor, her possessions and follows her own inclinations if she has sufficient determination." Contrary to accepted wisdom, the Native woman "is not necessarily the slave of the man." Rather, her work stoking the fires; making the food, tents, and clothing; and raising corn, beans, and pumpkins meant that "she is the conserver of life," a position that came with many privileges and was awarded due respect.[21] Now, Sitting Bull was telling Fletcher directly: Lakota women had more freedom and power than the white women of the West. He was also, in her rendering, asking Fletcher for help.

For Fletcher and other white feminists, assistance meant taking guardian-ship *over* people of color. Fletcher felt that Indigenous people were not doomed to be forever suspended in the barbarian stage of development. They could be saved, trained into the habits of civilized sex specialization. "It is good to think of the so-called dependent races as children," rather than through the lens of "savagery" or "barbarism," she corrected in 1900.[22] Natives were not frozen in prehistory, as her colleagues believed. They were in need of a mother—a white mother, who could raise the race into maturity.

Amelia Quinton, president of the Women's National Indian Association, put it best. "The Indian Question must become more and more a woman ques-tion," she instructed. "When all legal rights are assured, and all fair educa-tional facilities provided, the women and children of the tribes will still be a sacred responsibility laid upon the white women of the land."[23]

Despite Fletcher's limited experience—visiting two tribes for six weeks total, while reliant on translators—she was now ready to call herself an ex-pert in Native life writ large. And indeed, she had now acquired more first-hand experience with Indigenous tribes than had most other social scientists in the United States. Throughout the 1880s and 1890s, Fletcher pushed for assimilation with full knowledge of the loss of liberties Native women would experience. Men needed to labor in the fields while women took care of the home and children. In historian Louise Newman's words, Fletcher and other white women reformers believed that "Indian women were to be given the gift of patriarchy."[24] Her white feminist position explicitly and knowingly helped undermine Indigenous women's traditional authority—while simultaneously taking inspiration from them to realize her own budding professional and po-litical power.

~ ~

Zitkala-Ša arrived at White's Manual Labor Institute at nightfall in March 1884 after three days of hard travel. Already unnerved by the incessant gaping of strangers on the train, she now faced a new sensory onslaught: a whitewashed two-story building illuminated by blinding gaslight. The eight-year-old child hugged the wall for safety, but to her horror, "two warm hands grasped" her, and a "paleface" woman tossed her up and down in the air. Unable to communicate a word with any of the adults and unused to being "trifl[ed]" with as a "plaything," Zitkala-Ša burst into tears, tears that eventually carried her into sleep that evening.[25]

The first days were full of surprises: learning how to sit in a chair; "eating by formula" after a series of confusing bells and prayers; being stripped of her new dress, belt, moccasins, and all other objects from home and assigned a "clinging" dress and stiff shoes in their place.[26] Judéwin, whose limited knowledge of English nonetheless enabled her to understand adults who Zitkala-Ša felt were "deaf" to her concerns, caught wind of the afternoon plan to cut their hair. Zitkala-Ša was moved to rebellion. Hairstyle played a significant role in Dakota and Lakota culture, and short hair was the punishment for dishonored "cowards."

"No, I will not submit! I will struggle first!" she cried to her friends.

The teachers tied her to a chair, and soon Zitkala-Ša felt the "cold blades of the scissors against [her] neck . . . gnaw[ing] off" her "thick braids."[27]

Over the next weeks and months, Zitkala-Ša became acquainted with what she called "the iron routine" of "the civilizing machine." It was unrelenting, grinding from 6:30 a.m. roll call until the bedtime bell, and it paused for no one. White's Manual, like other off-reservation boarding schools, provided a strict industrial education. It emphasized cleanliness, promptitude, and Protestant Christianity. Sex-segregated training prepared boys to become carpenters, shoemakers, and farmers and taught girls the arts of domesticity. At White's, girls spent half the day working in eight areas of bourgeois housekeeping, including baking, handling and making dairy products, and maintaining the standards of the Victorian-era dining room and its dizzying amount of serving ware and cutlery. All pupils were forbidden from speaking unless it was in English. Fatal illness plagued boarding school children. Of the seventy-three youth removed from the Shoshone and Arapaho nations of the mountain West in the early 1880s, only twenty-six survived.[28]

Yet Zitkala-Ša continued to create little moments of resistance to express her anger. Sent to the kitchen as punishment for violating a school rule she found needlessly restrictive, she was assigned the task of mashing turnips, a vegetable whose very odor she found "offensive." Furious, she "bent in hot rage over the turnips" with such force that she shattered the bottom of the brown earthen jar. Dinner that day was turnip-free, and Zitkala-Ša "whooped in [her] heart for having once asserted the rebellion within."[29] Nearly twenty years later, she would pen these scenes for the most prestigious literary magazines of her day (and ours), such as *The Atlantic* and *Harper's*, of what befell her when, lured by red apples, she traveled east of Eden.

Zitkala-Ša's rage at the civilizing machine was well justified. Richard Henry Pratt took slavery and the prison as his models when he founded Carlisle Indian Industrial School, beginning off-reservation education. In his mind, enslavement had "forcibly transformed millions of primitive black people" into productive laborers through submitting them to "the care and authority of individuals of the higher race." He sought to do something similar. Removing Native children from their tribes and assimilating them into civilization as workers, he reasoned, would be the most effective way to assume control of Native lives and eradicate backward Indigenous cultures.[30]

When in 1879 Pratt approached the federal government for funding and the use of some military barracks in Carlisle, Pennsylvania, to establish a boarding school for Native youth, Indian commissioner E. A. Hayt jumped at this chance to hold the children of the Lakota Sioux and other resistant tribes "hostages for the good behavior of their people." It was only two years after the Black Hills War. While Sitting Bull and his band were evading capture in Canada, Pratt traveled throughout the Pine Ridge and Rosebud Reservations. He recruited pupils with false promises that his education would prepare the children of the Lakota to defend themselves so that a loss like that of the sacred Black Hills would not be repeated. Meanwhile, to fellow white reformers Pratt characterized the school as a fatal machinery that would bring about the "total annihilation of the Indians, as Indians and tribes."[31]

Yet it would not only be the military who benefited from taking Lakota and other Indigenous children hostage. Child removal proved to be a profitable career path for many white women. The civilizing machine required humans to run it: white women teachers. The boarding school movement presented them with significant new career opportunities. Middle-class white women in the mid- to late nineteenth century were still largely confined to the private sphere. But civilizing the West was deemed an appropriate extension of women's domestic duties. This "manifest domesticity," in scholar Amy Kaplan's memorable phrase, thrust white women's work into the center of the settler colonial enterprise. White women could respectably extend their own realm of power and influence through adopting a maternal attitude that saw Natives as children in need of their guidance. According to historian Margaret Jacobs, "the majority of boarding school employees nationwide" were white women.[32]

Reformers, especially white women, appointed themselves the task of upwardly evolving the Indigenous. Evolutionary theory in the late nineteenth century was overwhelmingly Lamarckian, meaning that everyone from Pratt and Fletcher to Charles Darwin believed that heredity was the result of repeated sensations and movements, not of a fixed, unchanging particle. They deemed childhood the most plastic stage of development, the period in which it was easiest to impress new traits into the flesh that would transmit down the generations. For reformers, environment during childhood, not inherent biology, determined heredity. Some schools thus removed Native youth from their parents at the astonishingly young age of three or four and only released them at the age of twenty-one in order to transform them, body and mind.[33]

The belief that physical traits resulted from childhood impressions granted white women a new and forceful kind of power over the population and its future. White women gained authority as civilizers by contrast with Native women, who were portrayed as backward creatures trapped in prehistory who dragged their children down with them. Breaking the tie between Native mothers and their youngsters thus seemed imperative to white reformers. Few reformers realized the truth Fletcher had discovered: that many Indigenous cultures were free from patriarchy, and women enjoyed considerable agency, responsibility, and freedom in their tribes.[34]

Boarding school children were acutely aware of the attempts to grind new experiences into their flesh through manual labor, physical beatings, and military-style discipline. A Sicangu and Oglala Lakota pupil whom Pratt recruited on his first trip to Rosebud, the writer Luther Standing Bear, later recalled, "The task before us was not only that of accepting new ideas and adopting new manners, but actual physical changes and discomfort had to be borne uncomplainingly until the body adjusted itself to new tastes and habits." Zitkala-Ša's accounts of her boarding school days are full of sensory detail bringing to life the trauma of her ordeal—an effective technique for enabling her readers to imagine that they, too, can feel the iron routine penetrating their flesh. She keenly apprehended both the scientific and military goals of Indian education. It is "heart rending," she later wrote to her lover, the Apache physician Carlos Montezuma, "to see a government try experiments upon a real race" that rendered boarding school children "practically prisoners of war."[35]

A year into Pratt's hostage experiment at Carlisle, Red Cloud, Spotted Tail, and other Lakota leaders traveled to Pennsylvania. They were horrified to discover their sons clothed in military dress, suffering from insufficient room and board, and subject to prison-style punishment. Spotted Tail's youngest son had been locked in solitary confinement for a week. While they all tried to bring their tribes' youth home, only Spotted Tail was permitted to withdraw his own children, and at his own expense.[36] More than three dozen Lakota children from Rosebud and Pine Ridge remained at Carlisle and would not be able to return home, even for a summer visit, until they had remained captive at Carlisle for three full years.

~ ~

Alice Fletcher's first paid position with the Indian reform movement was to accompany these thirty-eight Lakota children on their first trip back home to Pine Ridge and Rosebud three years later. She was also hired to recruit more children. Fletcher was returning to Sioux reservations she had visited the prior summer on her initial fieldwork trip, work that Pratt's boarding school had made possible, for she had been hosted by the family of a Carlisle student. But now in the summer of 1882 she served as Pratt's direct representative, the first phase of an alliance they maintained for decades. Fletcher then traveled south to the Omaha Reservation to round up more pupils for Carlisle and for Hampton (an industrial school for African Americans that recently had begun an Indian assimilation program). She removed at least three dozen children—more than had been planned. After escorting the children east to school she embarked on a lecture tour to raise the extra $1,800 in funds needed to accommodate the additional children; her event in Springfield, Massachusetts, drew a crowd of two thousand people. Pratt paid her $50 per month for her work.[37]

While at Red Cloud's Pine Ridge Reservation, Fletcher worked as both an employee of Pratt's and an unpaid anthropologist collecting for Harvard's Peabody Museum. She arrived in the middle of the Sun Dance, the most important spiritual festival among Plains Indians. It was announced as the last Sun Dance to be held at Pine Ridge: both the US and Canadian governments were outlawing the sacred ceremony, among others, in hopes it would help destroy Indigenous culture. The brutal white agents in charge of Pine Ridge were particularly intent on withholding food rations and prohibiting ceremonies as retribution for Red Cloud and his people's singular victory over US forces in the Bozeman War fourteen years prior. Over nine thousand people from the Oglala and Brule bands of the Lakota Sioux had gathered for this final Sun Dance, setting up their white tents in a circle three-quarters of a mile long that opened to the eastern sunrise. Red Cloud himself was adept at a mode of recruiting: when scientists entered his lands to dig for fossils or study his people, he tried to win them as allies in his own fight for survival. Fletcher was no exception, and Red Cloud informed her of the importance of the Sun Dance and its intention "to harden [our young men] to endurance" to fight their numerous enemies, both Indigenous and white.[38]

The Sun Dance ceremony involved four days of fasting, abstinence, and group prayer in preparation for the main event: two days of dancing around a cottonwood pole rising forty feet in the center of their circle. Two red banners and two rawhide effigies, one of a buffalo and another of a warrior with an erect penis, flew from the pole. One or more male dancers pierced their flesh with eagle or buffalo bone and tied themselves to the cottonwood; their dance gradually tore the bones from the flesh, creating ecstatic pain that sacrificed their bodies for the sake of individual and tribal protection.

Fletcher was determined to obtain the two effigies for the Peabody's natural history collection. The buffalo and warrior figure were prized elements of the ceremony wanted by many, but Fletcher secured the help of the white reservation agent and the local police force to win them for herself. When the police detached the penis before handing the rawhide figure to Fletcher, she balked and demanded its return, wanting as authentic a specimen as possible. To Fletcher, these weren't sacred or even obscene idols, but inert artifacts. She felt that collecting relics was necessary to preserve evidence of the primitive origins of society, which she was sure would soon vanish from the continent.[39] Preserving Native culture, however, worked through her method of choice: severance. In this case, she removed sacred phenomena from tribes and transformed them into static museum objects.

Fletcher didn't stop at removing objects. For years, she made friends with Native leaders and cajoled them to share the details of secret spiritual ceremonies such as the vision quest and White Buffalo feast. Most were extremely reluctant to divulge this information. But she usually prevailed, and one of her tactics was to convince leaders that if whites had better knowledge of Native lifeways, they would better understand and sympathize with Native land struggles. Hers was a version of Pratt's technique of persuasion. Both promoted the fantasy that better information, whether gained by Natives or settlers, would create a more equal power relationship between tribes and their colonizers. Yet data, like sympathy, do not break free of power: they are its result.

Fletcher's quest for knowledge knew few bounds, and she volunteered to have Indian graves dug up in order to extract skulls and skeletons from the Omaha and other tribes for interested friends back at the Peabody. Fletcher aimed to save Native culture, but as remnants of bodies and sacred objects preserved behind glass. In this act of theft, she had good company: over four thousand Native skulls amassed in East Coast museums during the period.[40]

Fletcher sought to place both Native objects and Native children under the guardianship of settlers, and she was a particularly enthusiastic promoter of Pratt's school. Over the next few years, Fletcher took men and women from Washington, DC, to Carlisle to observe firsthand the four hundred students learning to shoe horses, cook on wood-fired stoves, and march in military formation. When not organizing publicity trips to Carlisle, she lobbied to increase funding for the school and those like it. She sought to convince politicians that boarding schools were highly effective ways to assimilate Natives. Her efforts helped to double federal funding for Indian education in a few short years, and by 1885 the budget stretched to just shy of $1 million. By 1890, almost ten thousand Native children attended off- and on-reservation boarding schools that aimed to keep students for at least three years.[41] Off-reservation boarding schools remained in operation until the 1970s.

~ ~

After three years at White's Manual Labor Institute, Zitkala-Ša was eleven years old and permitted to return home for the summer. Perhaps she had been imagining a tearful reunion and days spent in companionable abandon in the hills. What she found, however, was that she "seemed to hang in the heart of chaos, beyond the touch or voice of human aid." The civilizing machine had ruptured her place in the world. Communication with her mother had become impossible. Her mother tried to soothe her daughter's anguish by giving her the one book in her possession, an Indian Bible. But Zitkala-Ša "felt more like burning the book." She was caught in the middle: unable to relate to her mother, yet "enraged" by the trappings of civilization that had penetrated her former idyll. A party on a moonlit night, as her friends gathered in their settler finery, only compounded her isolation. "They were no more young braves in blankets and eagle plumes, nor Indian maids with prettily painted cheeks," for they, too, had spent three years away at school.[42] Zitkala-Ša was desperate to join, but she had no hat nor close-fitting muslin dress trimmed with ribbons, and she had thrown away her hard-soled shoes in favor of moccasins. Excluded from her own peers, she cried and cried in the wigwam, to her mother's visible distress. Boarding school hadn't only changed her: it was changing the culture of her tribe.

Zitkala-Ša remained at home for a year and a half until her restlessness and love of reading and classical music pulled her back to boarding school for another three years. During her years back at school, the target of Zitkala-Ša's resistance began to shift. Increasingly, her frustration and rage were directed not at the civilizing machine but toward her mother, who now symbolized to her a preliterate, traditional way of life. For all its housetraining elements, White's Manual also taught Zitkala-Ša skills that opened her world, such as writing, oratory, and playing the violin and piano. Her critical power led her to continue to find fault with civilization, as well. She used her graduation speech, "The Progress of Women," as an occasion to voice her increasing feminist consciousness, objecting to the way women were relegated to a position of "subjugation" in white culture.[43]

Despite her mother's opposition, she enrolled at Earlham College, a coed Quaker institution located one hundred miles south of Wabash, where she excelled in public speaking. In 1896, she competed in the Indiana State Oratorical Competition as the official representative of Earlham. The evening contest took place at the city's lavish English Opera House, but Zitkala-Ša found it filled with "strong prejudice" and "worse than barbarian rudeness."

As the crowd of more than one thousand gathered, her fellow students whispered anti-Indian "slurs" throughout the hall. With a dry "burn" gathering in her breast, she took the podium to deliver her speech "Side by Side."

"The universe is the product of evolution," she began. "An ascending energy pervades all life." Like Fletcher, Zitkala-Ša was well acquainted with the evolutionary paradigm that governed turn-of-the-century intellectual thought, though she used the framework to insist that Natives were innately capable of progress. Hers was an assimilationist vision, but one in which both races possess equal capacity for progress and march "side by side" into the future that belongs to all.[44]

A group of students had coordinated their hostility in advance. When she finished, they unfurled a large white banner. "SQUAW," it read, with a racist caricature of an Indigenous woman. Ignorant drudge, sexless savage—this is the insult they hurled at her, "before [a] vast ocean of eyes."[45] Zitkala-Ša burned with anger, her teeth clenched. Yet she was to have some revenge, for she was awarded second prize in the state competition.

Fluent in two cultures, Zitkala-Ša pursued the one career path available to an educated Indigenous woman: teaching at an off-reservation boarding school. Illness and a need to make money prevented her from completing her Earlham degree, but she refused to go home. Though she was still "frail and languid," she traveled east to Pennsylvania, in 1897.[46] Now twenty-one years old, she saw boarding schools as providing beneficial education despite their militaristic ways and was eager to help civilize Indigenous people by teaching for Pratt at Carlisle.

Her misgivings began on the day of her arrival. Escorted to a small, "ghastly" white room whose insufficient windows were further covered by thick, dingy curtains, Zitkala-Ša sat in a stiff-backed chair in quiet horror, not even having removed her traveling hat when she heard a man's boots tramping down the hall. The "imposing" but "kindly" man greeted her after eyeing her up and down, with apparent disappointment.

"Ah ha! So you are the little Indian girl who created the excitement among the college orators!"

She knew at once he was Captain Pratt, and her sense of "ill fortune" grew stronger. When he left the room she cast her hat aside and collapsed onto the bed. It was an inauspicious beginning to another difficult period in her life.[47]

A month later, Captain Pratt summoned Zitkala-Ša to his office early one morning for a thirty-minute conversation during which only he spoke. At its close, one line rang in her ear.

"I am going to turn you loose to pasture!" Pratt was sending Zitkala-Ša west, home to Yankton, to recruit students for Carlisle.[48]

She went, eager for a reprieve from her labors at the school and for the opportunity to see her mother. Zitkala-Ša, as Fletcher had been, was now a paid recruiter for Carlisle. When she arrived back at the Yankton Reservation, conditions made her ill at heart. Her brother Dawée, once a government clerk earning good wages, had been replaced by a white man. His education had proven useless, and the family couldn't afford to purchase food.

While Fletcher's recruiting trips to the Omaha and Sioux had bolstered her commitment to child removal, Zitkala-Ša returned to Carlisle with a new cynicism. She began to see once more that the Indian education/war machine was the scene of cruelty. A colleague of hers abused a student by telling him

Zitkala-Ša, photographed by Gertrude Käsebeir. (Courtesy of Division of Work and Industry, National Museum of American History, Smithsonian Institution)

he was nothing but "a government pauper," which appalled her. Meanwhile, Carlisle continued to receive streams of white visitors eager to see the effects of their benevolence, though the trips were no longer organized by Fletcher herself. The publicity visits further aroused Zitkala-Ša's skepticism: she saw self-satisfied tourists looking to "boast of their charity to the North American Indian. But few," she cautioned, "have paused to question whether real life or long-lasting death lies beneath this semblance of civilization."[49]

Alone in her "white-walled prison" of a room, a new idea came to her. She left Carlisle for Boston in 1899, where she enrolled at the New England Conservatory of Music to study violin. A year later, she performed a solo at the White House for President William McKinley, and soon leading East Coast photographers sought to take her portrait.[50]

While in Boston, Zitkala-Ša published semiautobiographical essays about her childhood and teaching years in the *Atlantic Monthly*, which I have quoted from liberally. The finely tuned pieces made her a literary darling and earned her praise from the likes of *Harper's Bazaar*; two decades later, they were anthologized in schoolbooks across the East. Anxious to broadcast a former teacher's grand success, Carlisle's newspaper, *Red Man and the Helper*, reprinted the essays, qualified by a lengthy editorial note. "We regret that she did not once call to mind the happier side of those long school days, or even hint at the friends who did so much to . . . lead her from poverty and insignificance into the comparatively full and rich existence that she enjoys today," the editor's preface announced. Her literary success, the editor claimed, was due to the benevolence of boarding school teachers, while her "underlying bitterness" was a personal failing. Pratt vowed to stay publicly silent on the matter, choosing to vent his anger in a private letter. "But for those she has maligned," he seethed, "she would be a poor squaw in an Indian camp, probably married to some no-account Indian."[51]

Zitkala-Ša had worked for Pratt for two years, but she would have the final say about the boarding school. Writing in response to the *Red Man*'s editor, Zitkala-Ša clarified: "I give outright the varying moods of my own evolution" to stir political debate about boarding school education. "No one can dispute my own impressions and bitterness!"[52]

Zitkala-Ša's efforts to own her experience, in the midst of assimilation machines and well-intentioned white feminists who insisted that Natives were too immature to make their own decisions, can be seen as intersectional feminist acts. For her, agency was not primarily about her status as a woman, nor was gender her singular form of her political work: but her right to testify to her own experience as an Indigenous woman was central to her political struggle. She was the very first Native American woman to tell her story in print in her own voice, free of translation, editing, or other forms of mediation that framed other Indigenous narratives, such as those given by Sarah Winnemucca, Geronimo, and Red Cloud. As she told Carlisle's readers, she was in charge of her own story and her own feelings—she was not raw material to be transformed by others. In a boarding school system dedicated to ingraining new sensory impressions and habits into the bodies of students, Zitkala-Ša's resistance was targeted and direct. Her "evolution" and her "impressions" were hers alone.[53]

Her essays are at once an artistic rendering of her feelings that helped her express and find an authentic self, as well as, in their loose fictionalization, a group autobiography that brought a generation's worth of Indigenous children's suffering into the white middle-class eye. Her stories develop a singular voice to bring collective life to the page, as if she were writing the experiences of tens of thousands of unnamed children into narrative existence, rather than conveying her own story alone. Motifs like alluring red apples that cast her out of Eden brought her individual experience into the realm of the mythic—tales that would speak of a community, not just an individual.

Zitkala-Ša continued to use her literary talents to bring a Sioux perspective into settler culture. She spent the summer of 1901 gathering stories from her own Yankton Dakota tribe, published as *Old Indian Legends*, and wrote several short stories and essays for New York publishers. These pieces reveal a political commitment that intertwined women's rights with Indigenous self-determination and cultural renewal. In her stories, a warrior Native woman rescues her lover from otherwise certain death, untying him from captivity just prior to his execution by a neighboring tribe. A boarding school–educated son watches helplessly as his father dies of starvation, for he has promised to give up the hunt in favor of civilization. Pratt declared the latter story "trash" and denounced its author as "worse than a pagan."[54]

Zitkala-Ša's response? "Why I Am a Pagan," published in *The Atlantic*, articulates a spirituality born of listening to the Great Spirit as he spoke through the "eloquence" of rivers, flowers, and clouds. For Zitkala-Ša, land is family, not property. Native religion enabled her "to recognize a kinship to any and all parts of this vast universe" and to know that "both great and small are so surely enfolded in His [the Great Spirit's] magnitude that, without a miss, each has his allotted individual ground of opportunities."[55] Given her keen poetic eye, her language is surely deliberate. The Great Spirit, not reformers, allots opportunity, and he allots to all.

Even as she published in prestige venues, Zitkala-Ša situated her emerging voice within a tribal and pan-Indian network. Just before she began writing for national outlets, she had a disagreement with her half brother's wife, who chastised her for deserting the family by pursuing an education. She chose to drop the name of Simmons in favor of the self-given name Zitkala-Ša. "You can guess how queer I felt—away from my own people—homeless—penniless— and even without a name! That I choose *to make* a name for myself and I guess I have made Zitkala-Ša known—for even Italy writes in her language!" she exulted to Montezuma during their courtship days. Commissioner of Indian Affairs Thomas J. Morgan had decreed that all boarding school children be as- signed the surnames of their fathers, according to settler patriarchal custom. But Zitkala-Ša, as usual, chose to go her own way, confident in her powers of creation. The name means "Red Bird" in Lakota—not in her native Nakota tongue.[56] In her name and dress she drew on a mixture of Sioux and other Native languages and customs, an early effort to create a collective pan-Indian position that worked through coalition rather than identity. Collective politi- cal work uniting Indigenous people across the country, in fact, would become her central goal.

~ ~

Alice Fletcher was learning that to the Indigenous, land was not property but was life itself, a manifestation of the Great Spirit with whom it was a blessing to be in coexistence. The Lakota, for example, in this period defined commu- nal territory as "any place where they cultivated relations with plant and animal life," explains Lower Brule Sioux scholar-activist Nick Estes, and that included great expanses of hunting grounds and arid soils unsuited for crop agriculture.[57]

Fletcher had some respect for the Native worldview that saw Nature as sacred and humans as part of its rhythms, but she also found it immature.

Natives' relationship to land is "like the cry of a child rather than the articulate speech of a man," she wrote in a scientific paper.[58] To Fletcher and settler
culture in general, a modern relationship to land looked like transformation:
plowing the prairies, felling woodlands, damming rivers, and blowing holes
right through the middle of mountains for railway tracks. Because Natives
sought to live in amicable coexistence with the natural world, rather than to
extract, exploit, and capitalize on its resources as individuals, Fletcher and
other anthropologists believed that they would remain in barbarism, unable
to advance materially, mentally, or emotionally. To evolve as a people, nature
must be transformed into property.

The greatest political work of Fletcher's life was to sever Natives from the
lands with which they lived in reciprocal relation. To her, Native land was
worse than unproductive: it was a curse and a waste and prevented assimilation. "The landed wealth of the Indian has been his bane," Fletcher concluded.[59] To relieve Indians of their vast lands, just as to remove children from
their tribes, was for Fletcher an act of benevolence that would propel Natives
into the forward movements of civilization and pacify the bloody relationship
between Indians and settlers.

Fletcher, other reformers, and politicians seized upon a new strategy in
the mid-1880s: privatizing the reservations. They sought to divide up existing lands into farming plots assigned to heads of individual families and then
sell off the vast "surplus" lands to settlers.[60] Land division, also called allotment, aimed to eliminate communally held lands, destroying the power of
chiefs and Native ways of life. Privatization imposed a settler model of kinship
based on the patriarchal couple, modes unrecognized by Native tribes that
saw aunts and uncles, cousins, siblings of spouses, multiple lovers, and others
as immediate family.[61] Rupturing Indigenous gender roles and sexual customs
became a prime lever for rupturing Indigenous ways of life.

In 1883, Alice Fletcher became a special agent of the Office of Indian Affairs to survey Native lands across the country and determine their suitability
for division; she was also employed to divide the Omaha Reservation, with
Francis La Flesche as her interpreter. Fletcher had a characteristically gran-
diose idea of her mission. She romanticized her return trip to the Omaha as
an unprecedented barrier crossing that traversed time itself. "I go to the wild
life, and unknown future, where the unknown past may find a voice," she

pronounced.[62] The Omaha were to have a future, Fletcher decided, because she was to become their mouthpiece and their guardian.

The Omaha Severalty Act of 1882, which Fletcher had helped modify so that it ensured Omaha would have first dibs on some of their lands, divided up seventy-six thousand acres into 954 distinct parcels. The remaining fifty thousand acres were opened to purchase by white settlers. Some Omaha were eager to hold family-based titles to their land, thereby protecting it from squatting or other theft. But this group, which generally had a positive view of assimilation, comprised only one-quarter of the tribe. A full one-third of the tribe actively resisted allotment, insisting that land should remain legally held by the tribe as a whole, in keeping with their custom. Fletcher enlisted the help of the local police to round up rebellious Omaha and force them to privatize their land.[63]

Severing communally held land into private parcels assigned to male heads of family or to couples provided a perfect settler feminist opportunity. Fletcher would save the Omaha by imposing settler gender and sexual norms upon them. Omaha society was nonmonogamous; men were permitted to take more than one wife, though Fletcher and La Flesche noted that polygamy wasn't a common practice.[64] Two years prior, Sitting Bull had asked her, according to her own telling, to give Hunkpapa Lakota women a future. Now among the Omaha, she relished enforcing monogamous, patriarchal ways of life.

Allotment gutted collective tribal authority, reducing Native-held land to monogamous marriages and making women, for the first time, economically dependent upon their husbands. Fletcher knew that this would be a serious downgrade in status for many Native women. That same year, she acknowledged that a Native woman told her, "I'm glad I'm not a white woman!" when informed of married women's lack of rights to own property or custody of their children in Anglo America.[65] But Indigenous women's rights were of secondary importance to settler feminism. Of primary importance was rescuing them from barbarism, a rescue that simultaneously bolstered white women's authority. A decline in Native women's rights and agency was merely the price of progress.

Fletcher's work privatizing Omaha land became a rehearsal for extending the practice nationwide. Allotment became key to the US government's new approach to the West: now that the military had defeated the tribes, assimilation, rather than conquest, became the goal. Fletcher's expertise lent her a key voice in shaping this new agenda. Initially, reformers and legislators considered allotting land to tribes, not to individuals. But Fletcher rejected this plan. "Under no circumstances should land be patented to a tribe," she informed the annual conference of white Indian reformers in 1884, held on a flowery estate at Lake Mohonk in upstate New York. "The principle is wrong."[66] She suspected that tribally held lands would enable communal forms of governance and kinship to continue. Fletcher's civilizing agenda entailed full assimilation, and eventual citizenship, for Native Americans. That meant collective communities in ongoing relationships with the land must be divided into individual families holding private property.

In keeping with her settler feminist position, this rescue work was to be done *for* the Indians, not "side by side" with them, as Zitkala-Ša would endorse in her speech at the Indiana Opera House a decade later. Initial drafts of the allotment policy, named the Dawes Severalty Act of 1887, as well as an amendment passed by the House of Representatives, gave tribes consent over privatization: two-thirds of a tribe must endorse allotment, or it would not take place. Fletcher pushed back here, too. "The work must be done for them whether they approve or not," she insisted. "We have inherited the guardianship of the Indians[,] we must therefore act for the benefit of our wards." But some of her white allies felt that she went too far in imagining her maternal authority over Natives. "She has fallen into a wretched sentimental way of calling the Omahas her children—her babies," a fellow reformer complained.[67]

White women did not yet have electoral power, but women like Fletcher were beginning to wield significant political influence.[68] In the summer of 1885, Fletcher diligently researched what would become a 693-page report on the history and progress of "Indian education and civilization," which included updates on treaty obligations that remained unfulfilled by the US government. This research positioned her as an unparalleled authority, and she leveraged her power to convince Senator Dawes to rewrite his act so that allotments would be granted to individual heads of families and not patented to tribes at large. Later that fall, Fletcher lobbied Congress directly in support of her vision.

The Dawes Act was the first major Indian policy in a century, and no single individual had more effect on its final shape, Fletcher's biographer Joan Mark argues, than Alice Fletcher. Fletcher's agenda won out: no tribal consent, and land was divided up among individual families and assigned to heads of households rather than allotted to communities or even couples. A pathway to eventual citizenship—a key marker of civilized status—was the reward for privatizing land. All land in excess of the 160-acre family parcels, 80 acres assigned to single people over eighteen, and, in some tribes, 40 acres to children, was opened for sale. This sometimes meant breaking treaties, such as with the Sioux, for communal lands, an agenda Fletcher and other Lake Mohonk reformers eagerly embraced. Fifty percent of the Great Sioux Reservation was sold to white settlers within just twenty years.[69]

Fletcher carried out a significant portion of land allotments herself. In her ten years of work as special agent for the Bureau of Indian Affairs, she allotted land to 1.5 percent of the national Indigenous population—about forty-four hundred people. Typically, Fletcher surveyed the lands and chose the plots to be assigned, though she was a newcomer to the territory. Yet she did her work carefully, all too aware that much reservation land was arid and not suitable for dwelling or farming. Some of her most extensive work was among the Nez Perce in northern Idaho, a tribe largely resistant to privatizing land. For several springs beginning in 1889, Fletcher traveled to Idaho with her new domestic partner, the photographer E. Jane Gay. Gay took photographs, wrote, and kept house while Fletcher surveyed and privatized the land to male heads of households, against the majority of the tribe's wishes. All remaining lands were sold off to white settlers. As a result of Fletcher's allotment work, the Nez Perce lost 75 percent of their lands, a full half-million acres.[70]

It was the beginning of a long, most likely romantic, partnership between Fletcher and Gay. It may be tempting to call Fletcher's situation in Idaho ironic: here she was, imposing compulsory heterosexuality upon a tribe who maintained radically different romantic and kinship relations, all while freeing herself from those very same norms personally and professionally. Yet her situation wasn't ironic, for it wasn't the result of unintended consequence: it was by design. To Fletcher and other white feminists, white women were civilized, without question, and same-sex attachments among each other didn't jeopardize this status. Their moral authority was the backbone of moral progress, whether they lived with husbands or in the so-called "Boston marriages" that united upper-class white women in enduring companionship. Feminist scholar Jasbir K. Puar has named this problematic phenomenon "homonationalism": the fantasy that white gay life is inherently civilized and good for the nation, whereas Black, brown, and Asian nonheterosexual life is primitive, backward, and a threat to progress.[71] Puar was writing about the twenty-first century, but the dynamic reaches back to the late nineteenth and the women like Fletcher and Gay who used their location in the "frontier" to liberate themselves from patriarchal sexual norms while simultaneously imposing them upon others.

In 1891, Fletcher and Gay together bought a house in Washington, DC, where they lived with Fletcher's research associate Francis La Flesche for the next sixteen years. (La Flesche and Fletcher had been living together since 1884.) La Flesche was restricted to a portion of the house. Fletcher, committed as ever to the idea she was a mother to all Natives, attempted to adopt La Flesche when he was thirty-four years old. The adoption was never legally formalized because it would have meant he would lose his surname, but throughout their long working relationship she saw La Flesche as an assistant rather than as a valuable colleague with cultural and linguistic knowledge she would never attain. He may have had an entirely different relationship to the idea of adoption, for adoption as an adult was an accepted part of Omaha culture.[72]

La Flesche was also quite possibly a lover, completing the picture of this decidedly queer household. Fletcher destroyed all her personal papers, so few details are known of the relationship between Gay, Fletcher, and La Flesche, except for something of its tumultuous end. In 1906, Francis married Rosa Bourassa, a Chippewa woman who had attended Carlisle, and she moved in. Several weeks later, Jane, Alice, and Francis were all struck with illness. A dramatic confrontation, the content of which we have no records, occurred between Alice and Jane at Alice's bedside, and Jane moved out two weeks later, never to return. Francis and Rosa were divorced by the end of the year, and he and Fletcher continued to live together until her death in 1923.[73] Despite the absence of details, it is clear that Fletcher used her increased social standing to conduct her own domestic relationships however she chose—the very agency she denied to those she deemed less evolved.

Fletcher's continued anthropological work, much of it done with La Flesche, launched her into new professional heights. She published extensively on Indigenous cultural traditions, especially music and dance. In the

Alice Fletcher at her writing desk. (Courtesy of National Anthropological Archives, Smithsonian Institution)

fall of 1890, she was awarded a paid research position at Harvard's Peabody Museum that a wealthy benefactress created specifically for her. The new position was for Fletcher alone—La Flesche continued as her unpaid research assistant. At Harvard, the fellowship had limited reach, for she didn't have students of her own to train. But she was now a full-time professional scholar and the first woman to have an appointment at Harvard. To the community of middle-class white feminists in DC, her university position was a major victory, and she was now feted by the same kinds of societies she had helped to found twenty years earlier. Eight hundred people attended a lavish reception held by the women's clubs of DC to celebrate Fletcher; she spent five hours greeting guests in the customary receiving line.[74]

That winter, Fletcher was an invited speaker at the now annual National Council of Women conference held at Washington, DC's Albaugh's Opera House. Elizabeth Cady Stanton and Susan B. Anthony, who had founded the organization, were also on the agenda. Prominent suffragist and temperance reformer Frances Willard, with whom Fletcher had served as secretary and organizer of the Association for the Advancement of Women, introduced the anthropologist with fanfare. "We are particularly proud of her as a Fellow of the

Museum of the Scientific School of Harvard University," Willard announced. "She is the first bird of a flock."[75]

Fletcher's speech assumed her leadership among feminists, and it assumed all those feminists united behind the civilizing agenda. She began "Our Duty Toward Dependent Races" with a statement of equality: that all the world's races have a right "to exist," free of attempted "destruction by war, pestilence, or absorption." But true to the evolutionary hierarchy to which she was so committed, she argued that races were not equal in development. "It is plainly seen that the white race has led the march of human progress," she asserted, as evidenced by its monopoly of "the higher arts and sciences" and its superior land holdings. This posed a dilemma. "What shall we from our abundance give to those dependent upon us?" she asked her fellow reformers.[76]

But Fletcher's audience at the National Council of Women was not only composed of white feminists eager to bolster their own position through civilizing people of color. Others had distinct ideas of feminism's meaning, objectives, and vision for change. After all, like all social movements, feminism is less a fixed platform than a rotating scene of ongoing tensions, debates, and outright conflicts.

The next scheduled speaker was none other than Frances E. W. Harper. Willard didn't introduce Harper, who launched right into pointed critique: "While Miss Fletcher has advocated the cause of the Indian and negro under the caption of Dependent Races," Harper began, "I deem it a privilege to present the negro, not as a mere dependent asking for Northern sympathy or Southern compassion, but as a member of the body politic who has a claim upon the nation for justice."[77]

Justice, Harper emphasized, was a right pertaining equally to all, regardless of whites' self-serving fantasies that their "rights of property or the claims of superior intelligence" placed other races under their magnanimous care. "While politicians," she concluded, "ask in strange bewilderment, 'What shall we do with weaker races?' I hold that Jesus Christ answered that question nearly two thousand years since. 'Whatsoever ye would that men should do to you, do you even so to them.'"[78] While white feminists like Stanton, Stowe, and Fletcher consolidated around the civilizing project, despite their competing approaches to the cause, intersectional feminists like Harper, Harriet

Jacobs, and Zitkala-Ša threw off white women's aggressive benevolence and stressed their right to self-determination.

Four years later, Alice Fletcher was named vice president of the anthropology section of the American Association for the Advancement of Science, the first woman elevated to a leadership position in the nation's most prestigious scientific organization. Her search for the origins of women's oppression in Native society had propelled her into the status of the nation's leading woman scientist. Fletcher's influence would inspire a new generation of women scientists, physicians, and anthropologists in the decades to come. Her protégés included Susette La Flesche, Francis's half sister, who went on, under Fletcher's mentorship, to become the first Native woman to receive a medical degree. Anthropologist Margaret Mead likewise followed in Fletcher's footsteps, building on her work with the Omaha beginning in the 1930s.[79]

Meanwhile, land privatization was continuing apace. The Dawes Act included a provision that families could not sell their lands for twenty-five years, in an attempt to ensure the oncoming rush of settlers wouldn't swindle Natives out of their property. But most Natives ended up leasing their parcels to settlers, opting not to become crop farmers themselves, and this effectively led to losing their lands. By 1934, when allotment policy was radically changed under the Indian Reorganization Act, Native Americans had lost ninety million acres, two-thirds of the lands they had controlled at the act's passage.[80] The Dawes Act is now considered by many to be the most harmful federal Indian policy in US history.

Alice Fletcher's chosen method for political work, true to her settler feminism, was severance. Zitkala-Ša's, by contrast, was collectivizing, and her method of collective power turned the tactic of severance into an opening. Boarding schools were designed to eradicate tribal attachments. But paradoxically, as scholar Brenda Child argues, they also brought together children of tribes from across the country, creating the possibility of cross-tribal networks between Natives from disparate regions for the first time.[81] Zitkala-Ša was at the forefront of turning these relationships into real political power.

Despite her success in prestigious national venues, Zitkala-Ša walked away from individual literary and artistic pursuits in the early twentieth century, ceasing to publish. The clubwoman approach of professional attainment was not for her. She along with Montezuma was eager to contribute her talents to form a new pan-Indian political organization bringing together tribes across the country. But their visions diverged sharply: he wanted sex-segregated associations, and she was a feminist who wanted to work in coalition. "I feel like putting my hand forward and simply wiping the Indian men's committee into no where!!!" she wrote him. "Am I not an Indian woman as capable in serious matters and as thoroughly interested in the race—as any one or two of you men put together? Why do you dare leave me out?" Her outrage echoed disagreements between the two of them about a future marriage, in which she balked at his desire for her to play the supporting role of an assimilated doctor's wife, or what she called "a fine horse to draw your wagon!"[82] She soon ended the relationship and married Raymond Bonnin, a childhood friend from Yankton, in the spring of 1902.

While living in Utah with Bonnin on the Ute Reservation a decade later, Zitkala-Ša collaborated with Mormon composer William Hanson on an opera bringing aspects of the Sun Dance ceremony to the stage, the ritual Alice Fletcher had watched in fascination at Pine Ridge in the 1880s. After two years of joint work on the libretto and score, *The Sun Dance Opera* was first staged in Vernal, Utah, in 1913, featuring Ute singers and dancers. It is one of the very first Native-led performances in US theater history, and it brought to life a story of heroic resistance rather than the tragic pageants or sensationalized Wild West shows that formed the bulk of Native-themed entertainment. Zitkala-Ša's efforts to bring Dakota and Sioux legends and spirituality to broad audiences are acts of both translation and community preservation, though it was far from an "authentic" rendering of the dance. Yet perhaps this, too, was part of Zitkala-Ša's vision for her people: continued evolution, rather than a fossilized past. As Laguna Pueblo feminist Paula Gunn Allen underscores, eradicating culture and imagination is a central part of settler colonialism. "The wars of imperial conquest," she writes, "have been fought within the bodies, minds, and hearts of the people of the earth for dominion over them. I think this is the reason traditionals say we must remember our origins, our cultures, our histories, our mothers and grandmothers, for without that memory, which implies continuance rather than nostalgia, we are doomed to engulfment."[83] Zitkala-Ša used her education not to assimilate but to resist engulfment.

After nearly fifteen years in Utah supporting the Ute tribe, Zitkala-Ša began to realize her dream of national organizing on behalf of collective Native rights. She and her husband moved to Washington, DC, where she was active in Native American politics from the mid-1910s until her death in 1938. She took leadership in a variety of causes, some now sharply criticized as assimilation campaigns and others upheld as progressive models: advocating for access to US citizenship; combatting peyote use—a largely conservative movement that saw her working with Pratt as an ally; fighting to end Bureau of Indian Affairs control over Native tribes; and especially, fighting land theft and gross abuses of power enabled by the Dawes Act. She wrote extensively, yet no longer for the pleasure reading of a literary audience: she edited the Society of American Indians (SAI) *Quarterly Journal*, conducted long negotiations by letter with federal agents, and researched and reported land abuses from California to Oklahoma. In one six-year period, she gave four hundred public lectures, mostly to women's clubs to recruit allies for Indian citizenship. World War I particularly incensed her: a full 25 percent of Native men enlisted to fight for the United States, yet all were still barred from suffrage and access to courts. But "if he is good enough to fight for American ideals," she countered, "he is good enough for American citizenship now."[84] Natives in most states were granted US citizenship in 1924, though their reservations were still under the oily thumb of the Bureau of Indian Affairs. The work was far from done.

When SAI collapsed, Zitkala-Ša and her husband founded the National Council of American Indians in 1926, based in Washington, DC. Zitkala-Ša, now fifty years old, served as president. Under the motto "Help Indians Help Themselves in Protecting Their Rights and Properties," they represented forty-nine tribes, often via lobbying and testifying in congressional hearings, while also traveling up to eleven thousand miles per year across the Midwest and West to investigate tribal conditions and editing and distributing the *Indian Newsletter* among reservations. Through this leadership, Zitkala-Ša became the most prominent Native woman activist in the United States.[85]

One of Zitkala-Ša's most significant political achievements was her co-authored pamphlet, *Oklahoma's Poor Rich Indians* (1924), which earned a congressional hearing into the exploitation of Natives' oil-rich lands, such as settler men's kidnapping and raping Indian children to weasel control of their allotted forty acres. While the hearing had little immediate result, it is credited with inspiring Congress to authorize an investigation of abuses on reservations that, a decade later, led to the Indian Reorganization Act of 1934 (IRA). Also known as the Indian New Deal, the IRA was as large a shift in federal Indian policy as the Dawes Act had been fifty years earlier. But while the Dawes Act adopted the policy of conquest via assimilation rather than military defeat, the IRA moved toward Native sovereignty. The act terminated the still ongoing process of allotting land; restored unallotted lands to tribes, now recognized as semi-sovereign nations; and legalized Native religious practices, including the Sun Dance. Fifty years after Fletcher began allotting land in Nebraska and Zitkala-Ša first stepped foot onto the property of White's Manual, Zitkala-Ša helped end assimilation policy, restoring some measure of tribal self-determination. Back in South Dakota, she organized her tribe to resist the new IRA-imposed constitution, composing one of their own that prohibited federal control of tribal affairs.[86]

Yet when Zitkala-Ša died in impoverishment at sixty-two in 1938, what little remained of her legacy was largely obscured by the settler norms she so fiercely resisted. While the *New York Times* published a brief obituary mentioning "Mrs. R.T. Bonnin's" work in Indian rights, her own death certificate merely read "Gertrude Bonnin from South Dakota—Housewife."[87]

PART II
CLEANSING

CHAPTER FOUR
BIRTHING A BETTER NATION
Margaret Sanger and Dr. Dorothy Ferebee

When the history of our civilization is written, it will be a biological history, and Margaret Sanger will be its heroine.

—H. G. Wells

ON A STEAMY MID-JULY DAY IN 1912, JEWISH RUSSIAN IMMIGRANT JAKE SACHS FINISHED his shift driving trucks, returned home, and climbed up the dark stairwell to his third-floor apartment. The three rooms Jake shared with his wife Sadie and their young children in New York's notorious tenement district were much like their neighbors': lacking direct sunlight and running water. Windows opened only onto narrow, garbage-filled airshafts. On the Lower East Side, over five hundred thousand people made their homes in buildings initially designed for one-fifth that number.[1] But poverty left the Sachs family and those like them with few options. That day, a tragic scene befell Jake when he opened the door. Their three children howled with anger and fear as twenty-eight-year-old Sadie's slight frame lay prone on the bare floor. Pregnant once more, Sadie had sought the advice of neighbors. She couldn't imagine another mouth to feed, another body to clothe, on Jake's paltry earnings. She had tried drugs and purgatives, but they failed to relieve her of the pregnancy. Finally, she borrowed a sharp instrument from a friend, and inserted it into her uterus. The result was a raging case of sepsis, an often-fatal infection of the blood. By the time Jake arrived home, Sadie was unconscious.

Disinclined to go to a hospital, Jake called a doctor known to the neighborhood. The doctor brought along a nurse to help him save Sadie's life. It would be no easy task. All the water, food, medicine, and ice to keep Sadie's dangerous infection at bay had to be hauled up three flights of stairs in stifling heat. All the waste was carried downstairs to the toilet shared by the hundreds of people in the building. The nurse stayed three weeks, stealing only little snacks of sleep as "days and nights were melted into a torpid inferno."[2] Yet the neighbors were kind, coming every day to care for Sadie, bringing soups, entrees, custards, and drinks as she improved.

At the end of the three weeks, as the nurse prepared to depart, Sadie summoned the courage to ask, "Another baby will finish me, I suppose?"

Her nurse hedged, replying only, "It's too early to talk about that."

The doctor arrived to make his last call, and the nurse relayed Sadie's fear about becoming pregnant again. He minced no words.

"Any more such capers, young woman," he scolded, "and there will be no need to call me."

"But," she trembled, "what can I do to prevent getting that way again?"

"Oh ho." The doctor laughed. "You want your cake while you eat it, too, do you? Well, it can't be done." He picked up his coat and bag, and with a friendly pat on her back dispensed his official advice as he left the room: "Tell Jake to sleep on the roof!"[3]

Sadie and her nurse locked eyes. The nurse fought back tears as Sadie, in despair, pleaded for information—information Sadie knew was readily available to middle-class women, for they had many fewer children than she and her neighbors did.

"He can't understand, can he?" she implored. "But you do, don't you? You're a woman and you'll tell me the secret and I'll never tell it to a soul."[4]

The nurse, too, was now distraught. Despite her medical training, she knew of only two techniques, and she felt neither condoms nor the withdrawal method was likely to be of any interest to Sadie. The nurse had previously concluded that tenement husbands were quite disinclined to use contraceptive methods. She had nothing to tell Sadie, promising only to return in a few days.

But days turned into months. The nurse couldn't contend with the woman and her circumstances, though Sadie's face haunted her dreams.

Three months later, the nurse received a phone call just as she was preparing for bed. It was Jake, in full distress, begging her to come attend to his desperately ill wife. She had sought the services of a five-dollar abortionist who left her severely injured. The nurse was loath to return, but she took the subway downtown and climbed up the three flights of stairs. She found Sadie in a coma. Within ten minutes of her arrival, Sadie was dead. Jake was inconsolable, mad with grief.

"My God! My God! My God!" he wailed, pulling at his hair, pacing in circles through the tiny rooms.[5]

The nurse folded Sadie's thin hands over her breast and took to her own pacing through the city streets, walking for hours before she returned home uptown. From her own apartment window, she watched the sun rise and throw its glow onto the rooftops stretched before her. She felt a dawn breaking inside her, too. The nurse realized she "was finished with palliatives and superficial cures; [she] was resolved to seek out the root of evil, to do something to change the destiny of mothers whose miseries were as vast as the sky." The nurse flung her bag from her hands, tore off her uniform, and swore off nursing forever. She resolved to dedicate herself henceforth to what she saw as the true underlying cause of Sadie's misery: "uncontrolled breeding."[6]

Sadie's tragedy is Margaret Sanger's favorite vignette relating how she transformed from a part-time nurse into a full-time birth control crusader. In Sadie Sachs's story, Sanger artfully brings to life the suffering of an individual woman in order to move her audience, though the even more finely tuned protagonist of the story is Sanger herself—Sadie is the foil for Sanger's self-birth. This origin story is almost certainly apocryphal, likely a composite of various women Sanger treated when she worked as a nurse.

But what's more revealing than the somewhat self-aggrandizing vignette is the moralizing that frames it when she repeats the story in her second autobiography. Sanger makes clear that the poverty of the tenements disgusted her. "I hated the wretchedness and hopelessness of the poor, and never experienced that satisfaction in working among them that so many noble women have found," she divulges. When in the Lower East Side, among "the submerged, untouched classes . . . the utmost depression came over me . . .

I seemed to be breathing a different air, to be in another world and country where the people had habits and customs alien to anything I had ever heard about."[7] Sanger grew up working class in rural New York, one of eleven children. She frames the immigrant Lower East Side as a place utterly beyond the pale of her prior experience.

By regularly and forcefully locating her own birth as a contraception activist in the tenements, Margaret Sanger set the stakes of her work and legacy. She laid out the twin imperatives of her mission for birth control: enabling women's autonomy and preventing "uncontrolled breeding" among the poor and so-called unfit. These goals were intertwined, not merely adjacent. Sanger positioned birth control as a method of eugenics. She saw contraception as a technological asset and the "entering wedge" in the nefarious eugenics movement that aimed to strengthen the nation by regulating the alleged hereditary quality of its people. For Sanger, the arc of the universe was long, and it bent toward population cleansing, an endpoint contraception could hasten. "Birth control itself, often denounced as a violation of natural law, is nothing more or less than the facilitation of the process of weeding out the unfit, of preventing the birth of defectives or those who will become defectives," she explained. The "unfit" was a wildly capacious category, comprising the physically and mentally disabled, impoverished, ill, queer, alcoholic, and criminal, among others. Sanger believed that a full "one-fourth" of the US population was unfit, and progress depended upon preventing them from bearing children.[8]

This is the central tension of Margaret Sanger's white feminism: sexual autonomy for the so-called fit, reproductive violence for the so-called unfit. It has made her one of the most enduringly controversial feminists in history. And yet her birth control movement accelerated despite the internal contradictions of feminist eugenics.

Sanger's movement grew because she introduced a new strategy that became a standard feature of white feminism in the twentieth century. Her nineteenth-century predecessors had cloaked their supremacy in the soft folds of civilization. Women like Harriet Beecher Stowe and Alice Fletcher attempted to reform racial groups they saw as their inferiors by offering pathways to assimilation and opportunities for conversion. These were all forms of discipline yoked to state, capitalist, and religious power, guided by the belief that white culture was inherently superior. But they were forms of control extended with a soft smile and a sympathetic tear. Sanger helped inaugurate a different mode, one in which the cloak of sentimentality fell off, baring the wolf beneath. She insisted that "stupid, cruel sentimentalism" merely encouraged the proliferation of the mentally, physically, and financially unfit into the future, creating much needless suffering.[9] To her, eugenics was a modern, scientific version of reform that would neutralize social ills at their source, creating a more successful society.

Nor did she shirk from the grim implications of her eugenic vision, warning that "possibly drastic and Spartan methods" may prove necessary to stop the dangerous breeding unleashed by the pattern of benevolence.[10] Her approach inaugurated a shift in white feminist politics as a whole toward a model that sought to rid modernity of people deemed unworthy. In the nineteenth century, civilizing was the key strategy of white feminism, and it promised that anyone could be made useful to white society. But now in the twentieth, the strategy became cleansing, and with it came harsh consequences for those deemed to jeopardize the progress of civilization.

One morning in 1929, a Black boy named Johnny still too young for school took his two-year-old brother by the hand and walked him a few houses down Third Street in southeast Washington, DC. Their mother's job as a domestic servant required her to leave at six o'clock in the morning, so Johnny dropped the toddler off at a neighbor's who watched over him.[11] As they approached the neighbor's door, she slid her front window open.

"I can't take your brother today, I'm sick," she told him. "Go home."

Once back inside, the toddler began to cry. He usually had his breakfast at the neighbor's. When Johnny opened the icebox and found it empty, devoid even of ice, he, too, began to cry. How would he feed his brother? Remembering that some people in the neighborhood received milk delivery in the mornings, he stepped outside. Directly opposite, a fresh milk bottle gleamed from the step of the only white family on the block. Johnny watched the milkman disappear around the corner, and he ventured across the street. Cradling the quart of milk in his arms, he ran back toward his house when a policeman appeared, immediately suspicious.

"Hey, you there. Hey, you there!" the policeman called out. Johnny didn't say a word. "Caught you stealing, huh? Caught you stealing," the policeman declared, convinced the boy's silence confessed guilt.

"No, I'm not stealing," the boy protested. "My little brother is hungry."

"I don't care if he is hungry, you can't steal milk." Grabbing him by the neck, he steered Johnny down to Fifth Street and into the police station, where he instructed the booking agent to jail the child.

"Please call Dr. Boulding," Johnny pleaded. "She knows me and she will help." Dr. Dorothy Boulding had served her medical internship at Howard University's Freedmen's Hospital, a position that regularly dispatched her to Johnny's neighborhood—which was also her own. Though she was now a clinical instructor in obstetrics at Howard Medical School and was soon to become the head physician in charge of all women students at Howard, she was still widely available in the neighborhood. When she received the call at her Howard office, she hopped back into her roadster—a gift from a wealthy uncle when she graduated medical school—and headed down to the Fifth Street precinct. She found Johnny behind the counter and the booking agent and the policeman standing watch.

"They're going to put me in jail!" Johnny exclaimed to Dr. Boulding.

"What about this?" she entreated.

"Well, he's been stealing. We caught him stealing a bottle of milk."

"I wasn't stealing, I was getting some milk for my baby brother!" Johnny again explained.

"Do you mean to tell me that you would arrest a little boy who's trying to help his baby brother who's hungry?" Dr. Boulding inquired of the officer in her polite but commanding tone.

"Well, I don't care whether or not there's anything in the house," the policeman retorted.

The booking agent displayed more empathy and agreed to release the boy into her care. Dr. Boulding insisted on taking the milk with them, paying the seventeen cents the police requested. She took Johnny home, where they found his little brother distraught, howling and thrashing about in his bed. A plan took shape in Dr. Boulding's mind. "There's something wrong with this town," she realized. "Any time a child goes hungry, and the mother has to work and leave a child home like this, we need some place for children."[12]

Johnny's troubles—or, in another telling she gave the boy's name as Georgie—were Dr. Dorothy Boulding Ferebee's story of how she came to launch the Southeast Settlement House in 1929. Dr. Boulding, who married Howard University dentist Dr. Claude Ferebee in 1930, came from a prominent Boston family that specialized in law. Though her father's parents were born enslaved, her grandfather escaped to Philadelphia and later became a Virginia politician. Her uncle George Lewis Ruffin was the first Black graduate of Harvard Law School, and another seven of her relatives worked as attorneys. But Dorothy's calling was in public health, and she finished as the top student out of her class of 136 at Tufts Medical School in 1924.[13] Through the tool of medicine, she felt she could serve the needs of Black communities much less prosperous than her own and who were almost universally excluded from existing social services on account of their race. Her notion of public health was vast, encompassing nutrition, sex education, medical care, and child-rearing in a project of health equity. She maintained a private practice in addition to her instructional and administrative duties at Howard Medical School. Despite these professional pressures, she threw herself into the task of establishing a funded daycare for poor Black families in her neighborhood.

Savvily, Ferebee approached the board of directors of a well-resourced white daycare around the block, proposing they join forces and establish an integrated program, such as she had seen in Boston. "It was as if I had thrown a bomb into the room," she recalled. Everyone erupted at once: it was simply impossible to admit Black children to the Friendship House. "Well, will you help us?" she pivoted. Now her request for funds seemed like a conciliation, and a wealthy white woman immediately offered $1,000; her peers chimed in with smaller contributions. Ferebee already had secured $5,000 from a local seed agency, which was later reorganized as United Way, and had set her sights on an empty house on G Street. She organized a board of directors, negotiated down the landlord's price, and opened the Southeast Settlement House offering daycare and after-school programs, the first institution of its kind in the city serving Black youth. She served as president of its board of directors until 1942. By the time of Ferebee's death in 1980, the organization served more than twelve thousand people a year drawing on an annual budget of more than $2 million.[14]

As Ferebee saw it, middle-class Black women like her had a "responsibil-ity for promoting the physical, mental, and spiritual advance of the race."[15] She was among those of the educated Black middle class who endorsed the era's doctrine of racial uplift, in which they assigned themselves the duty of lifting up the Black poor into a higher stage of civilization. This was a char-itable ideology shaped by no small amount of elitism. Uplift doctrine had particular appeal for Black women reformers of the professional classes, who began forming hundreds of Black women's clubs around the country in the 1890s. While Black clubwomen embraced, and indeed developed, respect-ability politics, their societies were not mere counterparts of the apolitical, self-advancing white women's club movement that Alice Fletcher had helped launch in the 1870s. These clubs were overtly political, often devoted to large-scale reforms in childcare, housing, antilynching, healthcare, voting rights, and fair wages that reflected their understanding of the web of challenges fac-ing the millions of Black people living in poverty.

Both Sanger and Ferebee understood that racism left the Black poor in dire need of healthcare, including contraception. When Sanger committed to bringing birth control to Black southern women in the 1940s, she and Fere-bee would work together directly on the ill-fated Negro Project. Yet they had distinct agendas. Almost from the beginning of the birth control movement, these two feminist approaches existed side by side. Sanger embraced contra-ception as a technology that would transform the quality of the world's peo-ple, securing "fit" women's sexual autonomy and limiting the reproduction of the "unfit." Ferebee folded contraception into the broader goal of health justice, which included supporting poor women's reproductive choices and improving the living conditions of their children.

These two approaches were each a mixed bag: each celebrated women's sex-uality, but also incorporated eugenics to one degree or another. Yet only one, Sanger's movement for the right not to give birth, has gone down in history as a significant feminist achievement, and it's the one that most fully incor-porated eugenics into its agenda. The other, Ferebee's project for the ability to prevent pregnancy, but also for the right of poor women to have children and to parent them in safe environments—an approach Black activist Lo-retta Ross termed reproductive justice in the 1990s—barely gets a footnote.[16] But the history of birth control activism includes both Sanger's movement to prevent pregnancies as well as the counterhistory of reproductive justice. When we only remember the former, we participate in the white feminist fantasy that sex difference is the single axis on which the world turns, obliterating all other dimensions of social power that profoundly shape public health and reproductive choices.

～ ～

In the early twentieth century, New York became the nation's center of trade and finance, and its robust economy depended on cheap labor. Southern and Eastern Europeans streamed into the city, and its population more than doubled between 1890 and 1920. Among the immigrants were 1.5 million Yiddish-speaking Jews fleeing organized massacres within the Russian empire. By 1900, two-thirds of New York City's population lived in the tenements; 2.3 million people were facing living situations like Sadie's and Jake's. Jacob Riis had exposed to the world the dire conditions of the Lower East Side tenements in his famous 1888 book *How the Other Half Lives*, including the bone-chilling 10 percent infant mortality rate.[17]

Reformers like Sanger were desperate to alleviate the suffering of the poor. Many saw capitalism as the source of this severe social inequality. Sanger, the daughter of a free-spirited socialist, initially took this perspective and became quite active in the left-wing branches of the labor movement, including the Industrial Workers of the World. But her experiences as a nurse in the tenements she so hated impelled her to envision another culprit.

Sanger insisted that the central problem facing New York's immigrant class and the nation as a whole was not capitalism, but endless births that drained women's strength and produced "low-quality" babies, prone to defect. Civilization turned on one singular pivot for Sanger: the biological merit of its population. And birth control was the lever to manipulate it. For Sanger, many different types of people were unworthy of having children. In her words, the unfit included the following:

the physically disabled	morons
idiots	imbeciles
the feebleminded	the insane
psychopaths	diseased slum populations

unemployables	the criminal
the epileptic	the chronically poor
the sick	the alcoholic

Eugenicists and race scientists had invented the new terms "moron," "imbecile," and "idiot" to diagnose distinct levels of mental incapacity, terms that are now common today as everyday insults—a symptom of eugenicists' successes. Their term "feebleminded" was a broad diagnosis of mental and sometimes physical disability that was also applied to queer and poor women. As Sanger's list implies, "unfit" was also a capacious category, a melting pot gone rancid.

Eugenics and feminism may seem to be opposed agendas, but they take ready shelter together under the umbrella of white feminist thought, which reduces complex social hierarchies to the single dynamic of sex. Following this model, Sanger embraced a single-axis solution to broad political and economic inequality: improving the biological worth of the population by regulating the women who could give birth. "A Nation rises or sinks on the physical quality of its citizens," she believed.[18] Enabling women to have fewer children, and enabling the nation to eliminate the so-called unfit were two paths to the same destination: progress by way of a distinctly biological approach.

Unlike many other white eugenicists, however, Sanger was firm that unfit was not in itself a racial marker, that all races had fit and unfit members.[19] For Sanger, mental and physical disability were her targets. She believed, however, these traits concentrated among impoverished communities with high birth rates—a conviction that unmistakably and disproportionately brought immigrants and people of color under Sanger's regulatory gaze, even as she fought racism in other forms.

Sanger went to extraordinary measures to bring birth control to poor women, services that, regardless of Sanger's intentions, were desperately wanted. In 1916, Sanger opened the first birth control clinic in the United States in the storefront of a Brooklyn tenement building, distributing pessary cervical caps she imported from Europe. She was promptly arrested and cannily played her trial and jail time into media events that attracted considerable support. She also secured a significant legal victory: physicians could now prescribe contraception to married women. Birth control, under the supervision of the medical profession, was now available—but only for married women who could afford a doctor and only in New York state. For the next five decades, Sanger built the birth control movement to extend this victory across the United States, creating organizations forceful enough to take on both the medical establishment and the national hierarchy of the Catholic Church.

When Margaret Sanger coordinated the first national birth control conference in the fall of 1921, she chose New York's Plaza Hotel as her launching pad. Perched on Fifth Avenue at the southeast corner of Central Park, the nineteen stories of the Plaza—the most expensive construction of its kind when it opened in 1907—take a commanding view of uptown Manhattan. The First American Birth Control Conference brought reformers and eugenicists, politicians and socialites together at the landmark hotel to inaugurate the American Birth Control League. Sanger had been working relentlessly to build a movement and declined to join one of the several existing birth control organizations—she preferred to launch her own, with herself at the head. Over a six-month period earlier that year, she gave no less than forty-six public lectures; by the conference opening, she had amassed a contact list of over thirty-one thousand supporters. The opulent setting and prominent sponsors like Winston Churchill, then a member of British Parliament, and novelist Theodore Dreiser underscored that the days of storefront tenement clinics were long behind her.[20]

At the Plaza Hotel, Sanger opened the conference and announced the aim of the new American Birth Control League: to give the instinct of sex the same detailed attention civilized societies paid to the instinct of hunger.[21] Women's sexual pleasure was of profound importance to Sanger, a truly radical notion for her time. But she also saw sex as the seed of social ills. She explained to her audience that the crux of birth control was its ability to modernize sex and reproduction:

> We see the healthy and fit elements of the nation carrying the burden of the unfit. . . . We have erected palatial residences for the unfit, the insane, for the feebleminded,—for those who should never have been born, to say nothing of their being permitted to carry on the next generation. Now the time has come when we must all join together in stopping at its source misery, ignorance, delinquency and crime. This is the program of the Birth Control movement.[22]

The league resolved that children should be "conceived in love" and "born of the mother's conscious desire." They should be "only begotten under conditions which render possible the heritage of health," and the league endorsed both contraception and sterilization as necessary methods to prevent the reproduction of the unfit. From the very beginning, Sanger united voluntary motherhood and eugenics into the same white feminist agenda. Her vision of individual women's liberation was intertwined with the act of social cleansing. Birth control would free women from unwanted births while simultaneously freeing civilization from "delinquency, defect and dependence."[23]

The closing event of the conference took the league's missive out of the rarefied Central Park air, down to the people in midtown Manhattan's theater district. Sanger, a massively popular figure in the early 1920s, and her fellow league organizers, held a public birth control meeting at the recently opened Town Hall venue on West Forty-Third Street. The meeting drew tremendous interest—large enough that the police, at the urging of the Catholic archbishop of New York, shut it down just before it was to begin. The police captain ordered the doors padlocked, with a full-capacity audience of fifteen hundred people captured inside. Sanger arrived at a locked building while thousands more milled about in the streets. The police were forced to open the doors to free the trapped audience, and Sanger and others made their way inside and toward the looming stage. She hesitated, trying to figure out how best to address the crowd.

The decision was made for her. A strong man hoisted her onstage, thrust a bouquet of long-stem roses into her arms, and directed all eyes toward Sanger. The dynamic Margaret Sanger was made for just this kind of public speech, but she was arrested as soon as she took the podium, as was another scheduled speaker. The New York World reported that a lively crowd of three thousand singing "My Country 'Tis of Thee, Sweet Land of No Liberty" followed the two prisoners down Forty-Third Street to the police station on Broadway, where they were quickly released.[24]

The man who lifted Sanger up to the stage was the writer Lothrop Stoddard, the nation's most visible eugenicist and white supremacist. Stoddard belonged to the Ku Klux Klan, inspired Nazi conceptions of the inferior "under-man," and as late as 1939 praised Nazis for "weeding out the worst strains in the Germanic stock in a scientific and truly humanitarian way."[25] By this point,

Sanger had deliberately intertwined her movement for contraception with the eugenics movement, and that meant aligning herself with men like Stoddard. Stoddard himself served on the organizing committee of the conference, as well as on the board of the new league; Sanger also worked with two other notorious eugenicists, Henry Pratt Fairchild and Harry Laughlin. All three were globally influential white nationalists who embraced eugenics as a means to whiten the US population. Sanger's campaign for women's sexual freedom was underpinned by—not merely coincident with—her belief in eugenics.

The rediscovery of Austrian monk Gregor Mendel's experiments with the laws of heredity in 1900 and the subsequent development of genetics had paved the way to the modern eugenics movement. Heredity was no longer understood to be the result of experiences and environment. Increasingly, the new model of the gene framed heredity as fixed and unchangeable, and suggested that hundreds and thousands of traits and behaviors had genetic origins. Sanger and other eugenicists saw mental and physical disability, degeneracy, alcoholism, and poverty as conditions printed on the gene. The idea of innate, immutable hereditary material that transmitted disability and disease from one generation to the next, unaltered, led eugenicists to seize women's fertility as the best lever for steering the direction of humanity. They feared that letting the genetically "unfit" reproduce was to let them copy themselves manifold into the future, like error-ridden newspapers rolling off the printing press.

But what was the best method to ensure that the unfit couldn't reproduce, thereby poisoning the gene pool? Segregation was one approach. "Every feeble-minded girl or woman of the hereditary type, especially of the moron class, should be segregated during the reproductive period," Sanger advised. Yet segregation was not a foolproof method, especially among the degenerate. Wily women could easily escape their decades-long confinement, giving rise to "an endless progeny of defect." Sterilization was, therefore, preferable to segregation, and throughout her lifetime Sanger advocated that the state should take charge of the fertility of the "incurably defective . . . either by force or persuasion." Indiana had passed the nation's first eugenic law in 1907, granting the state government the right to forcibly sterilize the unfit, including "confirmed criminals, idiots, imbeciles, and rapists." Over thirty states soon followed and sterilized between sixty thousand and seventy thousand

women by the late 1930s. As late as 1950, when much of the nation had begun to recoil from eugenics in the wake of Nazi Germany's genocidal efforts
at population cleansing, Sanger recommended that unfit women who agreed
to be sterilized should receive state pensions of $75 per month on account of
their contributions to society.[26]

But sterilization, too, had its shortcomings. Surgical operations were costly
and lengthy; Sanger suspected sterilization was merely a "superficial deter-
ren[t] when applied to the constantly growing stream of the unfit." Contraceptives like condoms, pessaries, and douching solutions were much easier
to distribute, preventing more births among the "diseased and incompetent
masses" in the first place. She positioned birth control as the prime method to
eliminate people she referred to as "biological and racial mistakes."[27]

Sanger's approach to eugenics had key differences from that of seething
racists like Stoddard, scientist Charles Davenport, and other white male leaders of the campaign for so-called better breeding. Like all social movements,
eugenics comprised a network of distinct and often competing methods and
goals. Conservative male eugenics leaders had two objectives, only the first
of which Sanger shared: to reduce births among women they declared genetically unworthy, and to increase births among "fit" women. Conservative eugenicists railed against feminism and birth control, for they wanted women
like Sanger pregnant and at home, building the white race. By the turn of the
century, middle-class white women were beginning to obtain college educations and start careers in large numbers. The "New Woman" smoked ciga-
rettes, rode bicycles, and maintained a public life in town, thus they were less
interested in raising half a dozen or more children at home. Sanger herself is
a good example of this shift: she had three children; her mother had borne
eleven.

Social conservatives were furious with the feminist New Women uptown
who seemingly shirked the social responsibility of counterbalancing the
large immigrant families downtown. Sociologist Edward Ross coined the
term "race suicide" in 1901, condemning native-born middle-class women's
declining birth rate, in relation to immigrant women's increasing birth rate,
as the coming death of the white race. Teddy Roosevelt spread fears of race
suicide from his presidential bully pulpit, and the term spread like wildfire.
To promote more white middle-class births, eugenicists held "Better Baby"

and "Fitter Family" contests at state and county fairs across the country in the 1910s through the 1930s. In 1913 alone, the Better Babies Bureau examined over 150,000 children.[28] Contests awarded medals to families with good looks, high IQs, numerous children, and robust bank accounts.

Sanger agreed with conservative eugenicists that the high birth rate among the unfit was "the greatest present menace to civilization." But she objected to the second goal of the conservative approach, or what she called "orthodox eugenics," which encouraged wealthier women to birth more children. For her, a "cradle competition" in which wealthy women tried to out-reproduce the poor dangerously advocated that wealthier women match their rate of childbearing with "the most irresponsible elements in the community." Too many births, she insisted, drained mothers and their numerous children of health and vitality.[29] She had an almost nineteenth-century view that the body is possessed of finite force that gets diluted with each pregnancy. If wealthier women reproduced at the rate of the poor, she felt, they would end up birthing the unfit.

Sanger countered that birth control would in fact prove a valuable tool of eugenics. She and other feminists argued that the goal of eugenics was to use the achievements of science and technology to improve women's health and create and sustain a nation of better "quality." Across the English-speaking world, historians Susanne Klausen and Alison Bashford have argued, feminist birth controllers joined "hand in glove with eugenicists to popularize the notion of rational family planning." *Control* was at the heart of their movement: contraception meant "to direct, to regulate, to counteract," Sanger explained. Animals no more, the middle class could "civilize" sex itself, transforming basic instinct into a tool of women's liberation and scientific progress. "We must perfect these bodies," she enjoined, not weaken them, through regulating the birth rate.[30] Eugenic feminism sought not only to curtail the reproduction of the poor—it also hoped to optimize the women of the middle and upper classes.

As the American Birth Control League took off, it worked on all fronts: clinical services, legislative lobbying, research coordination, and educational outreach. They opened the nation's first legal birth control clinic, the Clinical Research Bureau, on New York's Fifth Avenue just west of Union Square in 1923. The office conducted research, provided education, and distributed diaphragms and jelly to married women—items originally smuggled from

Margaret Sanger, seated, surrounded by staff members of the American Birth Control League, ca. 1921. (Courtesy of Prints and Photographs Division, Library of Congress)

Holland via a ship docked twelve miles off New York's coast by Sanger's Italian neighbor, Vito, and her second husband J. Noah Slee. Two years later, a chemical engineer named Herbert Simonds, who was an occasional lover of Sanger's, obviated the need for this operation by producing diaphragms in the city.[31]

In addition to reaching poor women much less able to access contraception via private doctors, Sanger and her organizations continued to hold conferences, publish the *Birth Control Review*, organize research at the clinics, and train thousands of doctors and nurses. Their work also had policy aims, lobbying for the complete abolition of the Comstock Laws, which since 1873 had made it illegal to circulate contraceptives, abortifacients, erotic material, and sex toys—or any information about them—through the mail. Prior to the lawsuit she filed following her Brooklyn arrest, this ban had included medical information, prohibiting physicians from distributing material about sex and reproduction. Sanger cast her net far and wide to gain support for contraception access. Throughout the end of the 1920s and the decade thereafter, Sanger traveled extensively, both domestically and abroad. Speaking to audiences ranging from the women's branch of the Ku Klux Klan in Silver Lake, New Jersey, to farmwives in Brattleboro, Vermont, and the secretary of the Commissariat of Public Health in Soviet Russia, Sanger accepted any invitation she thought would advance her cause.[32]

In 1924, the bureau opened a clinic in the African American neighborhood of Columbus Hill in New York. It had few clients and closed after a few months. For the next decade, Harlem women had to travel downtown for bureau services, and they did so in large numbers—nearly two thousand of the bureau's seventeen thousand patients made the trip. This posed problems for Sanger and her associates downtown, who catered to white patients' pervasive racism even as they were determined to bring their services to Black women. Sanger wrote to a potential financial supporter, "If already three or four colored women are in the waiting room of the clinic, we have to distribute them to the upstairs doctors and sometimes postpone the visit of others so it will not look like a colored clinic . . . other patients are inclined to grumble." Ever ambitious, Sanger raised the necessary $10,000 for a clinic in Harlem, a neighborhood she was anxious to serve for it had the highest infant mortality rate in the city.[33]

Yet the long history of medical exploitation of Black people both during and after slavery made Harlem residents suspicious of the clinic's agenda. Once Sanger eventually accepted the guidance of the Harlem Advisory Board, made up of prominent Black citizens, on how to assure Harlem residents that the clinic was not an experimental research site or a plan for extermination, the Harlem clinic prospered. Sanger also eventually consented to another of the Harlem Advisory Board's recommendations: that the clinic no longer hire exclusively white staff. These changes represented significant victories for the Advisory Board members, who were relegated to a peripheral role in the operations of the clinic. As board member and nurse Mabel Staupers informed Sanger, "[It's time] you and your associates discontinue the practice of looking on us as children to be cared for and not to help decide how the caring should be done."[34] Both precedents—failing to see Black allies as equals and widespread mistrust of her agenda—would haunt Sanger's next major project with Black communities, a project in which she joined forces with Dr. Dorothy Ferebee.

Like Margaret Sanger, Dr. Ferebee broke taboos about openly discussing sexuality, taboos that were all the riskier for Black women to breach given long-standing tropes of Black women's hypersexuality that helped legitimate slavery and colonialism. Ferebee lectured widely and boldly on children's health and sexual health. In advance of a 1928 talk at the Women's Co-operative Civic League in Baltimore, her middle-class hosts balked at her title "Sex Education for the Adolescent"; in the presentation, Ferebee proposed that five-year-olds should receive basic sex education from their parents. She repeatedly endorsed birth control, broached the topic of abortion—something Sanger never publicly supported—and encouraged free discussion of sexuality. Yet when tragedy struck in her own family, she remained publicly silent. While her daughter Dolly was away at college in Plattsburg, New York, she died suddenly; Ferebee's biographer provides evidence that the cause was likely an illegal abortion, the only kind available in 1949.[35] Publicly, Ferebee cited the reason as a severe cold and pneumonia. Perhaps the bourgeois imperative of Black women's respectability was too strong to break when it came to the reputation of her own beloved daughter.

Ferebee's sexual health agenda also converged with eugenics, a nearly all-pervasive concern of middle-class reformers both Black and white. In discussions today, the term *eugenics* is often used as if it were a synonym of race science. The meaning of eugenics, in contemporary usage, is stretched to describe any scientific research that posits the inherent superiority of the white race and the inherent inferiority of all other groups. By this logic, Black eugenics would be nearly impossible. But that's not how eugenics was understood in the first half of the twentieth century. Eugenic science is a specific type of race science, one that focuses on ranking hereditary quality; it is the practice of treating the biological diversity of the human population as evidence of allegedly valuable or invaluable hereditary material. Unfit was not necessarily a mark of race—it was overwhelmingly used to condemn physical and mental disability, indigence, criminality, and queer sexuality as genetic contagions.[36] In the broader eugenics movement, the ranking of families as fit and unfit by elites thus cut across racial lines, even as Black and other communities of color were much more likely to be described wholesale as diseased and debilitated by white eugenicists. Black professionals often endorsed the eugenic belief so common in the interwar years that social progress depended on regulating hereditary quality.

While white reformers like Sanger generally emphasized cleansing allegedly unworthy heritable material from the gene pool, Black reformers of the professional classes overwhelmingly embraced eugenics as a method to improve the alleged quality of the Black population. Theirs was a third position, distinct from both white supremacists like Stoddard and Davenport, and Sanger's white feminist eugenics. Ferebee and famed scholar and National Association for the Advancement of Colored People (NAACP) founder W. E. B. Du Bois objected to violent, cleansing strategies like sterilization. For them, encouraging the reproduction of the fit was the most important aspect of eugenics, for it formed a tactic for uplifting the race. Dr. Ferebee, for her part, endorsed the existence of superior and inferior physical types and advised progressive women that it was their duty to proliferate the superior. At her 1928 Baltimore speech, her biographer Diane Kiesel relates, Ferebee "urged women to seek for themselves mates of the highest type in order that the best possible heritage might be handed down to posterity." It was a common sentiment among fellow Black elites: eugenic marriages would allegedly improve the physical and mental condition of the race. When Du Bois was president of the NAACP in the 1920s and 1930s, he funded the organization's antilynching campaign through hosting "prize baby contests" for middle-class Black families who birthed "fit" children. Within three years, over half of the three hundred local NAACP branches held these contests; within six years, the pageants raised over $80,000. At the same time, Du Bois protested sterilization and other measures of state violence that removed personal autonomy.[37]

In the 1920s and 1930s, Du Bois and Dr. Ferebee were two of the most visible Black campaigners for birth control, and both would join Planned Parenthood's Negro Project in the 1940s, which aimed to bring contraception to Black women in the South. For them, birth control and "better" marriages were part of larger public health and racial uplift campaigns. Yet eugenics by any method is deeply harmful, for it transforms human variation into the mark of "superior" and "inferior" hereditary material. That eugenics of any kind could be folded so easily into uplift ideology further points to the elitism lurking in the core of its doctrine.

Regulating birth was only one aspect of Dr. Ferebee's multipronged approach to racial uplift. She folded birth control into her broader goal of improving Black public health during a time in which she was one of fewer than

130 Black women physicians in the entire country. In addition to her clinical and instructional positions at Howard and raising her young twins, she felt a strong calling to serve the race in the Black clubwomen's tradition. In 1935, while still head of the board of directors of the Southeast Settlement House, Ferebee helped launch one of the nation's most significant efforts to bring healthcare to impoverished African Americans. Alpha Kappa Alpha (AKA), the prominent Black sorority to which she had belonged since medical school, hosted the Mississippi Health Project, a summer healthcare clinic for share-croppers in the Delta. Ferebee became the project's medical director and its principal steward, organizing fundraising, logistics, and volunteers while lob-bying local and federal health authorities to bring healthcare directly to field-workers in the middle of the Great Depression.[38]

In the summer of 1935, Ferebee recruited a dozen volunteers for the Mississippi Health Project's first trip south. They refused to ride in the soot-ridden Jim Crow cars, always located just behind the coal-fired steam engine, and instead drove a caravan of four vehicles over eight hundred miles south in the July heat. In addition to the lack of air conditioning, driving that distance through the segregated South was no easy task: restaurants, lodging, and even gas stations often refused to serve Black customers, and the roads deteriorated into gravel and mud the farther south they reached. The group stayed with friends or at Black colleges along the way and arrived in Holmes County four days after departing Washington.[39]

Ferebee's plan was to establish five temporary clinics in Holmes County, one of the poorest regions in the United States. But when they arrived, a dozen plantation owners learned of the project from county health officials and shut it down. Local health authorities complied with the wishes of the richest res-idents to prevent their workers from accessing basic medical care. "Here we were, in Mississippi," Ferebee recalled, "with all the materials and drugs that we had bought, all the things necessary for the health of young children, and [we] couldn't use them." One plantation owner did consent to allow the hundreds of people who worked his fields to receive healthcare services, but only on one condition: under no circumstances would the laborers be permitted to leave his property. In many respects, sharecroppers in the 1930s were no more free than their enslaved ancestors had been. Throughout the plantation South, more than 99.5 percent of Black adults had never even cast a ballot in an election.[40]

The AKA clinic would have to come to the cotton fields. The caravan from Washington now proved providential: the cars became the clinics and Ferebee and her team created the very first mobile health clinic in the United States. Six days a week, they left at five o'clock in the morning and set out on roads so poorly maintained that dust clouds obscured the car in front. Their first stop was the icehouse, to keep the vaccines cold. The local health services did not vaccinate African Americans, thus Ferebee's number one goal with the clinics was to inoculate Black children from fatal but now preventable diseases, especially smallpox and diphtheria.[41] When they arrived at a plantation site, they donned their white uniforms, hung draperies from trees to create privacy, and pinned health education posters with explanatory images hopefully legible to a largely illiterate clientele to a clothesline.

Ferebee and her team quickly ascertained the best way to recruit people to their mobile clinic: by talking directly with the local midwives. In Holmes County, Black midwives delivered 95 percent of all Black babies. Yet despite their crucial role in keeping Black women and children alive as the main link between rural poor Black people and medical care, Black midwives in Holmes County and across the American South comprised an extremely vulnerable population with little to no power in the white medical establishment. Dismissed as unsanitary, uneducated, and superstitious by white public health officials, Black midwives, who were also often sharecroppers themselves, were often blamed for the systemic issues that underpinned Black illness and mortality. Many became the targets of elimination campaigns led by, among others, white women nurses. While disapproving of some of the midwives' tactics, AKA did recognize their influence and authority.[42]

Soon, the group's dietician secured food donations from the secretary of agriculture, and Ferebee began holding cooking demonstrations of rice, dried apples, and dried potatoes—food unfamiliar to the patients. Sharecroppers were paid only in credits at the plantation commissary, and bosses restricted the available groceries to three low-nutrient carbohydrates: cornmeal, sugar, and flour, and for flavoring, fatback and salt. The sorority sisters learned to offer the food late in the afternoon, when people were too hungry and tired from waiting in line all day, sometimes three hundred people deep, to resist instruction and sustenance. That first summer, they were able to vaccinate more than twenty-six hundred children, conduct over two hundred physical

examinations, and hand out nearly seven thousand copies of health information. Most of the clinic's patients were children who had no other access to
the medical establishment. Over the seven years Ferebee ran the Mississippi
Health Project, they vaccinated nearly fifteen thousand youth.[43] They treated
thousands of adults as well, particularly screening for and treating syphilis
and other sexually transmitted diseases.

Dr. Ferebee and her colleagues were shocked by the conditions they found
on the plantations. Single-room shacks housed more than a dozen people
each. The deadly effects of poverty and malnutrition were palpable. She found
the children to be "diseased, deformed, aged and wizened all too soon," while
the adults were largely "a saddened, defeated, submissive lot" who stared out
at her with faces "stupid, vacant, and void of hope." Some of her reaction was
rooted in the clubwomen mentality—theirs was charity work, not solidarity
work, and they believed bringing bourgeois Black people down south would
nudge the poor closer to civilization. "Enlightened Negroes," AKA promotional material announced, "must go down, side by side with the humblest,
blackest, 'distorted and soul-quenched' Negro serf and elevate him by actual
contact."[44] Common racial belonging may stimulate sympathy among reformers, but it hardly creates equivalent experiences or generates an automatic alliance between college-educated professionals and the desperately poor. Just
as with sex, race is cut through with other dynamics of power, especially class
and dis/ability. The AKA women saw themselves as something of saviors who
had a duty to help the less fortunate. Nonetheless, this elitist attitude remains
a good distance from the attitude of sterilization advocates and others committed to preventing the reproduction of the "unfit."

Ferebee made sure that birth control information and devices were included in clinic offerings. This service enraged plantation owners. Planters
wanted sharecropping women continually pregnant issuing a steady supply
of unpaid labor into the future. Local white physicians catered to planters'
desires for wealth accumulation, not workers' health needs, and they not only
regularly denied Black women contraception—they also recommended Black
girls as young as twelve and thirteen engage in sexual activity. Even as planters eventually agreed that future generations of living workers were preferable
to dead children and permitted the clinics to come to their vast fields, they
surveilled the AKA's health project. Ferebee wrote that plantation owners

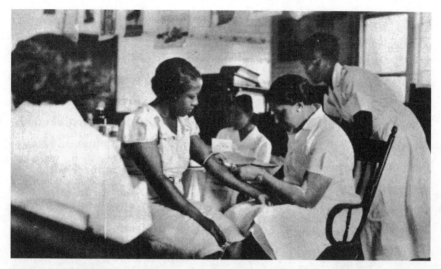

Dr. Dorothy Boulding Ferebee giving a blood test to a woman at the Alpha Kappa Alpha sorority traveling health clinic, Mississippi, 1938. (Courtesy of Sophia Smith Collection, Smith College)

posted "'riders' with guns in their belts and whipping prods in their boots; riders who weaved their horses incessantly, close to the clinics, straining their ears to hear what the staff interviewers were asking of the sharecroppers." This surveillance mission was in part based on a rumor that the sorority sisters were communist organizers fomenting a rebellion. But while terrifying, the riders were easy to dodge—AKA president Ida Louise Jackson reported with some glee that Ferebee and the nurses simply spoke in medical jargon when they needed privacy, and the white riders couldn't understand a word.[45]

Dr. Ferebee and her team were far from advocating redistributing planters' property to their laborers. Theirs was a professional-class reform mission that received glowing coverage in the pages of *Reader's Digest*, not a communist seizing of the means of production. But unlike Sanger's initiatives, Dr. Ferebee brought birth control to severely marginalized women as part of a broader healthcare initiative that addressed multiple needs. She made the case plainly: "People whose economic and health status is lowest have least access to the techniques of planned parenthood." Thus, she insisted that contraception information be folded into public health programs—not introduced via clinics that solely treated sexual health—and that public health programs adopt creative approaches to reach impoverished communities.[46]

Ferebee saw disease to be an axis of oppression that intersected with other forces of power in people's lives, rather than the singular measure of individual worth. The Mississippi Health Project, she wrote at its termination in 1941, "has graphically demonstrated the interrelation of every social and economic activity as a part of a whole. . . . The problem of health is one of many facets which link it to the entire social order; for disease is both the cause and result of many miserable social and economic conditions."[47] Health was not imprinted on a self-reproducing gene that humans were powerless to shape, apart from reducing childbirth among those deemed to lack it; health emerged at the crossroads of multiple, interconnected social structures such as segregation, poverty, and centuries-old plantation economies based on un-free labor. Dr. Ferebee's intersectional agenda that placed reproduction within a dense matrix of power was distinct from Sanger's approach that positioned the quality of children as the singular axis of civilization, even as they were both leaders within the feminist movement for birth control.

Beginning in 1937, Margaret Sanger and her oil magnate second husband J. Noah Slee lived most of the year in a house made of "adobe, trimmed in blue" in the arid Catalina foothills above Tucson, Arizona—about as far from the tenement districts of New York as she could get. Sanger and Slee occupied separate apartments within Casa de Adobe, accommodating her lifelong desire for as much independence as possible within marriage. The foothills estate was a place for rest and retreat, and hosting lavish parties attended by the likes of Elizabeth Arden and Eleanor Roosevelt, when she could convince penny-counting millionaire Slee to spare the expense. Now almost sixty, Sanger was removed from the day-to-day operations of the league and the Research Bureau. She served as the honorary president of the organization, renamed Planned Parenthood Federation of America in 1942. Sanger maintained a large presence in the global birth control movement through occasional travel and regular correspondence. She liked to devote her early mornings to writing movement letters, propped up in bed by a pile of fluffy pillows.[48]

Sanger's semiretirement was prompted by two major victories in contraception access she had won in the mid-1930s, following years of legislative lobbying work. One was a legal triumph: a test case of pessaries she had requested from contacts in Japan for use by the Clinical Research Bureau had, as intended, provoked a legal fight with the federal government. The Clinical Research Bureau's victory ensured that doctors could now engage in legal interstate and international trade of contraceptive devices and information, formalizing access that had already become increasingly possible de facto. Sanger's second victory was clinical. In 1937, the American Medical Association overturned national policy restricting contraceptive care to patients with sexually transmitted infection. It now endorsed contraception as an integral part of sexual health for all married women, a topic suitable for discussion in medical schools and deserving of further scientific research and stronger legal standing in the courts.[49] Contraception was becoming a standard component of healthcare, a sea change in public attitude Sanger had long hoped to achieve. The downside of this arrangement was that birth control access was still firmly under the control of the medical profession, something Sanger supported, and primarily available only to married women who could afford medical visits.

Nursing a failing gallbladder and an arm broken while promoting birth control in Japan, yet confident in her professional success, Sanger took reprieve in Tucson. Over the next few years, she chose to maintain a firm hand in just one of Planned Parenthood's various initiatives. It was a brainchild of hers that she trusted only her longtime secretary, Florence Rose, to put into action: the Negro Project. The Negro Project's stated goals were to demonstrate that a birth control program among southern Black working-class women would reduce maternal and infant mortality and disease as well as reduce state health and welfare expenditures. As with Sanger's general eugenic approach to contraception, the Negro Project leaders didn't frame their agenda as ensuring Black women's reproductive self-determination. Instead, they presented reducing individual women's fertility as a solution for relieving burdens on the community as a whole—a tactic that both reflected their own goals and was designed to appeal to white-led public health departments. Yet Sanger was particularly concerned about sky-high rates of maternal and infant death. Black women died during childbirth at nearly twice the rate white women did, and the mortality rate among infants was similarly skewed. A devastating 9 percent of Black infants didn't live to see their first birthday, 2.5 times the rate of white infant mortality.[50]

On a Sunday in early December 1939, Sanger wrote to her close associate Dr. Clarence Gamble, physician, philanthropist, leading eugenicist, and an heir to the Procter & Gamble fortune, about the Negro Project's design. She insisted that the federation hire and train a Black physician, rather than a white one, to promote contraception, a progressive move that Gamble had been resisting. "While the colored Negroes have great respect for white doctors they can get closer to their own members and more or less lay their cards on the table which means their ignorance, superstitions and doubts," she explained to Gamble in her concerned, yet patronizing, tone. "We do not want word to go out that we want to exterminate the Negro population," she wrote, "and the minister is the man who can straighten out that idea if it ever occurs to any of their more rebellious members."[51]

It has proven to be a fateful choice of phrasing. Today, "we do not want word to get out that we want to exterminate the Negro population" has been reverberating throughout the anti-abortion movement for more than twenty-five years. It ricochets across billboards, websites, pamphlets, documentaries, book-length exposés, and Supreme Court opinions, assassinating Sanger's reputation via a shot fired by her own hand. Over the decades, activists with politics as opposing as conservative author Dinesh D'Souza and leftist feminist Angela Davis have both cited the passage to indict the Negro Project as a plan for exterminating African Americans. Particularly to those familiar with Sanger's beliefs that one-quarter of the population should not be allowed to have children, beliefs that the pro-life movement circulates aggressively, her words seem entirely believable at face value. Yet the truth is more complicated.

Throughout the Negro Project's short run, tension simmered between its leaders about the true nature of the initiative. The Negro Project meant different things to the various people involved: Sanger, Rose, Planned Parenthood's white male leadership, the white southern affiliates, and the Black reformers Sanger and Rose recruited to play an advisory role—including Dr. Ferebee.

The arguments started in late 1939, before the project got off the ground. When Sanger returned from a short, rain-soaked Thanksgiving trip to Skull Valley in northwestern Arizona, she fired off letters from her first-floor quarters in the Tucson estate. Sanger insisted that the project launch as she initially intended: with a year-long outreach campaign conducted by a Black doctor and Black minister, trained "by the Federation as to our ideals," who would "arouse and educate the colored people." She knew white officials would never have the same effect that Black professionals could. "There could be an awakening in the South which would work like yeast," she enthused. Sanger envisioned a mass of activated people rising like fermented dough. Then, the project would open clinics to serve the demand. She also insisted that leading Black professionals be consulted in the project's development. There was "no use in asking the advice of . . . any white person" about bringing birth control to Black communities, Sanger emphasized. "They are always wrong."[52]

But Planned Parenthood's leadership, which was all white men save for Sanger, ignored her initial design for the project and instead opened three demonstration clinics straightaway, one in Nashville and two in rural South Carolina counties, Lee and Berkeley. Sanger threatened to call the project off altogether if the project hired white doctors, but the organization called her bluff.[53] The Berkeley County clinic was staffed by white nurses. Sanger was furious, and not only because they were white.

"I will never consent to nurses at this stage," she informed Planned Parenthood staff. Sanger wanted physicians. While she was much more of an antiracist than the vast majority of her white counterparts, she was wedded to expertise and authority. She operated within a top-down model that saw urban professionals, both Black and white, armed with superior knowledge and technologies, as saviors who would liberate rural Black women from unfettered births. Such rescue missions would be "lifelines to the mothers we are dedicated to free," Sanger wrote.[54]

Sanger and Rose created a National Negro Advisory Council to guide the project, appointing around thirty nationally prominent Black individuals to the board. The council was stocked with expertise and leadership, including Dr. Ferebee; W. E. B. Du Bois; Mary McLeod Bethune, who was then a member of President Roosevelt's "Black Cabinet"; and civil rights activist and writer Mary Church Terrell. Terrell in particular was a leading Black feminist who has since been recognized for developing one of the earliest formulations of the idea of intersecting oppressions. "A white woman has only one handicap to overcome—that of sex," she wrote in her 1940 autobiography. "I have two—sex and race. I belong to the only group in this country, which has two such huge obstacles to surmount." Yet despite this boundary-breaking expertise, the National Negro Advisory Council was not convened until months after the clinics first opened, and when it was finally under way, its members were relegated to a mere accessory function. It existed only to provide "moral support" to the Planned Parenthood staff and to be "extremely helpful in adapting the plans to the negro psychology," in the words of one member of Planned Parenthood's executive committee.[55] In true white paternalist fashion, Planned Parenthood tasked these national leaders strictly with providing insight into Blackness and propping up the egos of the white staff.

Some white project administrators were incensed when their Black colleagues appeared to play anything more than a purely decorative role. White South Carolina site director Dr. Robert Seibels blocked the distribution of a clinic promotional letter until Florence Rose revised a paragraph mentioning that the project was "guided by our Negro Advisory Council." Furious, Dr. Seibels admonished Rose and her colleagues, "in no uncertain terms . . . Southerners were not 'guided' by Negroes!"[56] For Dr. Seibels, Black expertise was merely a resource to be extracted for the benefit of the true southerners: its white population.

Tensions swelled to the surface at a 1942 advisory council meeting held at Planned Parenthood's gleaming headquarters on Madison Avenue. Members of the council were convinced that grassroots organizing, not deploying outside white or Black professionals to administer to the poor, would likely have better outcomes in recruiting patients. Black mothers, urged Shellie Northcutt, a national director of Black teachers in the South, would be best reached if birth control were introduced via organizations they already trusted—not brought by new clinics and professionals providing only that service. Only 11 percent of rural Black women in Tennessee even employed a physician when they gave birth, one member emphasized: their medical care was provided by Black midwives. As member after member chimed in, the advisory council was unanimous in its recommendation: integration. Abandon the single-pronged approach that positioned birth control as the singular purview of medical professionals, integrate birth control outreach work within local communities and other health initiatives, and racially integrate the leadership of Planned Parenthood by appointing Black advisors to all areas, not just the Negro Project.[57] But the advisory council had little power within Planned Parenthood to effect such a recommendation, and their counsel was ignored.

At the 1942 Planned Parenthood annual meeting, Dorothy Ferebee, who was by now also president of the Alpha Kappa Alpha sorority, took to the podium at the Waldorf-Astoria Hotel. She didn't hold back from criticizing the organization. Her goal with the Negro Project was public health. Family planning, she explained, reduced the high fatalities of Black mothers and Black infants by allowing severely ill women to prevent pregnancy and raised the standard of living. In common with her advisory council colleagues, she informed Planned Parenthood that the project's single-issue approach to promoting birth control alone was backfiring. Many poor Black people suspected that contraception was "motivated by a clever bit of machination to persuade them to commit race suicide," she advised, and others also found it to be immoral. White-led clinics devoted only to contraception services did little to assuage these fears. The solution, Ferebee proposed, was "the integration of this work directly into all public health services."

She concluded with even sharper criticism of Planned Parenthood's approach to Black outreach. "Negro professionals," she insisted, must be "fully integrated into the staff of this organization" and employed as field outreach specialists. Black professionals like herself deserved roles as full "participants" in the movement, not just the secondary "consultant" roles to which they were relegated.[58] For her, bringing birth control to Black women was just one element of a larger campaign for Black public health and racial justice, one that should be led by Black professionals. Yet again, however, this advice that Planned Parenthood abandon its single-axis strategy effected no change.

Some advisory council members, however, also advanced the eugenic agenda Sanger and some Planned Parenthood staff still maintained. To drum up support in the regions it served, the Negro Project circulated fifteen thousand copies of an article by Du Bois advocating family planning for Black families. Du Bois characterized Black working-class children in such brazenly discriminatory terms that notorious eugenicist Clarence Gamble copied one of his passages verbatim, but did not attribute it to Du Bois, in Negro Project funding appeals—appeals that scholars and activists have cited for decades since as evidence of the project's racist intent on extermination. Opined Du Bois (and later Gamble), "The mass of ignorant Negroes still breed carelessly and disastrously, so that the increase among Negroes, even more than the increase among whites, is from that part of the population least intelligent and fit. . . . They must learn that among human races and groups, as among vegetables, quality and not mere quantity really counts."[59]

Though a eugenic approach tendrilled its way throughout the birth control movement, some denounced the class hierarchy blooming in its core. A sociologist consulted about the Negro Project's plan wisely bemoaned, "Why, oh why, can't the birth control advocates stress the advantages of their prescription with regard to the individual and individual family, and then forget or shove into the background the song and dance they insist on giving about regional, national, and world progress."[60]

In the end, the Negro Project had minimal impact on southern Black women and their families. Over the test period, fewer than three thousand women visited the three clinics to obtain either a sponge and foam powder or diaphragm and spermicidal jelly. In two full years, the clinics treated fewer than one-fifth of the patients the Mississippi Health Project treated in its six-week-long summertime clinics. The advisory council concluded that African American women fundamentally mistrusted the clinics and steered clear of their services.[61]

Ferebee, her advisory council colleagues, and Sanger herself had predicted correctly that without reaching out directly to local communities, demand would be low. Staff in Nashville studied why some women who made an initial clinic visit nonetheless failed to keep follow-up appointments. Results revealed the intersecting set of hardships patients were facing. Women cited their lack of transportation, childcare, and "suitable clothes to appear in public"; some patients were as young as fourteen. Each of the first fifty patients was found to be suffering from "a serious health condition."[62] No single panacea, not even contraception, would transform the severe challenges poor Black women faced in the Jim Crow South.

Planned Parenthood closed the demonstration clinics as well as the Division of Negro Services in 1944. Upon the recommendation of a hired "Negro Consultant," the organization ceased segregated programming and attempted to incorporate limited educational outreach to Black communities into the larger aims of Planned Parenthood in 1944.[63] Yet it still maintained segregated advisory boards and insisted that bringing contraception to a limited number of Black women was the beginning to saving the race: "Better Health for 13,000,000," trumpeted the cover of the Negro Project's final report.

The Negro Project was *not* a plan for extermination. Sanger was an inte-
grationist committed to offering birth control services to Black women. Yet
she had simultaneously a eugenic vision, an assimilationist ambition, and a
feminist agenda. The project was born of the same strategy Sanger wielded
throughout her family planning advocacy: it treated contraception as the
linchpin for relieving vast social, economic, and political inequality. This approach is committed to social progress through biological measures, an overwhelmingly ableist agenda. In this approach, the birth rate and the alleged
mental and physical quality of children are figured as the primary solution to
economic and political problems. Yet Sanger's was a racially inclusive eugenics: she sought to assimilate Black women into the fold of women responsible
for safeguarding the nation's biological future. This outreach doesn't eradicate
the supremacy at the core of Sanger's approach, for she sought to fold Black
women *into* her eugenic vision. Her inclusive eugenics throws into relief the
limits of inclusion itself as a feminist strategy—for instead of trying to over-
haul an existing hierarchy, it seeks instead to diversify the status quo.

Sanger's "eugenic feminism" with the Negro Project, in other words, is
guilty of the same misapprehension of power that white feminism makes in
general.[64] Overall, the Negro Project promoted single solutions to deep economic and political oppression, committing the same miscalculation—that
power functions on just one primary axis—that white feminism makes over
and over again, century after century. The reproductive choice movement
treats pregnancy prevention as a panacea, isolating it from and elevating it
over all other women's health concerns. White feminism, more generally,
similarly fixates on the single issue of sex equality alone. Both strategies work
within, rather than against, other forms of systemic injustice.

∾ ∾

One hundred years after Elizabeth Cady Stanton helped launch white feminism, intersectional feminists kept developing agendas to interrogate multiple
structures of power at once. In the 1940s, Dr. Ferebee and other members
of the Negro Project's advisory council embraced a multipronged approach
to bringing birth control to Black communities that was separate from their
work with Sanger. They understood that for Black women living within
a nation where eugenic ideas gripped even civil rights leaders like Du Bois,

reproductive freedom must extend beyond the ability to prevent pregnancy—
it must also defend the right of all women *to have* children.

Under Dr. Ferebee's and Mary McLeod Bethune's leadership, in 1941 the
National Council of Negro Women (NCNW) passed a resolution recommending that every Black civil rights organization in the country incorporate contraception into its health outreach work. This was years before most
white women's clubs would publicly support birth control; NCNW became
the first national organization to incorporate family planning into its agenda.
The NCNW newsletter reprinted both the resolution in full and Dr. Ferebee's
speech to Planned Parenthood in its entirety, reflecting the importance of
this work to their mission. McLeod Bethune and Ferebee had an expansive
view of voluntary motherhood. Family planning, the resolution announces,
"aims to aid each family to have *all* the children it can support and afford, but
no more."[65] The italics make it plain: the National Council of Negro Women
wasn't recommending anything like sterilization or denying women the opportunity to birth children. They were supporting the right of poor women to
have children in the first place. Their recommendation stopped short of complete reproductive self-determination, however—the firm "no more" raises
as many questions as it answers. Yet overall, the resolution is a significant
step away from a single-minded focus on preventing pregnancy and toward
broader reproductive justice.

Today, the reproductive justice movement launched by Loretta Ross and
other Black feminist activists in 1994 fights on three fronts, rather than on the
single axis of pregnancy prevention and termination. Its first principle stems
from the pro-choice movement Sanger inaugurated: the right *not to have children*, via contraception, abortion, or abstinence. The second and third principles echo the approach Dr. Ferebee anticipated: the right *to have children*
and the right *to parent the children* in safe and healthy environments, involving
agendas that tackle white supremacy, economic inequality, sexual abuse, environmental racism, mass incarceration, queer and trans marginalization, and
related structures of power.[66] The movement fights structural inequalities that
harm reproduction at all life stages.

Sanger's association with the pro-choice agenda thus presents us with an
opportunity. Fully confronting Sanger's white feminism enables us to move
away from the reproductive choice movement, of which she is the founder

and remains its leading hero, and toward the reproductive justice movement. The key takeaway from Sanger's career for intersectional feminists today is not only her appalling insistence that children varied in their quality and thus value to the nation, but also her underlying political framework: that progress pivots on one axis. Sanger sought to liberate women and redress the nation's social ills by improving the biological quality of the population, a eugenic vision that doubled down on hierarchies of class and ability and further dispossessed the marginalized. But there has always been an alternative: protecting the rights of all people to have children, or to not have children, and to have access to environments that enable all children to flourish.

CHAPTER FIVE
TAKING FEMINISM TO THE STREETS
Pauli Murray and Betty Friedan

If [middle-class white women] find housework degrading and dehumanizing, they are financially able to buy their freedom—usually by hiring a black maid. The economic and social realities of the black woman's life are the most crucial for us. [Oppression] is not an intellectual persecution alone; the movement is not a psychological outburst for us; it is tangible; we can taste it in all our endeavors.

—Frances M. Beal, "Black Women's Manifesto"

IN THE DAYS LEADING UP TO THE AUGUST 1963 MARCH ON WASHINGTON FOR JOBS AND FREE-dom, civil rights activist and attorney Pauli Murray was furious. Head organizer A. Philip Randolph, an old ally of hers, had announced he would be giving a publicity speech at the National Press Club. News was made, not only reported, at the Press Club's speaking series; presidents launched policy proposals, and foreign leaders such as Nikita Khrushchev and Charles de Gaulle announced global initiatives from its podium. Yet the Press Club, the nation's premier organization of journalists, still barred women from membership. Women reporters were granted admission to events as spectators, but only as spectators—they had to sit in the balcony and were forbidden from asking questions.

The setup reminded Murray of a key moment in women's movement history. Taking to one of her favorite forms of activism, what she called "confrontation by typewriter," she fired off letters to Washington newspapers. "In 1840 William Lloyd Garrison and Charles Remond, the latter a Negro," she wrote, "refused to be seated as delegates to the World Anti-Slavery Convention in London" because women including Lucretia Mott and Elizabeth Cady Stanton were denied seats and relegated to "the balcony." She called for Randolph to do the same. Legal segregation based on sex was akin to legal segregation based on race, Murray insisted. "It is as humiliating for a woman reporter assigned to cover Mr. Randolph's speech to be sent to the balcony as it would be for Mr. Randolph to be sent to the back of the bus."[1]

Murray's intervention succeeded. The Press Club temporarily permitted women reporters to sit and speak among their male colleagues the day of Randolph's event. The Press Club, however, didn't change its policy to admit female journalists until 1971.[2]

For months in advance of the march, Murray and two of her long-standing allies—Anna Arnold Hedgeman, the lone woman on the March on Washington planning committee, and National Council of Negro Women (NCNW) president Dorothy Height—had struggled against the sexism of the male coordinators. Randolph, march coordinator Bayard Rustin, and other male leaders prearranged the march's front line to include only themselves, assigning Height, Rosa Parks, and other prominent women civil rights activists positions at their rear, alongside their wives. They permitted one female speaker, and only after consistent pressure from the trio. In the end, Randolph permitted Daisy Bates to speak for one minute and then grabbed her microphone away. The only sustained female voices heard at the March on Washington were those lifted up in song, most famously Mahalia Jackson's. "Our time," Rosa Parks whispered to Bates when she resumed her seat, "will someday come."[3]

The day after the march, Dorothy Height gathered a group of leaders from the eight-hundred-thousand-member NCNW at the organization's headquarters, which was then located on the first floor of Mary McLeod Bethune's private residence. There they would plot the next steps of the women's branch of the civil rights movement. NCNW was the largest Black women's club in the country, now largely dedicated to structural reforms. Height wanted to expand the purview of their organizing beyond racial discrimination lawsuits, and the others agreed. But as they brainstormed advocating for changes that would further transform the daily life of Black women and children, such as employment, housing, education, and childcare reforms, another, equally urgent agenda took over. Between policy priorities, emotion slipped in, mounted, and roiled. Together, they began confronting their anger at the entrenched patriarchy within the civil rights leadership, realizing that their individual experiences accumulated into a pattern of "second class" treatment.[4] The revelatory conversation spilled over into a later gathering at the Shoreham Hotel.

"We began to realize," Height later explained, "that if we did not . . . demand our rights, we were not going to get them [and we] became much more aware and much more aggressive in facing up to sexism" where they encountered it. "That moment," she recalled, of together naming the effects of the March on Washington's deliberate and exclusive focus on Black men "was vital to awakening the women's movement." Height's meeting could qualify as the first feminist consciousness-raising session of the 1960s, though that title is typically conferred upon the New York Radical Women, a largely white, middle-class group who initiated weekly sessions later that decade. Historian Carol Giardina argues that the feminist movement, much quieter since World War II had temporarily sent white women in large numbers into the workforce, was rekindled that day. Black women's time had not come—they were seizing it for themselves.[5]

Three months later, and just one week before President Kennedy's assassination, Pauli Murray addressed a crowd at the 1963 NCNW leadership conference in New York City. Women, she charged, were still simmering with frustration at their "secondary, ornamental" treatment during the march and must gather their forces to oppose the rampant sexism flourishing within the movement. Black women "can no longer postpone or subordinate the fight against discrimination because of sex to the civil rights struggle but must carry on both fights simultaneously," Murray entreated. The dual effort she outlined entailed resisting civil rights movement efforts to focus only on training and employment reforms for men, as well as forging an "alliance" with white women to fight the astounding legal and social prohibitions women faced in the 1960s United States. Dorothy Height recalls with admiration that Murray "lifted the situation to the context of equality," transforming private pain into a political issue.[6]

Among the activists incensed by the misogyny of the male March on Washington leadership, none were as prepared to fight institutionalized sexism as

Pauli Murray. One of the leading legal minds of the twentieth century, Murray brought Black women activists a political framework for understanding their experience: they were pinned to "the bottom of the economic and social scale" by the dual forces of "white supremacy" and "male supremacy." Sexism wasn't the result of individual male chauvinism, Murray argued. Rather, it was a structural phenomenon akin to racism that relegated women to legally, socially, and culturally inferior positions. She approached sexism and racism as analogous forces that converged and compounded in the lives of Black women—and in the process made a major contribution to the development of intersectional feminist theory.[7] In her extensive publications, Murray reframed sexism as a caste system sequestering power and capital in the hands of men, and she gave it a memorable name: Jane Crow.

Yet as feminist activism filled living rooms with meetings and boulevards with protestors over the next fifteen years, most journalists—and historians in their wake—saw an altogether different catalyst to the revival of the feminist movement. They agree that 1963 was the year that reignited women's liberation. But their dominant narrative thrusts the lit match into the hands of one woman alone: Betty Friedan. Friedan's explosive 1963 book *The Feminine Mystique* revealed the misery of the middle-class housewife, and her message spread like wildfire, making her name synonymous with the cause of women's rights. She soon thereafter cofounded the National Organization of Women (NOW), along with Pauli Murray and others, to bring feminism into the streets. Friedan liked to claim that she was a singular "Joan of Arc leading women out of the wilderness." Yet she was following in the footsteps of her Black feminist predecessors.[8] Her refusal to acknowledge that debt would appropriate Black feminist political skill, especially Murray's. Today, framing Friedan's revolt of the housewives as the impetus of 1960s women's liberation not only whitens movement history—it also hampers feminist understandings of the nature of sexism itself.

~ ~

In the summer of 1944, Betty Friedan (then Betty Goldstein) turned down UC Berkeley's most prestigious PhD fellowship and headed back east to become a journalist. Friedan had loved her undergraduate days at Smith College, where she shed the loneliness that had haunted her in Peoria, Illinois, and discovered a calling as an intellectual-activist and student leader. Back home, she had been excluded from the sororities that organized high school social life—they didn't admit Jews. At Smith, however, she made friends, publicly embraced her Jewish identity, wrote editorials opposing fascism, and discovered that new psychological theories attempting to grasp the complexity of the human mind in total made her "feel like some kind of mental mountain goat, leaping from peak to peak." Later in life, Friedan speculated with no small humility, "I probably would have loved law school, might have ended up a judge myself.... But it never occurred to me to want to be a lawyer, because Harvard Law didn't even take applications from women."[9]

But Friedan was fantastic at psychology. After a year working on a master's degree under leading developmental psychologist Erik Erikson at UC Berkeley she won the institution's most significant fellowship for scientists, becoming the first woman and the first student from the psychology department to do so. Her boyfriend, a communist physicist working on Robert Oppenheimer's atomic bomb project, fumed. "It's over between us," he announced as they walked through the redwoods that blanket the hills above the lab. "I'm never going to win a fellowship like that." Friedan's fear of continued romantic rejection likely combined with her own suspicion that academic life—if she could ever find a post, given that many universities banned Jewish professors from their faculties—was too far removed from the radical politics that electrified her.[10] Persistent asthma attacks, and the rashes that broke out over her body, further made it clear. Her body would not tolerate a solitary life of the mind.

Friedan would end up using her training in psychology to remarkable effect. Her marriage to the Left theater director Carl Friedan in 1947 found her performing the housewife role while also frequently drawing paychecks larger than her husband's from the women's magazine journalism she continued on the side. In preparation for an alumnae reunion in 1957, Smith College asked her to conduct a survey of her two hundred fellow graduates and write about the remarkable lives Smith women were living fifteen years later.[11] But, according to the narrative Friedan would repeat for years, what she found surprised her. Many of the peers with whom she had experienced her intellectual awakening were ignoring their training and sinking themselves into the unfulfilling role of Cold War housewives. And though they were miserable, they were suffering in silence, convinced their unhappiness was due to personally failing to live out the promise of the aprons-and-pearls lifestyle.

Friedan spent the next five years researching and writing about "the problem that has no name," or women's widespread yet unspoken misery on being denied access to the professions.[12] Her work exposing the condition of American women—by which she meant, specifically, housewives—was soon declared by her and mainstream media to be synonymous with feminism itself.

Pauli Murray was one of the twentieth century's most perceptive observers of the way racism and sexism shape the texture of everyday life, creating vast structures that penetrate deep into the individual psyche. Their cumulative effect not only prevents equality and justice—it also poses a fatal threat. Racism, she wrote about her youth in the Jim Crow South, was not often experienced as acute trauma. Rather, it was "the pervasive irritant, the chronic allergy, the vague apprehension which made one uncomfortable and jumpy," requiring constant vigilance. At times though, particularly when personal pressures mounted and stress tolerance dwindled, racism uncoiled and struck, materializing like "the fatal accident," "the blind railroad crossing," "the sharp curve rising suddenly in the darkness."[13]

One such moment for Murray transpired at age eight, in 1919. She and the aunt who raised her were visiting family in Baltimore when they received a late afternoon telegram from home announcing her grandfather's impending death. Rushing to the evening train as a thunderstorm soaked the streets, Aunt Pauline slipped and smashed her glasses. Her cheeks bled and her eyes swelled. In Norfolk, North Carolina, Aunt Pauline left young Pauline at the station's doors with their luggage while she went inside to inquire about their connecting train to Durham. She returned to find her niece frozen in place. Pauli was a specimen pinned in the middle of a circle of white men looming over her, their faces flushing red with anger. One man pursued them into the cinder-strewn, coal-smeared Jim Crow car, where long after his departure the pair remained too terrified to sleep. Their infraction? Aunt Pauline had been unable to read the "Whites Only" sign in the waiting room.[14]

Another occurred that fall, after her grandfather's death. Disoriented by grief, Murray's widowed grandmother Cornelia flashed back to the last time she had kept house without her husband, in her twenties. Then, she had regularly awoken to the sound of pounding hooves as KKK night riders encircled her cabin, flaming torches in hand. Now, every evening Cornelia would barricade herself and young Pauline in her upstairs bedroom by piling furniture and clothing floor to ceiling in front of the door and windows; once secure, she would roast potatoes and boil greens and salt pork at the fireplace that Pauline would be too scared to eat. Cornelia's own childhood had been marked by terror—she was born enslaved to a woman who was regularly raped by her enslaver, a prominent white lawyer. Slavery's long shadow stretched well into the twentieth century, clouding Murray's young life in the dawn of the 1920s.[15]

Chronic burdens erupt into fatal crises. Murray's father was institutionalized in a segregated, negligent mental hospital where twice as many patients left in body bags as were discharged. When Murray was still a child, a temporary guard beat her father to death. Racism, writes the contemporary prison abolitionist and scholar Ruth Wilson Gilmore, is not individual antipathy or hatred of people of color. Its greatest impact is not misjudging people by the color of their skin. Rather, it is a structure that generates continual proximity to the fatal; it is the "production and exploitation of group-differentiated vulnerability to premature death."[16]

The idea that racism materializes as vulnerability to early death can be put in productive conversation with the theory of biopolitics, which was initially proposed by the French philosopher Michel Foucault. Biopolitics refers to the modern system of governing that treats the central duty of society to be optimizing the population, particularly in a biological and economic sense. Eugenics, whether of the conservative, white feminist strategy or the Black professional variety, is a key tool of biopolitics, for it emblematizes the strategy of approaching politics as a matter of improving the alleged quality of the population. In biopolitics, mechanisms of state, capital, and culture mark some people, especially the white wealthy and middle classes, as the members of the nation who matter and who must be enabled to thrive. Resources like capital, education, and health initiatives flow to this chosen group on the belief that their flourishing will secure the success of the population. The same mechanisms simultaneously designate other people, especially people of color, the impoverished, and the disabled, as contagions best left to die once their labor has been extracted. In sociologist Ruha

Benjamin's terms, Black people in particular are "underserved" in order to "overserve" the chosen.[17]

The result is the uneven distribution of life and death: morbidity and mortality cluster among the racialized poor and/or disabled, in order that the rich, abled, and white may prosper. The impact of decades of biopolitical policies and practices can be seen most clearly in the drastically different life spans within urban populations in the United States today. Currently, in cities like Chicago and Washington, DC, people who live in the poorest zip codes die thirty years earlier on average than their neighbors in the wealthiest, whitest zip codes.[18]

Sexism, too, is a tool of biopolitics. Traditionally, institutions have designated white men to be the most deserving of flourishing due to their allegedly superior intelligence and economic productivity. White women are simultaneously relegated to a supporting role among the chosen. They are tasked with providing a charitable veneer to a system that is designed to let the racialized, poor, and disabled die, thereby smoothing out the contradictions of such a brutal structure of power. Through their presumed moral authority, emotional sympathy, and civilizing projects, they seemingly sanctify the whole structure. Women of color, by contrast, are cast as reproducers: dangerous breeders of the "unfit" who, at best, can be corralled into serving the families of the "fit."

White feminism works within biopolitics, rather than against it, to carve out a prominent place for middle-class women within these fatal dynamics. In the nineteenth century, white feminists like Elizabeth Cady Stanton, Harriet Beecher Stowe, and Alice Fletcher seized their assigned role as civilization's stabilizers to expand their own authority, insisting upon respect and status on account of the crucial work they provided to the structure of society. In the twentieth, white feminists developed a bolder agenda, claiming that white women belonged as full equals—not only as civilizing helpmeets—among the part of the population that must be cultivated. Their own growth, they insisted in increasingly biological language, would maximize their own potential and the "quality" of children, thereby improving the nation as a whole. One of their tactics, as was true of biopolitical governance in the twentieth century more generally, was to cleanse the population of people who seemingly threatened their success. This was most visible in eugenic feminisms like Margaret

Sanger's (and writer Charlotte Perkins Gilman's), but it was a consistent, if less apparent, feature of white feminism throughout the century. As president of NOW, Betty Friedan would undertake a cleansing project of her own.

~ ~

While white feminists seek to more firmly establish their place among those who deserve to thrive, intersectional feminists, by contrast, typically set out to eradicate the underlying logic that a society's advancement requires sacrificing the many. Murray exemplifies this tradition. As an adult, Murray, who had adopted the more androgynous name Pauli in her early twenties, didn't want only to personally escape segregation.[19] She determined to defang the snake of Jim Crow, weakening a lethal threat to Black lives. She had direct experience with the effects of the systematic devaluation of Black life, including inferior educational opportunities and wages so low she suffered from chronic malnutrition due to regularly not being able to afford to eat. After cramming two years' worth of college-preparatory classes into one year to meet entrance requirements her segregated high school in Durham hadn't fulfilled, and despite extensive breaks to work Depression-era diner shifts in Manhattan that didn't pay enough for her to eat regularly, nor would they provide meals to Black staff, Murray held a valuable degree from Hunter College.

Her diploma from what was known as the "poor girl's Radcliffe," combined with her pride in her descent from prominent white and Black southern families, gave her what she called a drive for "excellence." But a New Deal job with the Workers' Education Project radicalized her, as did her affiliation with socialist organizations. She saw the violence and poverty capitalism created and began to comprehend that "a system of oppression draws much of its strength from the acquiescence of its victims"—a conditioning she had heretofore accepted. Rights, Murray realized, should not come about by exceptional members of the race like her "proving" their worth. The goal should not be fighting your way to the top, becoming part of the population whose lives matter. Instead, rights should be won by a broad movement insisting that equal treatment was a birthright. Since racism was a systemic phenomenon, individually breaking through its barriers had little effect—it was structures of power that needed demolishing. "It is difficult to understand how revolutionary [this idea] seemed in the 1930s," Murray reflected near the end of her life. "For a

Negro to act on this conviction was considered almost suicidal in many parts of the South."[20]

Murray nonetheless attempted to splinter the all-pervasive structure of racism. In 1940, she innovated brand-new direct action techniques that would propel the civil rights movement forward fifteen years later: refusing to sit in the back of the bus and occupying lunch counters that wouldn't serve Black patrons. Her bus actions landed her and her girlfriend Adelene "Mac" Mc-Bean in jail; she also cofounded the Congress for Racial Equality with Bayard Rustin and others to engage in civil disobedience. Further pulled both by the desire to chip away at the edifice of Jim Crow and by fealty to Aunt Pauline, who was nearing seventy and needed support, she decided to return south. In the fall of 1938 Murray filed for graduate admission at the University of North Carolina, hoping to pursue a graduate degree with their race relations experts. UNC, as she knew, was a segregated institution, and she wished to initiate a change in their policy. But they denied her application to the Department of Sociology: "members of your race are not admitted to the University."[21]

The rejection singed with hypocrisy. Not only was the institution's important work on racism reserved for white people, but Cornelia's wealthy white aunt, who had also been Cornelia's legal owner, had funded scholarships for UNC students in perpetuity. UNC was still benefiting from wealth generated by the enslavement of Murray's own family. Murray's private application quickly became a public matter, for the US Supreme Court took up a case regarding whites-only higher education at state universities just a week after her submission. In the resulting furor, North Carolina's governor made the state's position clear: "North Carolina does not believe in social equality between the races."[22]

Murray's experience navigating the resulting media blitz encouraged her to pursue law school instead of sociology, as did her ongoing racial justice work that brought her repeatedly into contact with NAACP lawyers. By joining the legal field, she could attempt to alter the racist structures that so unevenly distributed the chances of life and death. But here she encountered further obstacles: to be chosen for flourishing, she learned, was also a matter of sex. On her very first day at Howard University's School of Law, in the fall of 1941, one of her professors announced that he didn't understand why women even pursued legal education. His insult, echoed in her classmates' laughter, triggered her drive for personal success: "he had just guaranteed that I would become the top student in his class."[23] Her response, however, was not only to try and rise above. Socialism had taught her to ditch the elitist approach of becoming the exception. Instead, the belittling she experienced at the nation's premier Black university, from the very people spearheading civil rights litigation, prompted her to identify a second, structural system of oppression in which she was caught: Jane Crow.

Despite the misogyny she faced, Murray had the confidence to invent legal strategy while still a student. Jim Crow segregation was authorized by *Plessy v. Ferguson*, the 1896 Supreme Court case that established the precedent of "separate but equal" facilities for Black residents. In the 1940s, lawyers' dominant strategy for challenging the effects of *Plessy* was exposing that segregated institutions were not in fact equal. Through this case-by-case approach, NAACP attorneys and allies demonstrated that the facilities Black people were forced to use were of vastly inferior quality, thereby violating the terms of the law. This approach resulted in incremental reforms. North Carolina, for example, had been forced to make some attempt at building graduate schools for Black students in the wake of Murray's application.[24] But Murray had a different idea.

Segregation itself, she argued from her classroom seat, was designed to "humiliate and degrade." The entire structure of Jim Crow, she insisted, was rotten; replacing moldering beams only reinforced the edifice. The new crop of civil rights attorneys Howard Law was producing, she announced, should challenge the legal merit of "separate" facilities in the first place by establishing that the core goal of segregation was to harm. They should incorporate psychological and sociological data demonstrating that Jim Crow eroded the self-worth and psychological health of Black people to make the case that segregation violated the Equal Protection Clause of the Fourteenth Amendment.[25]

It was a wildly unorthodox opinion. Her peers broke into "hoots of derisive laughter." Opposing the legality of *Plessy*, they argued, would end up backfiring and buttressing Jim Crow. But Murray was sure of herself and prepared a lengthy paper articulating her position. She made a $10 wager with Professor Spottswood Robinson: the Supreme Court would overturn the foundation of *Plessy*—that separate could ever be equal—within twenty-five years.[26] And though nobody would bother to tell her for decades, Murray's paper would play a role in that victory.

Jane Crow repeatedly prevented her from realizing her own legal successes. When Murray did, in fact, graduate from Howard Law at the top of her class in 1944 despite being the only female student in the school, she desired to follow the customary path of Howard's most successful graduates. That meant pursuing a master's degree in law at Harvard. The institution's response to her application, however, had a familiar ring: "you are not of the sex entitled to be admitted to Harvard Law School."[27]

Murray had run afoul of Jane Crow at Harvard, just as she had run afoul of Jim Crow at the University of North Carolina six years prior. Though women had been petitioning for admission since 1871, Harvard Law wouldn't admit women until 1950. (Two decades later, Harvard College merged with its women's college affiliate, Radcliffe, and admitted female undergraduates.) Murray had prominent supporters—she had begun a decades-long friendship with First Lady Eleanor Roosevelt during her Workers' Education Project days and President Franklin D. Roosevelt himself interceded on her behalf—but many of her Howard peers responded with bemusement, poking fun at her for thinking Harvard would admit a woman.[28] Jane Crow ran thick at Howard.

For her part, Murray struck a whimsical tone closing one of her ultimately futile appeals to Harvard Law: "Humorously, gentlemen, I would gladly change my sex to meet your requirements but since the way to such change has not been revealed to me, I have no recourse but to appeal to you to change your minds on this subject. Are you to tell me that one is as difficult as the other?"[29]

As is so often the case with humor, Murray's joke flirted with a deeper truth. Murray had not been sitting idly by waiting for the path to sex change to be "revealed." For the prior decade, and for a decade to come, Murray fought her doctors for access to testosterone. Her life in Harlem, then the site of a queer renaissance that included rollicking drag balls and sex-crossing stars like Bruce Nugent and Gladys Bentley, no doubt informed her quest for hormones. In 1939, she and McBean wrote the editor of a major Black newspaper thanking him for a front-page article about hormone therapy for effeminate men, praising the paper for highlighting the needs of this "minority of minorities." Of slight, boyish build, Murray kept her hair closely cropped and rejected blouses and skirts for collared shirts and slacks. Aunt Pauline affectionately referred to her as a "boy-girl"; Pauli labeled one of her most fetching, androgynous photographs "the imp" and occasionally signed letters as "Peter Panic." She had passionate affairs with "extremely feminine and heterosexual women," such as Peg Holmes, her girlfriend of five years with whom she hopped trains across the country in 1935, and she didn't identify with homosexuality. She "prefer[ed] experimentation on the male side," she informed a doctor at the Long Island Rest Home.[30]

Murray's letters and journals, particularly those during hospitalizations for mental and emotional breakdowns following breakups with girlfriends in the 1930s and 1940s, reflect her quest to understand her maleness, which she presented as "wearing pants, wanting to be one of the men, doing things that fellows do, hating to be dominated by women unless I like them." Her research into the new science of hormones led her to suspect a glands problem, and she convinced her doctors to search for undescended testicles or other signs that she was a "pseudo-hermaphrodite."[31] The results, which declared her anatomy and endocrinology to be sex-normative for women, disappointed her. For decades, her biographers detail, she pursued medical and scientific explanations for and treatment to enhance her strong identification with maleness. For this reason, scholars today consider Murray's life to be an important chapter in transgender history. (Following them, I use the female pronoun for Murray since that is how she referred to herself throughout her life.)

Murray's own quest for respectability, and possibly her inability to completely shake off her family's insistence that progress was to be earned through the "best of the race" leading the way, drove her to erase any traces of gender and sexual non-normativity in her public writing.[32] Her uneasy relationship to femaleness casts her own commitment to exposing and dismantling Jane Crow in a new light. She was devoted to ending sex and race discrimination, but not because she herself consistently identified as a woman. Murray's call was for structural justice, even when some personal truths seemed too vulnerable to expose.

In the end, Pauli Murray went to UC Berkeley to earn a master's in law, showing up on campus just a few months after Betty Friedan had left for the East.

Beginning in the late 1950s, Betty Friedan developed a diagnosis of her own, identifying the problem she extrapolated from the Smith College alumnae surveys. Women were suffering from the feminine mystique, she proposed, or the harmful fantasy that they would flourish only through sacrificing themselves to the needs of their husbands and children. Her 1963 blockbuster *The Feminine Mystique*—which sold three million copies in three years[33]—argued that popular culture, social science, and corporate advertising systematically devalued women's capacities to the point that housewives were suffering from an identity crisis so acute it was making them ill.*

Women, Betty Friedan insisted, are "sick," and they're sick from the drudgery of performing housework day in, day out. The housewife's lifestyle, she wrote, is "quite simply, genocide," for menial labor slowly poisons her organic right to grow and prosper—as if it were regular doses of anthrax, rather than vacuuming powder, that she sprinkles wall to wall. In other words, middle-class women, who Friedan felt deserved full membership among those chosen to thrive, were unfairly cast into the realm of premature death. Like any good doctor, Friedan dispensed her diagnosis along with a cure. Women, she prescribed, must be liberated from the endless stream of cooking, cleaning, and childcare so that they may assume careers that enable their "full realization of human potential" for abstract, creative thought. Side pursuits in politics and the arts did not count: only specialization did. "The amateur" or "dilettante," Friedan insisted, "does not gain real status by [their work] in society, or real personal identity." Professionals alone succeeded in securing respect and self-realization via the marketplace.[34]

As Black feminist theorist bell hooks pointed out back in 1984, Friedan's diagnosis of the feminine mystique misidentified the psychological condition of the educated white housewife as the universal condition of all women. One-third of all women *were* working for wages in the early 1960s, including most women of color, and they faced far more substantial inequities than being bored at home. This aspect of her critique is now well-known. But hooks didn't only expose the women whose existence Friedan forgot. She also revealed the women whose growth Friedan foreclosed. "White feminists" like Friedan, bell hooks argued, were not trying to redistribute wealth and power,

---

* "Identity crisis" was a new concept theorized by Friedan's graduate adviser, Erik Erikson.

despite their big talk. Rather, they "were primarily concerned with gaining entrance into the capitalist patriarchal power structure" themselves. The fundamental problem with Friedan's account of "the problem with no name" is not that she *ignores* all women except for the housewife. The problem is that she implicitly *sacrifices* all other women to the housewife's aspirations. hooks illuminated that working-class women and others who make up "the silent majority" not only fall out of Friedan's frame; they are pinned beneath it.[35]

Friedan recommends that the middle-class woman free herself from mere "biological living" and unlock her capacity to flourish. But this necessarily relies on outsourcing the incessant grind of sustaining life to the working class. What liberates middle-class women to become professionals is the essential labor blue-collar women provide. To free up time to pursue a career, Friedan praises the tactics of hiring "a three-day-a-week cleaning woman," ordering groceries via phone rather than shopping in person, and "sending the laundry out," along with asking husbands and children for "help." The advice is cursory, almost an afterthought in the final chapter—her focus was to free middle-class women from the trap of housework, not on those who would clean up in their place.

Friedan, in other words, advocated a form of biopolitics. She framed the chronic undervaluation of housewives as a biological threat to the vitality of the population. In Friedan's rendering, the feminine mystique was eroding the nation from within. The incapacitation of the housewife "is taking a far greater toll on the physical and mental health of our country than any known disease," she maintained. Women were sucked of their vitality; they were "walking through their leftover lives like living dead women." Weakened housewives, whom society depleted instead of enhanced, were producing "pathological" children—Friedan attributed the rising incidence of autism to mothers whose own arrested development resulted in immature children who lived only in a world of things and animals, walled off from human emotion. (The accepted etiology of autism at the time was "refrigerator mothers" who withheld affection from their infants, so Friedan was following established science in turning to mothers' conditioning, rather than physiology, for a cause.) She also attributed "the homosexuality that is spreading like a murky smog over the American scene" to housewives who must live vicariously through their children, resulting in "parasitical" attachments that prevent sons from maturing into heterosexual relationships. Housewives, she argued, were suffering from a "progressive dehumanization" so extreme that the split-level suburban home was akin to a "comfortable concentration camp" (an analogy she later regretted, and rightly so).[36]

But, she concluded, if middle-class women were freed of menial labor so that they could find self-fulfillment, society may reach "the next step in human evolution."[37] Like Sanger's, Friedan's goal was not merely women's freedom to choose the labor of social reproduction: it was also to improve the "quality" of women and the nation in a biological and social sense. This goal meant sacrificing the working class to domestic labor in order to cultivate the psychological and physical health of wealthier women.

In Friedan's book tour and many media appearances—she claimed to be one of the first authors to use the power of television to drive book sales—she would cast herself as a housewife wrapped in the feminine mystique like chiffon for a cocktail party. She elided the fact that she had been a working woman. Indeed, for six years after she departed Berkeley, Friedan had been a labor journalist covering strikes for the country's most left-leaning union newspapers—until she was fired for being pregnant. Her articles often highlighted the specific struggles of Black working-class women. She had even attempted to join the Communist Party in 1943, showing up to the New York office in pearls and pumps.[38] Her move from solidarity with the working class to sacrificing the poor to domestic labor in order to liberate the middle-class woman may seem jarring. Partly, the shift can be attributed to the increasing conservativism of the McCarthy era. But another reason lies in the structure of white feminist biopolitics, which she embraced to great mainstream success.

Friedan and other middle-class white feminists identify sex as the only thing holding them back from flourishing. Friedan saw "women as a class" unto themselves, uniquely marginalized in relation to middle-class white men. "My early political experience writing for the so-called working class," she contended, "had taught me that ideas, styles, *change* in America comes from the middle class."[39] The possibility of interrogating other vectors of power dropped away, and middle-class women became, in the tradition of white feminists before her, a single axis, a discrete half of an analogy, a population to be defended.

But Pauli Murray knew that Black women lived their lives at the confluence of Jim Crow, Jane Crow, and capitalism, and that if civil rights were to mean anything, protections from race *and* sex discrimination in employment and other arenas were necessary. In the mid-1950s, for example, Murray held two law degrees, and she had published an important book on state segregation laws that attorney and future Supreme Court justice Thurgood Marshall referred to as the "Bible."[40] She even occasionally spent weekends at her friend Eleanor Roosevelt's Hudson River retreat. On the strength of her creative writing, she had just become the first African American to be awarded a residency at the MacDowell Colony, where she befriended James Baldwin when he arrived at the famed artist retreat a few weeks later. Murray would publish her first autobiography, an account of her family's history, in 1956. Yet despite all this achievement, she simply couldn't find enough organizations willing to hire a Black female attorney, nor could she support herself as a writer and poet. She wasn't earning a living, so her literary agent found her work as a typist. Murray anonymously prepared the manuscripts of other authors.

In 1955 and 1956, Murray regularly typed for Betty Friedan.[41]

Murray worried that her legal education and her careful demonstration of how the structure of Jim Crow could be demolished rather than dismantled piecemeal had been "wasted effort."[42] After all, it was the typist skills she learned in her segregated high school that were paying the rent and purchasing her food. Murray wouldn't learn that her reasoning had in fact played a role in striking down segregation law until a decade after the fact. She had received a break in 1956 when attorney Lloyd Garrison, the great-grandson of the nineteenth-century abolitionist William Lloyd Garrison with whom Frances E. W. Harper, Harriet Jacobs, and Frederick Douglass had worked closely, offered her a position at his New York firm. The job relaunched her legal career.

Buoyed in part by this change in fortune, Murray dropped by Howard Law School in 1963. She wished to track down a copy of her two-decade-old paper. And, she hoped to collect the $10 her former professor Spottswood Robinson owed her for having lost her bet that *Plessy's* precedent of separate but equal institutions would fall within twenty-five years.

Pauli Murray in Petersborough, New Hampshire, 1955. "It's my most natural self, I think," Murray wrote on the back of the photograph before sending it to Eleanor Roosevelt. Photograph by Florence Goldman. (Courtesy of MacDowell Colony)

When she asked Robinson for her paper, to her astonishment he produced it instantly from files near at hand. As they waited for a secretary to make a carbon copy, Robinson remarked off-handedly that her paper "was helpful to us" in destroying *Plessy*. When preparing the briefs as part of Thurgood Marshall's NAACP team arguing the *Brown v. Board of Education* case, Robinson had remembered Murray's paper and dug it up from the law school's files. It was her framework that segregation caused lasting psychological harm, thereby violating the Equal Protection Clause of the Fourteenth Amendment, that led Marshall and his colleagues to their successful argument that separate educational institutions were inherently unequal and in violation of the Constitution. The Supreme Court decision had been unanimous: segregated public education "generates a feeling of inferiority" with enduring consequences;

separate could never be equal.[43] Her law school essay had influenced one of the most important civil rights victories of the century. She was stunned to the point of near speechlessness.

"Spots, why on earth didn't you tell me?" was all she could muster.[44]

Murray's political and legal work in the years to come similarly shattered long-standing justifications of discrimination. But this time she would receive credit for her contributions.

In the 1960s, "Help Wanted, Men" and "Help Wanted, Women" ads filled daily newspapers; bans persisted in preventing women from serving on juries, attending universities, or controlling their own credit cards and bank accounts; and "No Ladies," "Men Only," and "Only Escorted Women Will Be Served" signs were still posted in the windows of restaurants, clubs, and bars around the country like sentinels guarding the castle. Yet few considered women's subordinate status to rise to the level of legal segregation. Many white women considered their chief battles to have already been won: suffrage, contraception, and access to the professions. But Murray saw deep, structural inequality that cut across racial and class lines. Determined to expose the uneven distribution of power entrenched far deeper than voting rights, she built on her expert knowledge of prosecuting civil rights cases under the Equal Protection Clause of the Fourteenth Amendment to advocate another new strategy. Women's marginalization, she insisted, was similarly a violation of constitutional rights.

When some of the March on Washington demands to end Jim Crow materialized in the form of the new civil rights bill proposed in Congress in the winter of 1964, Murray found her opportunity to weaken Jane Crow. In the final hours of debate in the House of Representatives, the Virginia Democrat Howard W. Smith introduced an amendment to Title VII of the civil rights bill, the section that made discrimination illegal in the realm of employment. "Sex," he proposed, should be included among race, color, national origin, and religion as characteristics that employers were prohibited from taking into account when hiring. Smith was a segregationist who thought white Christian women would need protection from the rights Black people were gaining in the post–civil rights era. Most congressmen took Smith's suggestion to be a joke, and the sound of laughter rang throughout the chamber. The committee tasked with drafting the bill hadn't even considered including sex as a protected category. But surprisingly, the House passed the amendment and sent the civil rights bill on to the Senate. Murray was ecstatic at the inclusion of sex in the equal employment opportunity portion of the bill, whatever its origins. "As a Negro woman," Murray explained, "I knew that in many instances it was difficult to determine whether I was being discriminated against because of race or sex."[45]

Unlike discrimination on the basis of race, however, restricting access to jobs on the basis of sex was considered a significant progressive agenda. Back in 1908, labor activists had successfully pushed for sex to be a valid employment restriction in order to win worker protections. Significant labor victories such as ten-hour shift maximums for women workers were won on the basis of the *Muller v. Oregon* ruling that the state had a vested interest in shielding women from overbearing work because of their social duty to birth and raise children. In the 1960s, *Muller* still set precedent, and the most common sex-based restrictions that remained were those specifying the maximum number of hours women could work per week. The US Supreme Court continued to uphold "sex as a basis for legal classification" in a variety of arenas. A 1961 case affirmed that restricting the courtroom jury bench to men alone was constitutional given that women were tasked with the "special responsibilities" of taking care of their families and thus shouldn't be burdened with civic duties.[46]

Murray, however, was convinced sex-based protections did more harm than good. To help ensure that the clause prohibiting jobs-related sex discrimination would survive the wheeling and dealing over the civil rights bill sure to happen in the Senate, she returned to her typewriter. She drafted a provocative legal memorandum in its defense, issuing her response to leading senators, the attorney general, Vice President Hubert Humphrey, and the first lady. She stressed her innovative argument that the Fourteenth Amendment of the US Constitution guaranteed equal treatment before the law, even in the case of sex. "Title VII without the 'sex' amendment would benefit Negro males primarily and thus offer genuine equality of opportunity to only *half* of the potential Negro work force," Murray insisted.[47] A reply from Lady Bird Johnson's social secretary two weeks later alerted Murray to the success of her memo: the Johnson administration supported the sex amendment, and the

Senate soon did as well. Thanks in large part to Murray's intervention, Title VII of the Civil Rights Act of 1964 had achieved what the Fourteenth and Fifteenth Amendments failed to do a century prior—to prohibit discrimination on the basis of race *and* sex, in this case in the realm of employment. Murray won intersectional feminism's first major legal victory.

In the wake of her success, Murray joined forces with a white woman civil rights attorney, Mary O. Eastwood, on a scholarly article cum manifesto, "Jane Crow and the Law" (1965). Together, they set a legal agenda for intersectional feminism. Discrimination on the basis of sex is illegal under the Fourteenth Amendment and Title VII, they argued, correlating race and sex as "entirely comparable classes" in which the precedence of antidiscrimination law for one should set precedent for the other. Murray and Eastwood saw the doctrine of sex classification to be akin to race classification: both addressed "permanent, unchangeable, natural classes" that were "susceptible to implications of innate inferiority." Paternalistic labor protections like hours limitations and weight-lifting restrictions reinforced inequalities through "restrictions and confinement," they argued. These laws enacted "chivalry," not justice, and reproduced the logic of separate but equal.[48] Debasement on the basis of womanhood, Murray continued to stress as she had during the March on Washington battle, did not merely pose individual setbacks—sexism rose to the level of structural marginalization.

Soon Murray herself landed a major court victory against Jane Crow. In 1965, she and Dorothy Kenyon, a seventy-seven-year-old white lawyer, successfully argued on behalf of the NAACP that male-only, white-only juries in Alabama violated the Fourteenth Amendment. It was the first time a civil rights lawsuit simultaneously challenged race *and* sex discrimination together. It was also the first time a federal court ruled that the Equal Protection Clause applied to cases of sex discrimination.[49] Though the case set precedent only in Alabama, Murray was on her way to chipping away at Jane Crow.

Six years later, in a case testing the validity of an Idaho law barring women from serving as executors of wills, the Supreme Court established national precedent. *Reed v. Reed* (1971) declared that the Fourteenth Amendment prohibited differential treatment on the basis of sex throughout the United States. The promising gender rights attorney at the ACLU who represented the plaintiff made sure Murray got credit for developing this legal reasoning. When signing her brief, she added two more names, though these women hadn't been directly involved in the case: Pauli Murray and Dorothy Kenyon. The lawyer was Ruth Bader Ginsburg. Ginsburg's move to share authorship, Brittney Cooper writes, "is a model for how to solve contemporary issues among young feminists over white feminists' appropriation without attribution of the intellectual and political labor of women of color."[50]

Murray's insight that sexism was akin to racism considerably advanced the project of intersectional feminism. Her reasoning depended on analogies, a favored rhetorical strategy of white feminist theory. Yet in her hands analogy became a method of convergence, rather than separation. White feminist theorists like Stanton posed equivalences between groups of people in which one allegedly stands in for the other: the woman becomes the slave. Murray, however, interrogated multiple structures of power and showed how they worked in tandem. She didn't position the women's movement as a separate, autonomous campaign from other social movements, as Betty Friedan did: "The students were doing it. The blacks were doing it. It was time for us," Friedan reflected in 2000. These formulations insist on distinct, parallel identities that never meet, leaving Black women structural impossibilities. By contrast, as Cooper and others have argued, Murray created a conceptual framework for revealing the connections between sexism and racism. "Since the problems of race discrimination and sex discrimination meet in me," Murray wrote, "I must consider both as equally important." For those who live at the crosshairs, she revealed, these forces compound one another, multiplying in effect, such that it is Black women, not white, who experience the fullest brunt of sexism within Black and white spaces.[51]

Murray sits at a key historical juncture. Her legal work in the 1960s made significant progress achieving the agenda initially set by Frances E. W. Harper, Frederick Douglass, and others one hundred years prior—civil rights that simultaneously addressed the forces of racism and sexism as separate, but overlapping, forms of social power. Murray also laid the foundation for feminist theory in her wake. The term *intersectionality* was first coined by Black feminist legal scholar Kimberlé Crenshaw in 1989 to address the confluence of racism and sexism in the realm of law, and she cited Pauli Murray as a precedent.[52]

Intersectional feminism rejects white feminism's biopolitical mandate to advance oneself through dispossessing others. Instead, it focuses on the needs of the most marginalized as the best vantage to power in all its complexity. "If Black women were free," the Combahee River Collective theorized in 1977, "it would mean that everyone else would have to be free since our freedom would necessitate the destruction of all the systems of oppression."[53]

∽ ∽

Murray had helped ensure that the civil rights bill included the prohibition of sex-based employment discrimination. The "Help Wanted, Women" and race-segregated job ads were to become a relic of the past. Yet a piece of civil rights legislation is only as good as the institutions that enforce it and the social movements that hold those institutions accountable. In 1965, a new body was created to oversee the application of Title VII in the workplace, the Equal Employment Opportunity Commission (EEOC). Its leadership gave every indication that it would *not* be taking sex discrimination seriously. In a major speech, the EEOC executive director Herman Edelsburg declared that the inclusion of "sex" in the civil rights employment law was a "fluke," a bastard idea "conceived out of wedlock." Meanwhile, the EEOC's legal team further weakened the provision, arguing in law review articles for what Murray called an "unduly restrictive interpretation" of the sex clause.[54] The EEOC was not willing to take women seriously as workers in need of rights.

Murray perceived that in effect Title VII would offer no protection from sex discrimination. Unless strong outside pressure forced the EEOC to uphold the clause, women would continue to provide capitalism's largest supply of exploitable labor. "What will it take to arouse the working women of this country to fight for their rights?" she wrote to her network of feminist attorney allies. "Do you suppose the time has come for the organization of a strong national Ad Hoc Committee of women?"[55]

From the stage of New York's Biltmore Hotel, an upper-crust establishment whose bar didn't even admit women patrons, Murray made a more momentous recommendation. She was an invited speaker at the annual conference of the National Council of Women, an organization founded by Elizabeth Cady Stanton and Susan B. Anthony—and the setting where Frances E. W.

Harper had shut down Alice Fletcher's appeal for white women to civilize the so-called dependent races. Women, Murray counseled her genteel listeners, should prepare to demand that Title VII's prohibition of sex discrimination be enforced.

"It should not be necessary to have another March on Washington in order that there be equal job opportunities for all. But if this necessity should arise, I hope women will not flinch from the thought."[56]

Murray hadn't thought her speech particularly moving or radical, covering as it did the legal details of Title VII, and she returned home that evening to New Haven where she was about to become the first African American to earn a Yale doctorate in law. But she had underestimated her own effectiveness as a speaker, and her audience was largely white upper-middle-class women.[57] Murray's spirited provocation that ladies ought to revolt in the streets landed an account of her speech in the pages of the next day's *New York Times*.

When New York woke up and read their morning papers, Murray's phone rang. Betty Friedan was on the other end, and she wanted to talk. Friedan requested an interview for her new book, a follow-up to *The Feminine Mystique*. Friedan never finished that book, though she sold it to her publisher, wrote one-third of it, and gave it a memorable name: *Jane Crow*.[58]

"When I was fired for being pregnant, there were no words such as 'sex discrimination' in my vocabulary," Friedan later recalled. "Those words 'sex discrimination,'" in the air since the passage of Title VII, "suddenly threw light onto the murkiness. . . . I tracked down Pauli Murray at Yale and made a date to meet her. And I started down the road that would lead to the women's movement."[59]

Within months, Friedan, Murray, and a dozen others would join forces to launch the National Organization for Women. Together, they were instrumental in reinventing feminist activism for the civil rights era.

༄ ༅

Murray provided Friedan with considerably more than an interview and a manuscript title. By this time, Murray was well connected with other feminists quietly and not-so-quietly working for women's rights from positions within federal institutions and commissions. Pauli Murray "tuned me into the underground network of women," Friedan explained. "I didn't have to work underground, however. As the author of a best-selling book on women, I was often invited to the White House in the Johnson years, when token women were needed."[60] Friedan's visibility and independence were major assets to the underground network, however. Government employees couldn't fight government institutions, but journalists could.

The underground turned into a movement in June 1966, as Murray, Friedan, Mary Eastwood, and others attended the third annual conference of the Commission on the Status of Women, an organization established by President Kennedy to further women's rights. On the escalator of the Washington Hilton the first morning, Friedan ran into Murray and Dorothy Haener, a labor leader with the United Auto Workers. They were all concerned that Title VII's prohibition of sex discrimination in employment was about to be rendered meaningless. The EEOC was retreating from any enforcement of sex equality and had recently decided that sex-restricted job ads were permissible because they served "the convenience of readers." All three suspected the real reason: sex-segregated employment that confined half the population to lower-paying jobs served the interests of capital. White women made about fifty cents, on average, to every white man's dollar, and Black women made only seventy-one cents compared to white women. Jane Crow rendered women, Black and white, a tremendous source of surplus labor, for the value they produced for their employers far exceeded the value of their paychecks.[61] Murray and Haener successfully urged Friedan to host a meeting in her hotel room that night to strategize how women could push the commission to enforce Title VII.

From her position on the next morning's keynote panel, Murray made plain that the EEOC must act to protect workplace equity. But the commission refused to offer even a resolution recommending that the EEOC uphold Title VII—the commission's function was restricted to window-dressing for the Democratic White House. Angry and energized, at the conference lunch Friedan, Murray, and a dozen others whispered and traded notes plotting a new organization that could pressure government agencies into action. Together they named their new group NOW—the National Organization for Women—and Friedan sketched the first line of its mission on a paper napkin:

"to take the actions needed to bring women into the mainstream of American society now, exercising all the privileges and responsibilities thereof, in truly equal partnership with men."[62]

Betty Friedan became president of NOW and Murray one of its cofounders alongside Eastwood, Haener, and four dozen others, including March on Washington alumna Anna Arnold Hedgeman and Puerto Rican activist Inez Casiano. Over the summer, Murray joined a small group of seven who strategized building NOW into a permanent entity. At the founding conference that fall, she pushed the organization to address social injustice in all its forms, including poverty, rather than focusing exclusively on women's legal rights. Wealth inequality hit Black women particularly hard, Murray stressed. After Friedan drafted the full-length NOW mission statement, Murray replaced Friedan's narrower focus on individual "equal rights" with a nod to the wide-ranging nature of social power. "We realize that women's problems are linked to many broader questions of social justice," Murray inserted after striking through Friedan's words, and NOW would attend not only to "discrimination," but also "deprivation."[63]

Murray long advocated for Black women and white women to join together in coalition to fight the concentration of power in the hands of wealthy men. But Friedan's NOW would fail to be the Black-white alliance Murray sought, much less a broadly multiracial one. Despite a somewhat diverse leadership, the organization largely enacted Friedan's agenda: enabling middle-class women to thrive. Hedgeman was leading NOW's task force on poverty, but the bulk of NOW increasingly sidelined her, just as it dismissed Murray when she insisted that the organization fight the federal government to include jobs for women in its poverty remediation programs. NOW wanted to focus instead on middle-class women who were entering the workforce, emphasizing measures such as gaining access to public accommodations that still barred women, removing quotas on women's admissions to graduate school, and supporting federal childcare centers for working mothers. Poor women weren't on their agenda. Friedan championed passing the Equal Rights Amendment, a bill that Murray, at the time, didn't support because it would focus only on the rights of sex. Disappointed, Murray withdrew from the organization she had not only helped found but had helped inspire. The single-axis focus on the ERA, Murray wrote, pulling her name from the NOW board of directors nomination slate in 1967, would result in NOW's restricting itself "almost solely to 'women's rights' without strong bonds with other movements toward human rights." The hierarchy of sex NOW was adopting might even "develop into a 'head-on collision' with Black civil rights and other struggles," she warned.[64]

Many of its founders had established NOW as "an NAACP for women," but the organization was now pursuing white feminist politics rather than building coalitions to fight the intertwined forces of racism, sexism, and capitalism. Under Friedan's leadership, NOW treated women as a class unto themselves, held back by sex alone. Murray told her colleagues that she wouldn't participate in a platform that sliced her three ways, "into Negro at one time, woman at another, or worker at another."[65] She insisted that Black women had to fight on all fronts simultaneously.

For a moment, there had been a possibility that the counterhistory of feminism would productively transform white feminism, pulling it toward a more capacious notion of justice. But that moment was short-lived. White feminists

Betty Friedan speaking to reporters in 1967. (Courtesy of Prints and Photographs Division, Library of Congress)

continued to view Black women as resources to be tapped, rather than strate-
gists of true equality.

Friedan, meanwhile, helped build NOW into a powerful organization that
represented sex discrimination cases, conducted boycotts, organized pickets,
and fought for abortion rights. She "wanted young Black women" in the movement, "especially in the South," though she didn't always recognize the impe-
riousness of her wish—even after four decades to reflect. On a trip to Atlanta
in the late 1960s, she encouraged women in the Student Nonviolent Coordinating Committee (SNCC) to join the feminist movement and was dismayed
when many insisted their priority was affirming Black men, not strengthening
Black women. "Well, I wanted to spank them," Friedan reflected—in the year
2000!—"but they learned soon enough. They eventually came in." Yet the statistics tell a different story. In 1972, pollsters conducted a national survey to
gauge support for the women's liberation movement. They found that 67 percent of Black women agreed with the cause of women's rights, while only 35
percent of white women did.[66] Once more it was Black women, not white, who
led the way in feminist consciousness, just as they had in 1963.

~ ~

Under Friedan's leadership, NOW turned to the task of making women's liberation respectable. This meant cleansing the movement. For Friedan, infamously,
feminism had internal enemies who threatened the success of the movement
and must be eliminated, and those enemies were lesbians. She sought to build
an organization that would influence the people who she thought mattered—
heterosexual middle-class Americans—and the visibility of lesbians and lesbian
politics struck her as "the lavender menace." In the late 1940s and 1950s, Friedan and her socialist associates had been pursued by McCarthy's campaign to
cleanse government of the "red menace"; now, she was wielding a similar technique within the movement. Lesbians, to Friedan, were "radical man-haters"
who endangered her agenda of speaking "to and for and from the mainstream."[67]

When Friedan organized NOW's first Congress to Unite Women in 1969
to bring together multiple factions of the women's movement, she excluded
any out lesbian speakers, prohibited any discussion of lesbianism, and purged
lesbian groups like the Daughters of Bilitis, a middle-class club formed in
1955. Soon, she fired out lesbian Rita Mae Brown from her position as New

York–NOW's newsletter editor. Meanwhile, several deeply committed members resigned in protest of the organization's homophobia, including the first executive director.[68]

But lesbians wouldn't disappear quietly. Rita Mae Brown was determined to make clear that lesbian issues were integral to women's liberation. She and a group of about forty women staged a "zap"—a seemingly spontaneous, theatrical style of protest begun the year prior by the Gay Liberation Movement—at the opening event of NOW's second annual Congress to Unite Women. Inside the public school auditorium, one activist waiting backstage cut the lights and microphone. When she turned the lights back on, dozens of others popped out of the aisles and seats and tore off their blouses and tops to reveal purple T-shirts proclaiming "Lavender Menace." The Lavender Menace stormed the stage and challenged the audience to join them in their politics and passion. "A lesbian," the manifesto they circulated throughout the crowd proclaimed, "is the rage of all women condensed to the point of explosion."[69]

The NOW women, Brown later remembered, were nonplussed, unsure if they should "shit, run, or go blind." Brown would soon establish the Furies, a lesbian commune in DC, and publish the twentieth century's most widely read lesbian novel, *Rubyfruit Jungle*. But for the next thirty years, Friedan would maintain that the Lavender Menace action, along with the "radical lesbian fringe" more generally, was the work of undercover CIA agents akin to those in the Black Power movement trying to "alienate" the movement from the mainstream.[70]

Friedan aimed to "restructure professions, marriage, the family, the home"—not by dismantling those institutions, but by changing women's position inside of them. She wanted middle-class women to be free to pursue a career. That essentially meant one thing: convincing bourgeois white people, both women and men, that housewives deserved to flourish. That meant lesbians had to go, because they jeopardized her mission to transform mainstream sex roles and social inequality between women and men. This emphasis on Friedan's antagonistic posture toward other women is no exaggeration. Friedan herself characterized NOW's early days as beset by "the enemies without and the enemies within."[71]

Friedan was pushed out of the NOW presidency in 1970 by term limits and the repercussions of her own ego and temper. Aileen Hernandez, an African

American civil rights activist and labor leader who had earlier resigned her position as an EEOC commissioner in frustration with its refusal to act on Title VII, assumed the helm. Friedan remained a central influence, however, and served as the figurehead of the wildly successful 1970 Women's Strike for Equality that drew tens of thousands of women to the streets to commemorate fifty years of (white) women's voting rights—an event she mentioned for the very first time during the NOW press conference publicizing that Hernandez was assuming the presidency. "When she announced it, I almost fell off my chair," Hernandez reflected—though the faux pas wouldn't have mattered much, for all cameras were trained on Friedan. Her bombshell had done the trick of keeping her center stage. In 1971, NOW adopted a resolution that lesbianism was "a legitimate concern for feminism." At the end of the decade, however, years after Hernandez stepped down from the presidency, she lamented that NOW "has been silent on almost any issue that deals with the inequity of society more than the inequity of being female."[72]

The result of these white feminist politics was that white women, and white women alone, flocked to the organization in the tens of thousands. In 1974, an internal survey revealed that NOW's members were 90 percent white. The results were never released to the public, and NOW doesn't appear to have studied its own demographics in the forty-five years since.[73]

Yet Friedan wasn't the only person openly worried that lesbian politics would weaken NOW's ability to effect institutional change. During a self-aggrandizing account of her role in the women's movement for a 1973 issue of the *New York Times Magazine*, Friedan took the opportunity to lambast lesbians for attempting to "manipulate" feminism "into an orgy of sex hatred." A flurry of letters to the editor followed from prominent feminists like Ti-Grace Atkinson and Toni Carabillo, the national vice president of NOW; all those published criticized Friedan's position on homosexuality, except for one. Pauli Murray, though grieving the death of her partner Irene Barlow just two weeks earlier, sat in front of her typewriter and fired off a letter to the *Times*. Friedan's article, Murray upheld, was "mellow, well-reasoned and fair," an opinion she authorized with her own credentials as a feminist initially encouraged by "the late Eleanor Roosevelt" to contest Harvard Law's ban on women students back in 1944. "A lesbian take-over" of the movement, she agreed with Friedan, would only strengthen its opponents. "Birchites, racists, segregationists and arch-conservatives" knew "that Friedan and her cohorts are far more of a threat . . . than the so-called revolutionary feminists" because they worked to reform the system from within. Lesbians, Murray concluded, "are only a minority" of women. "Problems of equality peculiar to lesbians" thus did not rise to the level of "feminist problems." Murray and Friedan spoke in unison: homosexuality was a "private personal matter."[74]

Murray and Friedan's shared belief that homosexuality was not a valid political issue for feminism likely stems in part from their common roots as activists. Both first came into social movements through labor and socialist organizing, which generally saw economic issues as the baseline of all political relations, the only structure that counts. Both Friedan and Murray made significant innovations to the Old Left framework, pushing it into the realm of sex justice, and for Murray, racial justice, too. But homosexuality, for this pair, did not have a history, and was not connected to structural uses and abuses of power: it was a bedroom concern.

At a Kansas City event in 1981, a lesbian audience member approached Friedan after her lecture about reinventing the family.

"Why don't you talk more about gay families and lesbians?" she asked.

"That's sex, not politics. Or it should be," Friedan replied.[75] The irony of her own work to exclude lesbians from the movement—the very definition of politics—seems to have escaped her.

While Murray and Friedan shared a public attitude in common, each had very different personal stakes in the role of queerness in feminism. In Murray's own writing, she often inserted the term "social minorities" alongside victims of race and sex discrimination as the constituents for whom she fought—a likely innuendo for those, like her, who fell outside sex and sexuality norms. Once, in a letter in 1977 criticizing an Episcopalian bishop for speculating about her sexuality, Murray interrogated his authority to speak about queerness at all: "What do you really know about sexuality—heterosexuality, bi-sexuality, homosexuality, transsexuality, unisexuality? What do you know about metabolic imbalance? . . . The varieties of approach to mental health?" It was about as close as she would ever come to publicly associating with trans people. But Murray crossed out the lines and then never mailed the letter.[76]

In public, Murray remained haunted by her own leanings to keep the movement and her own biography solidly within the boundaries of sex respectability. And she was likely denied an important opportunity to change institutions from the inside, her preferred agenda, on account of her queerness. Though she was nominated to the EEOC in 1966, she failed to pass the FBI's security clearance—and was deeply spooked by what the agency possibly learned about her sex identity, romantic relationships, socialist affiliations in the 1930s and 1940s, and history of mental health breakdowns. When Murray wrote her second autobiography in the early 1980s, as she was dying, she scrubbed any mention of her romances and her persistent self-knowledge that she was more male than female. She refers to her life partner, Irene Barlow, only as one of her "dearest friends." Gender and sexuality were not public issues, for Murray, and thus not part of her account of the intersections of power, even as she consistently pushed against social expectations of binary male/female and binary Black/white identities she saw as "rigid molds" constraining her.[77]

Friedan, for her part, remained hostile to the role of sexuality in feminism throughout her life—except for when she chose to write about her own sexual liberation and her passionate feelings for men. Perhaps this very public heterosexuality made gay rights less threatening to her personally as time went on. She came to endorse lesbian rights as a distinct cause, lending surprise support at a crucial moment. When the 1977 National Women's Conference in Houston debated a highly controversial resolution supporting lesbian rights, Friedan took the floor to announce, "I am known to be violently opposed to the lesbian issue. . . . Now my priority is in passing the ERA. And because there is nothing in it that will give any protection to homosexuals, I believe we must help the women who are lesbians."[78]

～ ～

Pauli Murray was ill-suited to the radical politics of the late 1960s and 1970s. As a professor of American Studies at Brandeis University, she offered some of the nation's first women's studies courses emphasizing African American feminist thinkers. Relatedly, she only earned tenure after mounting a characteristically fierce battle against the tenure review committee's criticism that her research lacked "brilliance and conceptual power." But she clashed with students in the rising Black nationalist movement. Just as she had wanted alliances between Black and white feminists to fight for institutional change, Murray wanted integration between Black and white society rather than distinct radical movements. She was also profoundly uncomfortable with the reclamation of the term "Black," insisting on the identity "Negro." Both positions infuriated her students. When Murray opposed their demands for an Afro-American Studies program in 1969, one of her star undergraduates stormed out of class, shouting "Black solidarity" as she went. The student was Patricia Hill—soon to be known as Patricia Hill Collins, the scholar most responsible for carrying the theory of intersectionality out of the realm of law and into feminist movements.[79] Murray helped train the next generation of intersectional feminists, even as they clashed against her old-fashioned ways.

But neither academia nor the book of poetry she published was to remain Murray's destiny. She still had other barriers to demolish. Irene Barlow's

Reverend Pauli Murray. Photograph by Susan Mullally. (Courtesy of the artist)

death from cancer in 1973 left Murray bereft. As Murray knelt before the cross and placed her hands on the coffin of her "silent partner" and "spiritual mate," she felt a current of energy pulsing through her. Active in the Episcopalian church since the age of thirty, a faith she had shared with Barlow for nearly fifteen years, Murray knew that spirit become palpable was no coincidence: it was a call to serve. The Episcopalian church, however, still refused to ordain women to the ministry, a position it shared only with Catholicism. But Murray took an 80 percent pay cut and entered the seminary anyway, and in 1977, at the age of sixty-six, became the first African American woman to be named an Episcopalian priest, and during the same month the church first ordained a woman. For her first service administering the Holy Eucharist, an event CBS broadcast on its evening news, Murray chose a church with profound personal significance. She held service at the North Carolina parish where her grandmother Cornelia, then enslaved, had been baptized.[80]

Murray's departure from law and academia for the priesthood was a significant shift in her political tactics. But it wasn't necessarily a change in strategy. Throughout her life, Murray was guided by deep faith and wrestled with power in myriad forms, fighting institutional, legal, and organizational battles against injustice wielded in the name of race and sex. Her turn to spiritual life can be understood as an extension of her fundamental engagement with power, in all its forms. Power, for Murray, was not strictly secular: it extended to the universe itself. In uniting her politics with faith, she continued a long tradition of feminist activism that cultivated a relationship with the divine as the ultimate arbiter of justice. As theorized by activists from Frances E. W. Harper, Harriet Jacobs, and Zitkala-Ša through Murray, intersectional feminism negotiates a new relationship to power both material and divine, extending beyond the "rigid molds" of the flesh. To that end, she published some of the first work bringing Black theology and feminist theology into relation.[81]

"When I say that I am a child of God—made in his image," Murray sermonized before a congregation in 1975, "I imply that 'Black is beautiful,' that White is beautiful, that Red is beautiful, [and] Yellow is beautiful. I do not need to make special pleading for my sex—male or female, or in-between—to bolster self-esteem."[82] All were connected to the divine and all were equally valuable, including those who defied the binary of biological sex.

By contrast, white feminist politics generally restricts itself to the material dimension, emphasizing secular rationalism, scientific modernity, and capitalist hierarchy as ways to optimize human existence. In the white feminist agenda, power is something to be seized to maximize opportunity and quality. Its horizon becomes biopolitics, the twinned movements of enhancing the health and earning potential of the few while extracting, depleting, and disposing of the many.

CHAPTER SIX

TERF GATEKEEPING AND TRANS FEMINIST HORIZONS

Janice Raymond and Sandy Stone

To encounter the transsexual body, to apprehend a transgendered consciousness articulating itself, is to risk a revelation of the constructedness of the natural order. . . . As the bearers of this disquieting news, we transsexuals often suffer for the pain of others. . . . Though we forego the privilege of naturalness, we are not deterred, for we ally ourselves instead with the chaos and blackness from which Nature itself spills forth.

—Susan Stryker, "My Words to Victor
Frankenstein Above the Village of Chamounix"

IN APRIL 1973, FIFTEEN HUNDRED WOMEN—SIMULTANEOUSLY ANGRY AND ECSTATIC— converged among the brick and palm trees of the UCLA campus. "It's beginning. FAR OUT," an organizer named Barbara McLean enthused backstage in her pocket journal as a Friday night concert opened the West Coast Lesbian Conference. "I feel as though I'm plugged into an outlet," she relished, looking out at hundreds and hundreds of short-haired, bra-less, free-spirited, mostly white women clad in androgynous plaid filling all the seats and clogging the aisles of Moore Hall.[1]

McLean and her co-organizers created the largest queer women's gathering yet held in the United States aiming to consolidate a unified political agenda for lesbians. To be a lesbian-feminist signified far more than whom one dated—it was a deep excavation of patriarchy from one's body, desire, and community. Many lesbian-feminists aimed to construct a radically new mode of inhabiting the world, one perhaps coming to life that night at UCLA. The West Coast Lesbian Conference, however, would become famous for the roiling conflict that nearly broke it apart and foreshadowed decades of discord to come.

Two hours into the event, white folk singer–songwriter Beth Elliott walked onto the stage with her acoustic guitar slung across her torso. Beth was a twenty-one-year-old member of the conference steering committee who had served as vice president of the San Francisco chapter of the Daughters of Bilitis, the oldest lesbian organization nationwide. She loved the playfulness, freedom, and aesthetics of lesbian-feminist culture, the way it nurtured deep love for women and their art and cultivated a sense of humor in the midst of rampant misogyny. "Well if you like sexist music" she crooned in one song, "then country music's the best. The women sing of how men are king and how it's fun to be oppressed."[2]

But not everyone agreed that Elliott had a place in the movement. As she took her seat onstage, two women rushed the platform, grabbing her microphone away.

"He is a transsexual and a rapist!" one yelled. "He has no right to perform!"

"You're wrong!" another woman protested. "She is a woman because she chooses to be a woman! What right do you have to define her sexuality?!"[3]

A melee quickly consumed the auditorium. A few women jumped the stage to attack Elliott, but two performers intervened and absorbed the blows themselves.[4]

Eventually, a small group took the stage and drew the line: "If Beth Elliott can't perform, then no one performs."[5] To settle the crowd, an organizer polled the audience on whether or not Elliott would be permitted to play her set. One of her many allies sat next to her, holding her hand. The crowd overwhelmingly chose for her to continue.

Elliott began to strum her guitar. But a vocal faction caused an uproar, drowning out her sound. Once more, her right to be on stage was subjected to popular vote. Once more, the audience voted for her to perform, this time three to one. Elliott's sweet voice rang throughout the auditorium even as her body shook and ninety angry women stormed out in protest.[6]

One member of the crowd was particularly incensed by Elliott's presence at the Lesbian Conference: former child star Robin Morgan, famous for her writing on sisterhood. Morgan was to deliver the conference keynote the following day. In her view, "one smug male in granny glasses and an earth-mother gown" sowed discord in the middle of lesbian utopia. Morgan stayed up half the night rewriting her keynote. It was an important speech for her, intended to help set the political agenda of lesbian-feminism, and she joked the text was to be kept for posterity "in a secret safe deposit box guarded night and day by the spirits of Stanton and Anthony."[7]

Morgan's speech was held outdoors the next morning on the campus quad, her podium perched one-third of the way up an imposing set of eighty-seven stairs. She insisted on her own credentials as a "political lesbian," though she was married to "a Faggot-Effeminist."[8] She deserved a place in the lesbian movement, she assured her audience. But Beth Elliott did not.

"No, I will not call a male 'she,'" Morgan inveighed. "Thirty-two years of suffering in this androcentric society, and of surviving, have earned me the name 'woman'; one walk down the street by a male transvestite, five minutes of his being hassled (which he may enjoy), and then he dares, he dares, to think he understands our pain? No, in our mothers' names and in our own, we must not call him sister. We know what's at work when whites wear blackface; the same thing is at work when men wear drag."[9]

Morgan had invented a new iteration of white feminism's favorite rhetorical structure: the Black/woman analogy. In this version, racist mockery is equated with gender transition. The analogy would stick.

"I charge him as an opportunist, an infiltrator, and a destroyer—with the mentality of a rapist," Morgan denounced. "You can let him into your workshops—or you can deal with him." Her speech ran twice the length of her allotted time.[10]

The Gutter Dykes, a transphobic group from Berkeley, blocked Barbara McLean from her hosting duties at the mike and continued Morgan's screed.

Trans-exclusionary radical feminists (TERFs), who object to transgender rights in any form, had arrived at the lesbian-feminist revolution. Accounts of the showdown at the West Coast Lesbian Conference soon spread across the lesbian press, helping to kick off a firestorm that would burn for years. Many, like organizer and writer McLean, insisted upon Beth Elliott's rightful place in the women-loving-women community. Others, especially those like Robin Morgan who had access to audiences far larger than readers of the photocopied newsletters produced by lesbian-feminist collectives, drew battle lines, framing Elliott as an enemy of the movement. Even as Betty Friedan came to gradually endorse lesbian rights, a new specter had emerged within white feminism: the transsexual woman.

TERF anger soon shifted from Elliott to another target within the women's music scene. In the mid-1970s, the beloved lesbian music collective Olivia Records invited a recording engineer named Sandy Stone, a trans woman, to join their community.* Stone's presence at Olivia became a point of violent contention, revealing the extent and depth of TERF opposition to trans women joining the lesbian-feminist movement. None of the objectors were as influential as Janice Raymond, a nun turned academic, who released a notorious study of transsexuality that set the TERF agenda for decades.

Though transsexual rights was a new topic in the 1970s, its opponents within women's liberation drew on the long tradition of white feminist politics. Rallying around the fantasy that sex discrimination is the main factor that shapes women's lives and that women are united by this shared experience, TERFs conceived of a starkly binary universe in which men only oppress, and women are only oppressed. Because trans women did not suffer the allegedly universal experience of growing up female, they maintained, they were, therefore, men and oppressors. Updating white feminism for the gay liberation era, TERFs developed a new cleansing agenda: removing trans women from the women's movement and especially lesbian separatist communities.

But, as at UCLA where the majority of the crowd twice voted that Beth Elliott remain on stage, the TERF position was far from universally embraced within feminism. Today, 1970s feminism is often, incorrectly, understood to have been overwhelmingly transphobic. To this day, TERFism threatens to drown out the existence of the counterhistory, disappearing the role trans

---

* The terms *TERF* and *trans women* are twenty-first-century coinages. I project them backwards because the ongoing struggle for trans rights requires recognizing the consistency of anti-trans and pro-trans feminisms and communities over time.

women themselves played in the movement and flattening a period of struggle into a single, white feminist history. Yet while trans women and their allies had far smaller platforms than Morgan and Raymond, they fought back against TERF insistence that there is only one way to be a woman.[11] The more expansive accounts of sex, gender, and power they developed form an important current of intersectional feminism.

⁓ ⁓

Two years after the West Coast Lesbian Conference and 350 miles to the north, a group of lesbian musicians from Los Angeles walked into a Santa Cruz stereo repair shop. The Wizard of Aud was a lesbian hangout, more of a collective than a store. Flyers adorned the walls and women draped on the sofa, catching up on each other's lives. The shop owner, a polymath and technology whiz named Sandy Stone, taught the collective's members how to repair audio equipment. In those days of cheap living on the California coast, fixing five stereos a month would enable them to make rent; selling used equipment brought in additional revenue.

Stone, buried in a stereo behind the counter, nonetheless felt eyes boring into her from the front of the store. A small sign hung above her: "Psychiatric Help 5¢."

"Can I help you?" she asked, looking up at the small group of women, white and Black.

"We're from Olivia Records, and we hear that you're a recording engineer. We're looking for a woman to engineer some music for us. Would you like to try doing that?"[12] Olivia Records had been cofounded by members of the Furies when the DC house with Rita Mae Brown and others dissolved. Now it was the largest women's music label in the country and a pillar of the lesbian separatist movement. Linda Tillery, Judy Dlugacz, and several other collective members had recently learned of Stone's engineering prowess from Leslie Ann Jones, the first woman engineer hired at ABC Studios, so they drove up north to meet her.

"Yeah!" Stone affirmed. Olivia members had called her about a week prior, so she had been expecting the visit. "But I think I should tell you before we go any further that I'm a transsexual."

"Yeah, we know," they replied nonchalantly.[13]

Stone was a spectacular recording engineer. She had started about eight years prior, in 1968, when she bluffed her way into a job at the newly launched and soon-to-be legendary Record Plant studio in Manhattan. The studio needed a technician to repair their state-of-the-art equipment, and though Stone had never seen anything like their Scully twelve-track, she had a gift for technology. She had been part of a team building some of the first solid-state computers when fresh out of high school in 1955 and had also worked as an auditory researcher at the famous Menninger Clinic in Topeka, Kansas, teaching myna birds to stutter. In her early thirties, she wanted to break into rock 'n' roll recording. She speed-read the twelve-track's manual during her Record Plant interview, using a skill she had taught herself while still in elementary school. When she walked over to the machine, it took her two minutes to fix it. Once owner Gary Kellgren collected his jaw from the floor, he hired her on the spot. Stone had just arrived in New York to pursue her dream and didn't yet have a place to live, so she slept on Jimi Hendrix's old capes in the basement.[14]

Three weeks into her Record Plant gig, the head engineer recording Hendrix's "Stone Free" and other songs fell sick in the middle of a shift. He insisted Stone take over. Though she was just the repair guy, everyone in the studio had seen her watching, rapt, while they recorded and mixed. When Stone sat at the console, she was electric. She felt that sometimes other people, including Jimi, could see the blue energy radiating off her.[15]

Eventually, Kellgren wanted her to head a subsidiary company, but Stone wanted her hands on the music itself. At an acid-fueled party in upstate New York, a well-heeled Timothy Leary supporter solicited adventurers interested in heading west, right then, in his chartered jet. Sandy raised her hand, and as she came down off the acid the next morning, she found herself sitting on the curb at the San Jose airport. She stayed in California and her engineering career took her to San Francisco and LA, where she recorded and mixed Crosby, Stills, and Nash; Jefferson Airplane; and Van Morrison's album *Tupelo Honey* and did gigs with the Grateful Dead, The Byrds, and others, often under the name of Doc Storch.[16]

Doc Storch had realized his rock 'n' roll dreams, but he was still sleeping on the floor regularly.* And, he couldn't shake a gnawing feeling that he would die

---

* I use the male pronoun here in accordance with Sandy Stone's groundbreaking theorizing about refusing the gender binary and the erasures of passing, as explored below.

in his body if he didn't finally take action to address a knowledge he'd carried within him since the dreams that began when he was four or five years old: he always appeared as a girl. She began to transition, with the support of Marty Balin, founder and vocalist of Jefferson Airplane, and especially David Crosby and Graham Nash, along with other musicians she worked with. But needing a wider queer, feminist community, Stone moved north to famously free-spirited Santa Cruz in 1974. She found quick and easy work repairing stereos at a home electronics chain store in the town mall. When she carefully explained to her employers that she was transitioning sex, they immediately fired her. She responded by opening the Wizard of Aud right across the street. Within two years, she and her burgeoning collective put the corporate shop out of business. "They had multiple factors going against them," Stone later reflected. "One of them was that no one went to them to have anything repaired anymore."[17]

Olivia Records was a far cry from the Record Plant. Despite the epic, drug-fueled recording sessions with Hendrix and others, the Record Plant's formal structure was more or less like a regular business, and its clients were among the country's best musicians. Olivia, on the other hand, was a true collective, forging communal lesbian life among themselves while also circulating lesbian music around the country. Olivia Records rented three houses on a block of LA's Wilshire neighborhood, where members lived and recorded, sharing all expenses and profits as well as rotating cooking and cleaning duties. The politics of their music, and the material conditions in which they produced and distributed records, were as important as the sound itself. This resulted in tracks with quiet, muddy instrumentalization, even as Olivia's cofounders Meg Christian and especially Cris Williamson had resonant, luminous voices—Bonnie Raitt remarked that hearing Williamson sing for the first time "was like hearing honey dripped on a cello."[18]

After that initial meeting at the Wizard of Aud, Stone began a yearlong trial period with Olivia Records, recording an album by the all-women rock band BeBe K'Roche, remixing Williamson's breakout album *The Changer and the Changed*, and staying at Olivia's LA houses.

At first, Stone, unused to making politics and music at the same time, kept saying the wrong thing in the studio.

"Well if she can't play, we should get somebody who can," she remarked during a recording session.

"Sit down, and shut up," collective members replied.[19]

The sisterhood wasn't new to her—Stone was part of a lesbian outdoors group called the Amazon 9 adventurous enough to be dropped by airplane north of the Arctic Circle in Alaska and kayak for thirteen days down the Kobuk River. But she hadn't been able to combine her recording talents with her commitment to women's culture, until now. Soon enough, Stone embraced what she saw as the Olivia ethos: "Learning the spirit of sisterhood was more important than technical perfection." In 1976, having passed her vetting period, the collective developed a new vision together. Stone would convert one of the house's living rooms into a school, and she would train a new generation of women recording engineers in sound design as well as developing and building recording equipment.[20]

Olivia Records made lesbianness itself a felt reality at a time when most gay life of any kind was conducted behind closed doors. Homosexuality was only removed from the *Diagnostic and Statistical Manual* of psychiatric pathologies in 1973, the same year the collective was founded. Yet Williamson's sensual, woman-loving *The Changer and the Changed* was one of the nation's top-selling independently produced albums for the next twenty years. Members took their role as liaisons for the lesbian sisterhood seriously. One crushed-out fan recalls writing an impassioned letter, at age sixteen, to singer and collective member Teresa Trull and receiving a lengthy letter in reply—full of Trull's recommendations to the women's bookstores in the teen's region.[21]

Lesbian-themed folk songs like "Wise Women," "Leaping Lesbians," and "Ode to a Gym Teacher" reclaimed as erotic and political what the mainstream saw as monstrosity in the eyes of the patriarchy. But folk was far from the only output at Olivia. With Black singers like Linda Tillery among its early members, the collective pushed women's music beyond its acoustic comfort zone, releasing jazz, soul, gospel, funk, and poetry by white and Black musicians. Black lesbian Pat Parker's 1976 spoken-word LP directly confronted the white feminist myth that the only oppressors were men. "Sister," her narrator corrects her white girlfriend, "your foot's smaller. But it's still on my neck."[22] One show created a scandal. Teresa Trull wore lipstick onstage, an allegedly unacceptable mark of women's oppression.

Olivia's prominence meant that Stone's presence became a lightning rod. One day, the collective received an eleven-by-fourteen manila envelope, the kind containing a college acceptance packet or a court summons. Janice Raymond, a former Catholic nun and now a PhD candidate in ethics at Boston College studying under famous feminist theologian Mary Daly, had mailed a chapter of her dissertation on transsexuality. Raymond's chapter painted transsexuals—which for her meant men masquerading as women—as dangerous dupes of stereotypical sex roles and of an exploitative medical establishment. She alleged that transsexual lesbians in separatist communities were akin to rapists who possessed women's bodies and invaded their spaces. Collective members were disgusted but quickly dismissed the writing, as Stone did, as "another weirdo writing a pseudoscientific paper."[23]

But the envelope was a bellwether. Soon, Olivia Records began to receive hate mail. The initial letters stuck to a common theme: the new Olivia albums were awful because they had a "male" sound—the mixes included prominent drums, which writers found to be objectionable "throbbing male energy." At first, Stone laughed at the preposterousness of the idea of sexed sound, for the entire collective was proud of the quality of the records they were releasing. The mail piled up as the months went on, however, reaching as many as forty to fifty letters a day. And the tone shifted. Increasingly, letters threatened Stone with death and pledged serious violence to the dozen women comprising the collective.[24]

A coordinated, elaborate effort to run Stone out of Olivia Records had begun. Olivia was about to launch its first national tour—the first national tour of lesbian music, period—hosted and staged entirely by lesbian separatist communities. To save costs, Stone had built most of the touring equipment herself, including microphone stands and mixing boards. Before their departure, the collective received the most specific threat yet: the Gorgons, a radical lesbian paramilitary group, would be coming to the Seattle show to kill Sandy Stone.

Again, Stone laughed, unable to find credible danger in a transparently ridiculous scenario. But again, as the collective asked around, their mirth was soon edged out by raw fear. The Gorgons, who wore camo gear, shaved their heads, and packed weapons, were a serious threat. Meanwhile, Stone felt forced to inform the collective of a private matter: she had not yet been able to afford surgery, though she was approved for the process at Stanford's Gender Dysphoria Program. The collective quickly pulled together the remaining funds so long as Stone kept her treatment a secret, and she went under the knife just one week before the tour's departure.[25]

In Seattle, Olivia hired security muscle to screen and remove weapons from audience members—another women's music first. Stone was nonetheless terrified that she would be shot. In the middle of the event, while Stone sat at the engineering console, someone called out "Gorgons!" Powered by visceral fear, she flew under the table, every hair on her body standing guard. Fortunately, the show continued without incident, but stress, fatigue, and needed time for postsurgical healing pushed Stone to the brink. Soon after, she collapsed from exhaustion.[26]

The attacks on Stone continued as the tour traveled south. In Berkeley, Olivia held a meeting with lesbian community members concerned about Stone's role in the women's music community. The collective thought an open dialogue would enable them to understand and defuse the rising hostility directed at them. They were to learn that such a goal was futile: TERFs, including the Gutter Dykes, wanted blood, not conversation, and they were organized. A group had even flown in from Chicago to rail against Stone's role at Olivia.

The Gutter Dykes and their allies opened the Berkeley meeting with a lengthy statement full of incendiary accusations such that trans women were men raping the women's community. No one at Olivia had prepared a statement, and the collective looked to Stone to respond. Flustered and on the spot, she sputtered out the first thing that came to mind: "That's all bullshit!"[27]

The room exploded in anger: Stone, many screamed—some while standing on chairs—had exhibited stereotypical male behavior. They demanded she leave. Though the collective initially insisted that she stay, they consented to Stone's desire to leave in hopes that dialogue might be possible, that there was a rational response Olivia could make that would resolve this fracture jeopardizing its future. But the remaining eight or so collective members found that dialogue was impossible, period. To TERFs, Stone was a man, men were always the enemy, and Olivia had committed treachery.[28]

Lisa Vogel, cofounder of the fiercely anti-trans Michigan Womyn's Music Festival, coordinated an open letter condemning Olivia for working with Stone and found twenty-one women to cosign. Olivia responded with a lengthy letter to the lesbian community; both letters were published in the West Coast feminist magazine *Sister* in June 1977. "Sandy met [the] same criteria that we apply to any woman with whom we plan to work closely," Olivia Records affirmed. And they rebuffed the repeated charge that the collective had been treasonous in not announcing to the women's music community that they were working with a transsexual. "To us," they insisted, "Sandy Stone is a person, not an issue." But TERFs had created a firestorm. For nearly two years, articles and letters attacking or defending Stone's right to be in the community appeared throughout magazines like *Sister*, *DYKE*, and *Lesbian Connection*. Emotions ran high. "I feel raped when Olivia passes off Sandy, a transsexual, as a real woman," one reader conveyed, while one of Stone's many, many supporters insisted, "Women can be big enough to accept a convert. I thought we were out to convert the world!"[29]

TERFs threatened to organize lesbians into a nationwide boycott of Olivia Records. Stone decided to leave the collective in 1979, for even a small drop in sales would threaten the livelihoods of Olivia members and recording artists. She moved back north to Santa Cruz but found TERF opposition there, too. Around fifty women convened to determine her right to be "allowed into 'women's spaces.'"[30] The vote was decisive: fewer than three women insisted on excluding Stone, and those few stormed out of the meeting in a fury when they were defeated. The detractors had been vehement enough to trigger the meeting in the first place. But their numbers were tiny.

The 1970s lesbian-feminist movement wasn't overwhelmingly anti-trans—it was rather that TERFs tried diligently, yet often failed, to overwhelm the movement. Stone resumed her place in the Santa Cruz lesbian world, returned to the Wizard of Aud, soon met Beth Elliott at a local goddess conference, and became an integral part of the northern California neo-pagan spiritual community. She maintained close friendships with many Olivia collective members that persisted for decades.[31]

Sandy Stone, the person, moved on. But Sandy Stone, the fictive rapist of women's spaces, continued to exert a magnetic draw for some feminists. The fallout would transform the direction of trans politics in the United States.

～ ～

In 1979, Janice Raymond published a revised version of the dissertation excerpt she had mailed to Olivia Records. It was now a chapter in her first book, an academic polemic against trans women. Getting the book published had been difficult—many editors wanted nothing to do with her, whom they called "the Anita Bryant of the transsexual movement," referring to the singer turned anti–gay rights activist. But Raymond had support throughout her writing from prominent feminists including Robin Morgan, Mary Daly, and writer Michelle Cliff; poet Adrienne Rich read multiple drafts of the entire manuscript. When it was released, *The Transsexual Empire: The Making of the She-Male* was immediately influential, earning glowing reviews from humanitarian psychiatrist Thomas Szasz in the *New York Times* and Gloria Steinem in the pages of *Ms. Magazine*.[32] This early reception set a precedent. Raymond's book would become the TERF bible for at least the next thirty-five years.

In *The Transsexual Empire*, Raymond lambasted sex transition as a pinnacle of male objectification and control over women. Transsexuals, she proclaimed, "are not women. They are *deviant males*." Surgeons and the psychiatrists and other specialists who collude with them, she argued, have consolidated into an "empire" that creates false women out of the flesh of men. Transsexuals themselves, who for Raymond are almost always trans women, exist only because they are foolish yet dangerous dupes of sex roles and of modern medicine. Deluded into believing there is an individual therapeutic solution to the problem of restrictive sex stereotypes, "transsexually-constructed" women, she alleged, are merely men who fail to adjust to the social expectations of masculinity. Instead of rebelling against sex role stereotypes altogether, they cling to the most retrograde ideas of femininity and find a ready medical industry willing to "mutilate" them to satisfy their backward desires. For Raymond, "male-to-constructed females" are obsessed with heels, "frilly" dresses, makeup, and the desire to be housewives, behaviors that fetishize, objectify, and fragment real women. They are akin to the atavistic, subservient robot women of the *Stepford Wives*—Frankensteinian products of scientific modernity that nonetheless rumble to life in order to drag society backwards to the rigid social roles of the 1950s. But as men in disguise, these robots are rapists, not sex toys. "All transsexuals rape women's bodies by reducing the real female form to an artifact, appropriating this body for themselves," Raymond charged.[33]

Though Raymond claimed to have interviewed fifteen transsexuals as part of her research, she seemingly hadn't encountered someone like Sandy Stone, who foreswore the apron and kitchen for the mixing board and feminist collective. Except that Raymond had encountered Stone, at least in the lesbian press. Transsexuals, Raymond claimed, were invading and destroying lesbian-feminist communities. Her primary example was Sandy Stone, who she claimed "inserted" himself into Olivia Records, a space "he" now "domina[tes]" and "divide[s]." While at first a paradoxical charge, given her earlier implication that all transsexuals mimic June Cleaver and Donna Reed, Raymond maneuvered around this apparent contradiction by arguing that transsexuals are drawn to women's spirit and women's creativity. Since women's energy is embodied most of all by the lesbian-feminist, the transsexual is vampirically drawn to her. He "feeds off woman's true energy source, i.e., her woman-identified self," she accused.[34]

But bloodsucking is the least of their crimes. Stone and other lesbian-feminists, Raymond insisted, seek to subdue and control women and their spaces. "The transsexually constructed lesbian-feminist, having castrated himself, turns his whole body and behavior into a phallus that can rape in many ways, all the time," Raymond extrapolated with barely subdued self-satisfaction.[35]

A biological binary motors the TERF universe: men are always the oppressor and women always the oppressed. Trans-exclusionist feminists adhere to a single-axis model of power in which sexism is the basic, underlying, most fundamental social inequality. Capitalism and colonialism, and the racism that fuels their engines, lay relatively inert. Instead, maleness or femaleness alone pins one's place in the social hierarchy and determines individual behavior. In this simplified cosmos, rape and assault are the primary crimes, and women have a common experience of marginalization, assault, and abuse at the hands of men. Exposing and fighting men's violence against women was an important element of feminisms of the era, from nighttime marches reclaiming the streets to winning legal recognition of marital rape for the first time. Intersectional feminists also emphasized the pervasiveness of the violence women faced, which was rooted in poverty, overpolicing and other forms of state violence, and lack of healthcare, in addition to individual relationships.

Anti-trans feminists, however, seized upon men's abuse and exploitation of women as the sum total of the violence women faced.

As a result, TERFs argued that liberation can only take place if men are absent. Theirs is a white feminist separatism—instead of aspiring to occupy the social positions held by white men, as did Stanton, Fletcher, and Friedan, they seek to replace those roles altogether with their own institutions. Lisa Vogel's annual Michigan Womyn's Music Festival, for example, which ran from 1976 to 2015, not only banished all men and trans women from the week-long event, but also removed male children over the age of four from their mothers and sisters and sent them to a separate campground. The rationale was that young girls needed a safe space.

The TERF framework Raymond outlined depends on a familiar underlying premise: that sex oppression is the primary form of oppression. Morgan, Raymond, Vogel, and their allies developed a new iteration of a long political tradition that fantasizes that there is such a thing as a universal female body and experience that has unfairly, and unilaterally, been prevented from flourishing. In the TERF worldview, race, capitalism, and family are all distinctly secondary to the primary fact of sex identity, an identity it insists flows transparently from the body at birth. In this updated version of white feminism, being a girl or a woman is biological, self-evident, and creates a unified political class unto itself. The false universal "woman," rooted in allegedly similar biology and experience, lies at the center of TERF politics.

In keeping with twentieth-century white feminism, TERFs insist that women must be allowed to thrive and threats to their success must be removed. Thriving, for TERFs, depends on spaces, such as the feminist collective, or today, the public restroom, reserved strictly for women who were born and raised as girls. Spaces populated only by cis women are by definition safe spaces, TERFs fantasize, free from harm and violence, that allow women to heal from traumatic pasts. Anyone who has ever lived as a male is cast as a threat, violating the sanctity of a world sealed off from men and, therefore, allegedly from the most fundamental forms of violence.

Raymond wielded the bluntest weapons in the safe space arsenal. She branded transsexuals as threatening specimens of the "various 'breeds' of women that medical science can create," shadowing transsexuals with the specter of race while simultaneously positioning them as fabrications of a decadent medical empire. Lesbian-feminists must banish transsexual women like Stone, she insisted, for they are not "like [us] in quality, nature, or status."[36] Real women are only those with XX chromosomes, she declared, flying in the face of two decades of sexology that identified at least six distinct, sometimes conflicting components of sex, such as hormones and genital appearance.

Raymond's essentialist position differed widely from that of non-TERF lesbian-feminists in the 1970s. In 1974, a group of socialist Black lesbians in Boston began developing an "integrated analysis and practice based upon the fact that the major systems of oppression are interlocking." The Combahee River Collective developed a simultaneous analysis of race, gender, heterosexism, and capitalism, and they did so while citing inspiration from nineteenth-century Black women including Frances E. W. Harper. Trans studies activist and scholar Susan Stryker has emphasized that the Combahee River Collective specifically opposed sex essentialism in their famous 1974 statement, finding it contrary to their intersectional politics. Lesbian separatism, they explained, "completely denies any but the sexual sources of women's oppression" and assumes that "biological maleness" is itself a threat. "As Black women we find any type of biological determinism a particularly dangerous and reactionary basis upon which to build a politic," the women of Combahee counseled.[37]

By contrast, double essentialisms characterize the TERF position: biological essentialism and experience essentialism. The former assumes that women have a common embodiment and the latter that women's experiences of those bodies are likewise shared. Both positions are two sides of the same white feminist coin. Raymond declared that trans women were "not our peers, by virtue of their history."[38] But what is this singular history of woman? Was Harriet Beecher Stowe's experience in her body anything akin to what enslaved women like Harriet Jacobs endured, whose bodies became sexual targets and reproduction machines? As Pauli Murray underscored, it is actually Black women, not white women, who are more fully forced into the caste system of sex, for racism compounds the effects of sexism, within both Black and white spaces.

Or, as Audre Lorde took pains to explain to Mary Daly in an open letter addressing Daly's racism in the spring of 1979, women do not experience the stresses of female embodiment identically. "Surely you know that for non-white women in this country," Lorde wrote, "there is an 80 percent fatality rate from breast cancer; three times the number of unnecessary eventrations, hysterectomies and sterilizations as for white women; three times as many chances of being raped, murdered, or assaulted as exist for white women."[39] Daly's myth that common biology drives a generic female experience fractures in the face of race and class.

But Daly, for Janice Raymond, was feminism incarnate. Daly played a powerful role in her mentee's life and work, as Raymond's unusual dedication in *Transsexual Empire* attests. "For Mary Daly," the book begins, "Who has moved me to the Moors of the Mind. . . . Who has taught me to feel with all my intellect and think with all my heart. . . . With Gratitude, Awe, and Love."[40] This steamy inscription—to her adviser—has led observers to speculate that Daly and Raymond were romantically involved while Daly supervised Raymond's PhD.

Whether or not this love was consummated, the romance pulsating off the vitriolic pages of *Transsexual Empire* sounds a larger truth: TERF politics has an erotics. The fantasy of sameness, of universally shared biology and history, is shot through with desire. In this universe, sex difference alone matters; the penis is the primary apparatus that wields power. Extracting the penis, the alleged principal cause of violence to women, thus enables true ardor. TERFs, if we extrapolate from this schematic, not only belong to a safe space—they belong to a sexual space, a refuge in which desire, freed of the violence allegedly inherent to male genitalia, can kindle.

In Raymond's vision, trans women haunt feminist space with the "phallus." By expelling trans women, the TERF sisterhood recommits to white feminism's fantasy cosmology in which sex is all that matters. In this cosmology, trans women, just like women of color, working-class women, disabled women, and many others, do in fact rupture the white feminist fantasy that all women are identical, that women hold a body and history in common, that the sisterhood has sanded the sharp corners of power all the way smooth, leaving only soft, safe, homogenous desire.

Convinced that transsexual medicine foists robot-rapists onto society at large, Raymond refused one of its key contributions: the concept of gender. Before the mid-1950s, gender referred solely to the grammatical concept of class or type, such as the practice of calling boats "she." Gender didn't take on the meaning of cultural ideas about sex roles until sexologist Dr. John Money and his associates proposed the term in the course of their investigations into intersex and transsexual patients. The first time the term *gender* appeared in this modern sense in the *New York Times*, for example, was in announcing the 1966 opening of Money's Gender Identity Clinic at Johns Hopkins University, the first program of transsexual medicine in the United States.[41] In the 1970s, feminists including Ann Oakley, Gayle Rubin, and Andrea Dworkin wrested "gender" away from the patriarchal sexologists at the clinics and transformed it into the vehicle for a feminist analysis of power. But to Raymond, "gender" was suspect on account of its medical origins and its association with transsexuality. It betrayed a therapeutic dimension, allegedly created to enable doctors to solve sex role problems through training and surgeries. Women, not the phenomenon of gender, were the heart of her feminism.

To protect lesbian-feminism and women at large, Raymond proposed a simple solution. "The problem of transsexualism," she concluded, "would best be served by morally mandating it out of existence."[42] For Raymond, sex roles and the medical empire were the causes of transsexuality; limiting medical access to transition procedures would reduce the numbers of trans people.

In 1980, the Reagan administration gave Raymond the opportunity to help bring about that dream. In the case of some extremely persistent patients, Medicare policies and state courts had sometimes deemed sex transition procedures medically necessary and paid the associated bills, as did some private insurance companies. But under Reagan, the National Center for Health Care Technology reviewed the efficacy of mandated Medicare coverage, looking to cut costs by shrinking the health services available to the poor. Trans healthcare came under scrutiny. The center asked Raymond to participate in the preparation of a report on transsexual surgery. Her task was to produce a paper on the social and ethical aspects of medical transition, a paper intended to determine whether sex transition procedures were "reasonable and necessary" and so appropriate for Medicare (and other insurers') reimbursement. Raymond unleashed her argument: insurance coverage of trans healthcare was "controversial" and "unnecessary," for transsexuality wasn't a legitimate medical condition as sexologists argued—it was the perverted spawn of society's restrictive sex roles and a form of "mutilation." Medical transition merely subdued deluded individuals into accepting these stereotypes, much like heroin functioned as "a pacifier of black people," tranquilizing them into accepting a racist system.[43]

The National Center for Health Care Technology's final report closed the door trans people were fighting so hard to keep ajar. Drawing on the work of Raymond, other experts, and other organizations compiled in the center's report, at the end of the decade the Reagan administration withdrew Medicare coverage of transition healthcare and gave insurers permission to deny the procedures on account of their "controversial" nature and lack of medical necessity. Private insurance companies followed suit, glad to have a federal blessing to reduce their liability. Meanwhile, state Medicaid coverage of trans medicine had been eroding since 1979. For the next twenty-five years, almost all US insurance companies refused to cover trans medicine in the private or public market, making sex transition healthcare available only to those wealthy enough to pay out of pocket, often by flying overseas. Transgender studies scholar Cristan Williams underscores the fatal impact of this policy change. Multiple studies, she emphasizes, demonstrate that access to transition dramatically reduces trans people's rates of suicide.[44] To restrict access to medical transition, for some, is to make life unlivable. The policy wasn't reversed until 2013, when a provision of the Obama administration's Affordable Care Act set a new precedent for federal, state, and private insurance coverage.

But trans people didn't disappear quietly just because medicine was far more expensive to access. Trans medicine doesn't produce trans people—the dogged insistence of trans people themselves led to the development of trans medicine. Gender transition clinics only came into existence in the first place after decades of "intense and unremitting pressure of trans-sexuals," as radical British sociologist and trans scholar Carol Riddell pointed out while refuting Raymond's book in 1980.[45]

Similarly, even as medical access retracted in the late 1980s and 1990s, transgender politics and theory pushed forward. And one of the most significant innovations in conceiving of trans politics as a multifaceted critique of power that addresses the intersections of sex, gender, capital, and colonialism, came from Sandy Stone.

When Sandy Stone moved north to Santa Cruz in 1974, she set out on a mission to find transition healthcare. She knew it was now possible to access sex transition in the United States. While earlier generations of trans people needed to travel to Copenhagen, Casablanca, Tijuana, and other international cities for hormones and reconstructive surgeries, rising domestic demand had led to the opening of trans clinics at US universities. But the clinics didn't exactly advertise in the daily newspapers, and Stone had never met a transsexual person. After multiple phone calls—and a guided tour of trans sex workers' poverty-stricken apartments in San Francisco's Tenderloin neighborhood, intended to scare her off—she found the Stanford Gender Dysphoria Program, now six years running and located just over the Santa Cruz Mountains.

But it wasn't a homecoming. She'd been warned by other "transies" that Stanford preferred Christine Jorgensen types, the tall, willowy, hyperfeminine blonde who became the first person famous for being transsexual back in the early 1950s. Stone knew her short, androgynous, Jewish body might pose a problem. In common with some other gender identity programs, Stanford ran grooming sessions to train preoperative trans women in delicate comportment, ladylike dress, and subservient heterosexual dating behavior that staff psychologists deemed appropriate to femininity.[46] Their goal was to admit and treat patients who they were certain would pass as genetic females. Stone had a choice: she could stage a performance that would satisfy Stanford's demands, or she could confront the clinic's sex stereotypes head-on.

Stone walked into her first appointment with plastic surgeon Donald Laub, who directed the clinic, wearing her traditional uniform of jeans, heavy boots, and a beard grazing her chest. Surgeon and patient sized one another up.

"I am interested in a sex change," she announced, in Doc Storch's deepest, most authoritative rock 'n' roll sound-guy voice.

"To what?" Dr. Laub replied.[47]

Stone gained admittance into Stanford's two-year presurgery program, but at subsequent appointments she met further obstacles. Allies she met in the clinic's waiting room, however, encouraged her to join them in refusing the rigid binaries the physicians imposed.[48]

"Why aren't you dressed like a woman?" Dr. Laub interrogated, surveying Stone's jeans and T-shirt.

"I *am* dressed like a woman," she informed him.

"No, you're not," he insisted.

"Have you looked out the window recently?"

The tension came to a head at Stone's final presurgery appointment. "Are you 100 percent sure that you want surgery to change sex?" Laub asked.

"No, I'm not," she replied. She distrusted absolutes and suspected that being 100 percent sure of anything actually demonstrated insanity, not sound conviction. She felt 99 percent sure.

"I'm an adult," Stone assured him. "I can take responsibility for my actions. This is informed consent. If I made a mistake, it's my fault, not yours. Let's go."

"I'm sorry," he told her. "You're not eligible" for surgery. And Stone drove back over the mountains to Santa Cruz.

Three months later, Stanford's program coordinator called Stone to redo the interview. When reviewing the transcript, the coordinator realized the impasse was procedural, not substantive. She drafted a script for both surgeon and patient to follow so that Stone would meet clinic qualifications.

"Are you ready for surgery?" Dr. Laub asked when Stone returned to the Palo Alto offices.

"Yes!" Stone confirmed. She was approved.[49] But it would be another few years, when Olivia Records contributed the balance due in a last-minute rush before their national tour, before Sandy received surgery.

A decade later, Stone pulled this experience into her next career: as an academic feminist theorist. At the age of fifty, she entered the University of California–Santa Cruz's famed interdisciplinary PhD program, History of Consciousness, a paradigm-busting department whose faculty included Angela Davis and Donna Haraway. It was Haraway who encouraged Stone to join them at the sprawling redwood-filled campus on the bluff overlooking town. Haraway was in the midst of writing her soon-to-be famous "Cyborg Manifesto," which demolishes the "antagonistic dualisms" between human and machine, human and animal, the natural and artificial, and man and woman to envision a feminist world organized by affinity rather than essentialized identity. "There is nothing about being 'female' that naturally binds women" together, she insists, launching her critique directly at white feminism's attachment to the fantasy that to be a woman is to have suffered identically at the hands of patriarchy.[50] And there is nothing inherently threatening about the new machine age, she urged. While late capitalism powered Reagan's launching of the Cold War into the stars, feminists and socialists could appropriate human-techno relations toward preventing, rather than enabling, unending war and massive wealth disparity.

Among the academics breaking conventional frameworks of thought, Stone had at last found her home. Working with Haraway, and alongside department colleagues like Gloria E. Anzaldúa—who was drafting her book *Borderlands/ La Frontera*, one of the essential texts of intersectional feminism—Stone built on these theorists' work on mixture and hybridity to confront essentialism where it pierced her most directly: in myths about transsexuality. She now knew how to confront Janice Raymond. In 1991 Stone published the essay "The *Empire* Strikes Back: A Posttranssexual Manifesto" challenging Raymond's portrayal of the transsexual empire head-on. Stone was still completing her dissertation, and she and Haraway worried it would destroy any possibility of a future career in the academy. Her essay had the opposite effect. "The *Empire* Strikes Back" became the founding document of a brand-new academic field: transgender studies.

The manifesto did something much bolder than merely refute Raymond. Stone overturned the dominant narrative, supported by trans medicine and by many trans people at the time, that to be trans meant to be "born in the wrong body." Instead, she articulated the radical potential of trans lives to break through binary notions of sex in which to be male was the polar opposite of female. Emphasizing self-determination over biological determinism and developing nuanced analyses of gender, race, and capitalism, Stone's manifesto joined a vibrant tradition of pushing back against the confines of white feminism—and extended intersectional feminist analysis into the realm of transgender politics.

Drawing on decades of published sex change narratives, "The *Empire* Strikes Back" eviscerated the standard accounts of trans identity promoted by physicians and patients alike. In these tales, radical transformations cleave a male past from a female future. Surgeons enact divine resurrection, first putting to death a heterosexual male and then animating a passive, delicate, high-voiced, femme fatale who awakens from surgery an entirely new person. In these magical journeys from one pole of sex experience to the other, Stone illuminated, "the male must be annihilated or at least denied, but the female is that which exists to be *continually* annihilated."[51] For femaleness in these texts is marked by a subservience so extreme that trans women are devoid not only of agency but of their very bodies; their corporeal form is mere putty formed in the wake of the surgeon's scalpel.

"No wonder feminist theorists have been suspicious" of transsexuality, Stone observed. "Hell, *I'm* suspicious." It was a gesture of generosity to TERFs—one that simultaneously risked undercutting fellow trans people.[52]

Janice Raymond was absolutely right that leading sex transition psychologists such as John Money and Robert Stoller insisted upon retrograde, antifeminist gender roles. But since Raymond understood trans people only as artificial products animated by trans medicine—not as fully fledged agents of their own lives—she couldn't see that trans people, too, resisted these roles. Sometimes that resistance took the shape of *inhabiting* gender stereotypes.

For years, Stone related, trans people advised one another on how to navigate gender clinics' strict requirements: study the manual of transsexuality that the doctors themselves used to assess patients' likelihood to succeed in society as feminine women—Dr. Harry Benjamin's 1966 *The Transsexual Phenomenon*—and perform the type, down to a T. Clinic staff were so eager to codify transsexuality as a new mental health disorder defined by identical characteristics that their own needs for objective, reproducible, standardized criteria made them highly gullible. It took the surgeons and psychiatrists years to figure out that they'd been had.

For Stone, the clinics offered a fascinating example of how gender is constructed in real time. Dr. Benjamin identified "born in the wrong body" as the defining self-understanding of transsexuality. Since his manual was the clinics' manual, patients repeated this refrain year after year in order to access transition care. Even after physicians realized that their patients, too, read Benjamin, they continued to pose questions that screened out any ambiguity, as Stone herself had experienced. Through these rote scripts, performed by doctor and patient alike, transsexuality solidified into the state of passing from one side of the sex binary to its alleged opposite, a transformation that demolishes any body or experience that came before. In physicians' hands, transsexuality reinforced, rather than broke down, the gender binary.

The "wrong body" narrative solidified into orthodoxy. In the 1970s, Stone shared, clinics even instructed transsexual women to invent a "plausible history" of their earlier lives.[53] They were to fabricate new childhoods as if they had always been female. In the medical discourse, to transition was not only to erase one's own past—it was to masquerade as an imaginary person.

"But it is difficult to generate a counterdiscourse if one is programmed to disappear," Stone objected. Universal, unrelenting passing is not the goal, she urged. Never-ending passing is a form of assimilation—an acquiescence to the status quo. Passing internalizes, rather than resists, the harmful structure of binary gender that delineates masculinity and femininity, man and woman, as fundamentally at odds. She argued that to pass perpetually, in all circumstances and interactions, forecloses the center of a person's individual power, the complexities, ambiguities, and nuances of actual life experience. And while passing admits one to the realm of gendered respectability, it means being forced to found relationships on lies, instead of on the truths that transsexuality exposes: that all bodies are malleable texts inscribed by power.[54]

Instead, Stone urged, "in the transsexual's erased history we can find a story disruptive to the accepted discourses of gender . . . which can make common cause" with other oppressed groups. She called this new identity the "posttranssexual"—the monstrous body reclaimed, in all its complexity. Closing her manifesto with a thrilling turn, Stone wrote collectively to other academic transsexuals—an audience she had to dream into being in 1991. Stone asked "us" to write our complex realities into history instead of being scripted as monolithic caricatures by physicians, feminists like Raymond, and even ourselves. Refusing assimilation is radical politics, "begun by reappropriating difference and reclaiming the power of the refigured" body—turning transsexuality into a site of resistance and alliance. She called for "solidarity" with queers and people of color—not individual, stealth access to the status quo through the edifice of binary sex. "Although *individual* change is the foundation of all things," she concluded, "it is not the end of all things."[55]

Trans lives, for Stone, became a jumping-off point for interrogating gender—the social dimensions of sex—and forging collective resistance to racism, capitalism, and colonialism. By contrast, trans-exclusionary feminism honed its project into one goal alone: liberating women from the oppression of men.

The singular identity "women," removed from the reality of all other so-cial forces besides biological sex, became a mythic category that actually obscured, rather than pried open, the workings of power. But gender—a term many TERFs and "gender critical" feminists today deem tainted by transsexuality—usefully exposed the process through which the identities of man and woman are assigned meaning. The concept of gender provided an angle onto the way social institutions shape personal identity and experience. Trans feminism like Stone's helped advance intersectional feminist analysis, and she was far from alone.

~ ~

The UC Santa Cruz campus nestled among the redwoods wasn't the only place cultivating intersectional trans politics. The narrow streets and dark piers of lower Manhattan, too, had been providing potent ground for those who defied the rules of binary sex.

In June 1973, just three months after the West Coast Lesbian Conference, trans activist and sex worker Sylvia Rivera mounted the stage at the Christo-pher Street Liberation Day rally clad in a long-sleeved sparkly bodysuit. Ri-vera wasn't on the scheduled list of speakers on this fourth anniversary of the Stonewall antipolice riots, but she commandeered the mike anyway, causing a commotion onstage and off. She was greeted by a raucous mixture of jeers, boos, and some applause.

"Y'all better quiet down!" Rivera began in frustration. Leaning into the mike, putting the full force of her thin body into her voice and keeping time with her right index finger as if the crowd were her orchestra, Rivera gave them a piece of her mind. "I've been trying to get up here all day for your gay broth-ers and your gay sisters in *jail* that write me every motherfucking week and you don't do a god damned thing for them!" Drag queens and trans women of color, including Rivera and her friend and ally Marsha P. Johnson, had led the Stonewall rebellion—but now the gay and women's liberation move-ments wanted nothing to do with sex workers. Rivera herself first lived on the street and turned tricks to survive at age eleven. To keep trans, gender nonconforming, and queer kids of color from a similar fate, Rivera and Johnson had organized Street Transvestite Action Revolutionaries (STAR) for the past three years. The pair were squatting a trailer in Greenwich

Marsha P. Johnson, left, and Sylvia Rivera, right, at the Christopher Street Liberation Day March, 1973. Photograph by Leonard Fink. (Courtesy of the LGBT Community Center National History Archive @ lgbtcenternyc)

Village, stealing food, and soliciting johns to support a group of street youth Rivera called her "children." Their solidarities were clear: "We share in the oppression of gays and we share in the oppression of women," STAR declared. But gay liberation and the women's movements wanted nothing to do with Rivera, Johnson, and their band of outcasts. "I have been raped. And beaten. . . . I have been thrown in jail. I have lost my job. I have lost my apartment for gay liberation and you all treat me this way?" Rivera exclaimed. She built to a crescendo: the true potential of gay power manifest when it acted in solidarity with "all of us," not when it shrunk into the "middle-class white club" that "you all belong to!" In closing, she led the crowd of thousands in a rousing cheer of GAY POWER.[56]

For Rivera and her allies, gay liberation was meaningless unless it allied with the most marginalized. The effects of homophobia weren't most apparent among the white middle class, who often had economic resources to fall back on even when their families kicked them out, or worse. The brutal workings of racism, capitalism, binary sex, and state violence intensified homophobia, making homophobia itself most potent where multiple forces of power converged in the lives of individuals. Child and adult street queens weren't exceptional cases that gay liberation could ignore: they were prisms that refracted and magnified the vectors of power itself. If a social movement didn't include the most marginalized, then it was reinforcing, not undermining, the structures that make inequality immensely profitable for the few.

STAR, in other words, began to articulate a nascent, trans version of what Pauli Murray was writing from her Brandeis office, what the Combahee River Collective would outline in its famous statement four years later, and what Black law scholar Kimberlé Crenshaw would develop as the theory of intersectionality in 1989. All were arriving at a similar conclusion: the best vantage onto the true workings of power is from below. To be a Black woman, these theorists argued, was not only to experience racism, sexism, and capitalist inequality. It was to experience them in their full intensity. To understand and confront how power aims to accumulate wealth and power in the hands of the few, they argued, movements must put at their center those lives that show the full force of oppression in all its brutal strength: those on the bottom of multiple hierarchies.

From a variety of locations across the country, intersectional feminist analysis was consolidating, and collectives were putting it into action in the 1970s and 1980s. From classrooms, movement meetings, demonstrations, advocacy, and downtown squats, a new form of politics interrogating multiple structures of power from below—rather than seeking to gain individual access to the status quo—gained strength.

ﾟ～ ～ﾟ

Lesbian white feminism had hardly exhausted itself, however. In the late 1970s, its reductive, single-axis account of power—men oppress, women are oppressed, and femininity is the mark of that oppression—consolidated around a new set of targets: pornography and prostitution. Prostitution wasn't an altogether new concern of feminists; social purity crusaders had policed working-class districts throughout the late nineteenth and early twentieth centuries on the grounds of preventing "white slavery." But 1970s feminists gave it a new spin. In the hands of figures like Robin Morgan, Susan Brownmiller—who drew on the myth of the Black male rapist—Catharine MacKinnon, and Janice Raymond, sex industries became the emblems of patriarchy's addiction to exploiting and harming women. In the 1980s, fights between antiporn feminists, who saw sex industries as untrammeled exploitation, and pro-sex contingencies, who saw erotic material and sex work as elements of women's sexual agency, escalated. The "sex wars" consumed much of feminism in the decade, especially among white women—whether or not they supported white feminist politics. By the early 1990s, the sex wars had largely come to an end. Pro-sex feminists emerged victorious and women's right to the erotic became integral to third-wave feminism.

But while antiporn feminists like Morgan and Raymond lost the sex wars, they did not disappear. They went "underground," in the words of a prominent activist, until it was safe to reemerge. Safety materialized in the 1990s in the form of the anti–sex trafficking movement, which by the early 2000s blossomed into a major international NGO force.[57] And from 1994 to 2007, Janice Raymond served as co–executive director of the most prominent feminist antitrafficking organization, the Coalition Against Trafficking in Women (CATW).

At first blush, anti–sex trafficking work seems to be a rock-solid agenda. Who could support a global network forcing women into sex work against their will? Yet antitrafficking discourse like Raymond's makes little distinction between those who voluntarily enter sex work—constrained though that set of choices may be—in their own countries, and those forced to migrate across international borders to become pawns in an industry of sex. Instead, it frames all prostitution as a sprawling industry that compels women into sexual exploitation, and it typically portrays these victims as brutalized teens. Antitrafficking accounts collapse the real, but infrequent, incidents of cross-border trafficking—which typically abduct women into household and other nonsexual forms of labor—and the flourishing domestic sex trade into one phenomenon, with one set of male perpetrators. Trafficking becomes a parallel of Raymond's empire of transsexual medicine: a vast patriarchal enterprise to steal and sell women's bodies, and in which participants are passive victims stripped of any agency. The title of a book by Raymond's ally, the Australian feminist Sheila Jeffreys, underscores the point: the sex trade produces *The Industrial Vagina*.

Raymond and other antitrafficking feminists see prostitution as the cornerstone of an empire of exploitation that subjects all women to a culture of violence, including rape and battery. Remove prostitution and pornography, they argue, and the edifice of patriarchal violence will crumble. But their work is simultaneously strengthening another power structure. To eradicate prostitution, they lean into policing and mass incarceration.[58]

Raymond and other antiprostitution activists "protect" women by coordinating with police, extending prison sentences, and reinforcing international borders to punish men who solicit and organize paid sex. "Our responsibility is to make men change their behaviour by all means available," Raymond declares, and those means include the punitive apparatus of the state. It means working in coalitions with police and other groups, such as evangelical Christians, who are no longer feminist enemies. These coalitions elevate one tactic above all: lengthy imprisonment. Successfully reframing pimping in the US courts as "domestic sex trafficking," the charge now extends the possible prison sentence from ninety days to ninety-nine years.[59]

Sociologist Elizabeth Bernstein studies Raymond's CATW and other feminist antitrafficking groups, such as local NOW chapters, and has coined a new term to characterize their embrace of criminal justice as a tactic: "carceral feminism." Carceral feminism names the white feminist strategy of turning to police, the courts, and the prison system to protect women from violence. It operates on the fantasy that police and prisons end violence—rather than proliferate it. In the words of writer Victoria Law, carceral feminism "does not acknowledge that police are often purveyors of violence and that prisons are always sites of violence."[60]

The consequences of the white feminist push for increased arrest, prosecution, and imprisonment of so-called sex traffickers have been stark for the usual targets of state violence: Black and Latinx people. Bernstein reports that between 2008 and 2010, African American men made up 62 percent of sex trafficking suspects, and Latino men another 25 percent. These numbers are wildly out of proportion with the percentage of Black and Brown US residents. They are, however, in keeping with the racial disparity of the criminal justice system. While male clients are the target of antitrafficking feminists' punitive goals, women sex workers often get caught up in the resulting over-policing. According to a recent study conducted in Baltimore, incarcerated women sex workers faced high rates of exposure to violence from both police and clients, as well as increased risk of exposure to HIV and other sexually transmitted infections. Among those studied, Black female sex workers were at the greatest risk for being jailed. These statistics are compounded by the fact that women are the fastest growing incarcerated population in the United States.

Similarly, the much touted Violence Against Women Act of 1994, sponsored by then senator Joseph Biden, works within the logic of carceral feminism. Its passage implemented mandatory arrest in cases of suspected domestic violence, increased the prison sentences of those convicted, and allotted $1.6 billion toward preventing and prosecuting violent crimes against women.[61] The vast majority of this funding was funneled into the criminal justice system, contributing to the highest incarceration rate in the world.

Sandy Stone argued in the 1990s that the ultimate significance of Raymond's *Transsexual Empire* lay in its method, not its topic. Raymond, she explained, "demonstrate[d] that one can cloak a radically conservative position in liberal language."[62] Stone's claim bears out in the politics of Raymond's antitrafficking work. Raymond's white feminist politics not only attempted to cleanse the movement of trans women; in a misguided attempt to protect cis women, it works with cops, courts, and the prison system to cleanse society of sex work.

The trajectory of Raymond's career makes the political context of trans-exclusionary radical feminism clear: just like carceral feminism, trans exclusion is part of the tradition of white feminist politics. Anti-trans politics crystallized among an ongoing struggle between white feminists who insist that women share an identity, biology, and universal experience of oppression and intersectional feminists who illuminate the multiple vectors through which wealth and power accumulate in the hands of a few. In the rampant inequality of late capitalism, the divide between the two forms of feminist politics becomes even more stark: carceral feminists who support the prison industrial complex and those who form coalition with street queens and sex workers, prison and gender abolitionists, and trans activists.

When intersectional transgender politics—and the new term *transgender* itself—fully flowered in the 2000s, it emerged at the juncture of Sandy Stone's posttranssexual manifesto and Marsha P. Johnson and Sylvia Rivera's work organizing street queens. The term *transgender* emerged in the 1990s specifically to de-emphasize the role of surgery and other medical interventions. Rather than a diagnosis and embodiment "created" by medicine, as *transsexuality* marks, *transgender* encompasses a range of binary-defying modes of life that may or may not include medical treatment. The term underscores the agency of individual trans people, defying beliefs like Raymond's that trans identity and embodiment are the invention of a medical empire. Like Stone had urged, many trans activists refuse the "born in the wrong body" narrative and instead emphasize that all bodies, trans or cis, are in continual states of transformation.

Trans-exclusionary radical feminists, however, continue to wage war against trans women and the notion of gender itself. In 2014, Australian Sheila Jeffreys (author of *The Industrial Vagina*) issued a new book, *Gender Hurts: A Feminist Analysis of the Politics of Transgenderism*. She argues that transgender identities are merely animated sex stereotypes; that "male-bodied transgender" people threaten women's safety in restrooms, showers, and prisons; and that gender itself is a harmful ideology that works to subordinate women.[63] The back cover of *Gender Hurts* features two blurbs by two influential feminists: Robin Morgan and Janice Raymond.

Meanwhile, the campaign to deny trans healthcare has built many allies. In the first three months of 2021 alone, over eighty bills were introduced in state legislatures seeking to roll back trans rights, especially blocking youth access to healthcare and organized sports.[64] The dangerous idea that transition healthcare mutilates bodies and that trans people jeopardize the safety of others is no longer a niche concern of some white feminists—it is a major national agenda.

Yet the counterhistory also builds strength, on the street and on the university campus. In 2011, Susan Stryker—who turned transgender studies into a flourishing field—held a conference at Indiana University–Bloomington to commemorate the twentieth anniversary of Stone's essay "The *Empire* Strikes

Back." Nearly five hundred people attended, many of them trans. During a panel discussion, Stryker asked Stone to read aloud the final paragraph of the manifesto. Long a professor at University of Texas–Austin and the European Graduate School, Stone focused on media arts and was accustomed to delivering renegade performances in front of large audiences. Yet as she read her text and looked out over the crowd, humility, fear, and exhilaration overcame her. Sobs interspersed her words. She had dreamed of one day being part of a community of trans theorists—and now she was among hundreds and hundreds. "It's been a long road," she reflected. "We're not near the end yet, but we're all clearly on our way."[65]

PART III
OPTIMIZING

CHAPTER SEVEN

LEANING IN OR SQUADDING UP

Sheryl Sandberg and Alexandria Ocasio-Cortez

Always ally yourself with those on the bottom, on the margins, and at the periphery of the centers of power. And in doing so, you will land yourself at the very center of some of the most important struggles of our society and our history.

—Barbara Ransby, *How We Get Free*

SHERYL SANDBERG NEEDED A BETTER PLACE TO PARK. ONE WINTER MORNING IN 2005, ONgoing morning sickness kept the heavily pregnant tech executive at home in front of the toilet until the last possible minute. She was now late to meet a prospective client at Google, where she headed the burgeoning sales and operations team. But the vast parking lot at Google's Mountain View, California, headquarters brimmed with cars, and Sandberg was forced to take a spot in its outer reaches. Lumbering across the asphalt expanse only sent her stomach back into her throat. While extolling the value of buying targeted advertising on Google—a product that was turning the company from the red into a rapidly growing profit juggernaut—she prayed "that a sales pitch was the only thing that would come out of [her] mouth."[1]

That night her husband, Dave Goldberg, remarked that his workplace Yahoo! reserved close-in parking spaces for pregnant workers. Inspired, Sandberg walked into the Google founders' office the following day and posed her

request directly to Larry Page and Sergey Brin. Google pregnancy parking
was born. The travails of one woman executive eased the way for all future
pregnant employees.

The parking anecdote is one of Sandberg's favorite examples of her vision of
feminist change. Her trial as a pregnant, nauseous executive traversing the oce-
anic Google lot opens and closes *Lean In*, the white feminist manifesto she published to much fanfare in 2013. It's a disarming introduction to Sandberg, one
of corporate America's richest and most powerful women. Opening the book's
glossy cover emblazoned with her face and hair half-lit and softly focused as if
she were an actress in a romantic comedy, I hardly expected to find her crouched
over a toilet on the very first page. Yet the folksy story, as with the intimate
close-up of Sandberg on *Lean In*'s cover, is key to the image she crafts. Imperfect, inspiring, relatable, and above all, normatively female, she presents herself
through the appealing combination of remarkable competence and quirky, all-
too-human weaknesses and vulnerabilities. Faced with a gender inequity that
compromised her sales pitch and her dignity she nonetheless solved it handily,
for herself and her colleagues. Let women like Sandberg rise to the top of corporate America, she tells her readers, and the sexism women face in the workplace
everywhere will diminish. "More female leadership will lead to fairer treatment
for *all* women," she insists.[2]

While *Lean In* doesn't discount the systemic barriers women face, such
as unequal pay, a lack of family leave, and a deeply sexist culture, the book
proclaims that these institutional factors have drowned out other feminist
approaches. "Too much of the conversation is on blaming others, and not
enough is on taking responsibility ourselves," she later explained to a *New
Yorker* journalist. The book thus turns away from structural solutions and instead emphasizes "internal obstacles," illuminating the ways that women hold
themselves back from career success. Women make individual choices, day in
and day out, her book claims, that compromise their own potential and keep
them out of positions of power. Sandberg encourages women readers to stop
underestimating their talent, lean in to their professional ambitions, and negotiate themselves all the way into the executive suite—where they'll make
sure those who follow in their stiletto footsteps have an easier path to tread. In
the allegedly postracist, postfeminist days of President Obama's second term,
Sandberg's emphasis on personal solutions to structural problems struck a

ready nerve. Her ally Oprah trumpeted Sandberg as "the new voice of revolutionary feminism"; Gloria Steinem, another personal friend, aptly anointed
her "feminism's new boss."[3] Four million copies flew off the shelves.

Sandberg helped usher in a twenty-first-century mode of white feminist
politics. In this new form of feminism, the key strategy has become optimizing: striving for a streamlined efficiency in which personal health and
happiness and feminist empowerment are indistinguishable from capitalist
productivity. Her executive career, Sandberg relates, is compatible with motherhood because she rises early—sometimes at 5 a.m.—schedules her office
time to end by 5:30 p.m.; rushes home for dinner, play, and bedtime; and runs
from the crib back to her laptop to resume her workday, which includes being
an inspiration to her female underlings. The worker, mother, and activist fully
dissolve into one another, arriving at an allegedly "revolutionary" feminism
whose central message is to work harder, smarter, and faster, even after you've
reached the executive suite.

Sandberg's feminism has much in common with the contemporary ideal of
the optimized woman, who as essayist Jia Tolentino writes, is perfectly toned,
coiffed, and salaried. This feminine ideal, Tolentino explains, reflects the val-
ues of the twenty-first century in which "work is rebranded as pleasure so that
we will accept more of it" and women are encouraged to "understand relentless self-improvement as natural, mandatory, and feminist—or just, without
question, the best way to live."[4] Parenting, executive leadership, and empowering women all become jobs to be performed with maximum efficiency and
maximum results. Improving the self, and lifting up some other women from
those lofty heights, has become white feminism's ultimate goal.

White feminism began in the 1840s with Elizabeth Cady Stanton and
others' fight for white women to possess the rights and privileges afforded to
white men, including the right to own property and to hold careers. By the
2010s, it had become a push to optimize one's potential in every aspect of life.
This represented a shift from the priorities of twentieth-century white feminists like Margaret Sanger and Betty Friedan, who largely campaigned to secure middle-class white women's status among those chosen to thrive in part
through cleansing society of those whom they deemed threatening to their
cause, such as the poor and/or disabled, lesbians, and trans women. But now,
in the twenty-first century, the idea that white women deserve to be among

the chosen is becoming more secure—even if the reality of gender equity in the office remains a distant dream. As fewer people object to the presence of middle-class women in the professions and in government, removing so-called undesirables from the movement and the nation has become less of a priority for white feminism as a whole. TERFs, now joined by "gender-critical feminists" who similarly rail against trans rights, remain fiercely committed to the cause of cleansing and are gaining power. But at the same time, many white feminists have turned inward, finding the greatest enemy to their own success to be nestled within their own psyches and habits. Regulating the community has given way to a relentless self-discipline. Self-optimizing, for white feminists today, is the hallmark of liberation.

The contemporary capitalist imperatives for efficiency, endless work, and the pursuit of excellence apply to professional-class men as well as to women. But white feminists saddle themselves with an extra burden. In a new kind of civilizing project arising out of white women's traditional role as stabilizers of society, they set out not only to conquer the corner office—but to make reforms to capitalism itself. Success, for these women, entails both individual advancement and making corporate capitalism appear to be inclusive. Their task is not only to self-regulate; their duty at the top of Fortune 500 companies is to redeem capitalism, turning cutthroat companies like Google into the kinds of places with pregnancy parking spots.

Yet while parking lot reforms bring about needed equality among corporate workers, corporate workers, especially in Silicon Valley, bring about massive wealth inequality for the country and the world. The conditions of the employee lot at Google HQ have zero ramifications on the vast majority of people who come into contact with Google. Google, after all, primarily exists not as an office complex in Mountain View, but as a data-hungry behemoth trawling the questions, personal correspondence, and business communications of its two billion users to assemble psychological profiles it can sell to advertisers. Thanks to this Big Tech business model Sandberg brought from Google to Facebook when she became chief operating officer of the social network in 2008, she is now a billionaire. Sandberg may draw a paycheck from Facebook, but, whether we realize it or not, we all generate revenue for Sheryl Sandberg.

Sandberg's status as a self-made feminist billionaire makes palpable that white feminism doesn't just embrace the rising wealth inequality of the twenty-first century—it's part of engineering it. The existence of feminist billionaires throws the contradictions of optimizing feminism into high relief, for feminism ceases to have any meaning at all when explosive, extractive wealth becomes its measure. Yet even white feminism's most vehement detractors find it difficult to avoid the optimizing trap. The demand that we devote ourselves to continual work and continual success has been laid for us not only by corporate feminists but by the penetration of capitalism into nearly every area of our lives.

A few weeks after Donald Trump's election to the presidency of the United States in November 2016, New York bartender Alexandria Ocasio-Cortez and two friends drove west. They joined the more than one thousand water protectors blocking the construction of the Dakota Access Pipeline at the Standing Rock Lakota Sioux reservation.[5] The pipeline would tear through Lakota Sioux burial and prayer sites at a spot three hundred miles north of where Zitkala-Ša grew up in Yankton Sioux territory 135 years prior, endangering the water supply of the entire region. In response, members of more than three hundred tribes gathered in Standing Rock to prevent its construction. Zitkala-Ša had created the first pan-Indian movement of Native tribes working together in coalition; Ocasio-Cortez was now an ally of its most recent iteration.

She was stunned by what she saw: "A corporation had literally militarized itself against the American people," attacking the Indigenous-led protest camp with rubber bullets, mace, teargas, and pepper spray. The need for dramatic, systemic change led by the most vulnerable themselves became palpable to her. She hoped to play a role in the struggle. "Lord, just do with me what you will," she prayed at Standing Rock. "Allow me to be a vessel." As she drove off the reservation, she received a phone call from an unknown number asking her to run for Congress—her brother had signed her up—and she said yes.[6]

A year and a half later, Ocasio-Cortez defeated the fourth-most powerful Democrat in the House of Representatives, Joe Crowley, to win the Democratic primary nomination for New York's Fourteenth Congressional District. Her extraordinarily unlikely win and her social media acumen soon propelled her to visibility rivaling that of the most famous American women in politics, even before she secured the House seat in the general election in November 2018. Increasingly disgusted by the belief that "we can capitalism our way out of poverty," she ran as a Democratic Socialist. Yet she also advanced a broad critique of power that pushed fierce critics of capitalism—many of whom tend to focus on economics alone—to reckon with racial, gender, and social injustice. "I'm not running 'from the left.' I'm running from the bottom," Ocasio-Cortez declared on Twitter, a medium she commands. The multiracial, largely working-class Fourteenth District she represents, which encompasses parts of Queens, the Bronx, and the notorious prison Rikers Island, is "like the epicenter for an intersectional argument for economic and social dignity," she later explained. "There is no such thing as talking about class without there being implications of the racial history of the United States. You just can't do it."[7]

America had an intersectional feminist politician, now beloved on the Left and notorious on the Right as AOC. Intersectional feminism teaches us that the best way to confront the uneven distribution of life and death is to examine the lives and conditions of those pinned to the very bottom and to work together in coalition, across positions and identities, to dismantle it. Ocasio-Cortez's alliance with three other progressive women of color elected to the House of Representatives at the same time—Ayanna Pressley, Rashida Tlaib, and Ilhan Omar—whom AOC affectionately dubbed the Squad, works to bring coalitional feminist politics' view-from-below into the highest ranks of government.

In the 2020s, it is not Sheryl Sandberg but AOC and the Squad who for many embody the future of feminist leadership. Their distinct theories of social change have correspondingly opposing relationships to power: leaning in to the center or aligning yourself with those on the margins. They also have distinct momentum: one version of feminism is stumbling, the other surging as more and more people reckon with the racial and economic violence that built the United States and call for radical transformation. *Lean In*–style feminism promotes privatized, top-down solutions to structural problems that depend on siphoning capital upward, such as corporations that provide their high-level employees with generous maternity leave and lavish healthcare including egg-freezing, but subcontract low-level employees to poverty wages. The Squad instead endorses a revamped notion of the public sphere in which resources are broadly spread downward. "In a modern, moral and wealthy society, no person in America should be too poor to live," AOC makes plain.[8]

Yet the very popularity of AOC and the Squad's appeals for structural change activates the demands of optimizing feminism. AOC's preternatural mastery of her job is key to her appeal: her Twitter clapbacks, beguiling videos, and eloquent, unscripted speeches from the campaign stage or House floor, even twirling on her haters in front of her congressional office door and applying makeup while insisting "femininity has power," are all delivered with fiery passion and captivating millennial glamour.[9] She is a seemingly tireless social media presence. Cooking black bean soup in the evenings or catching the train back to the Bronx on the weekends, Ocasio-Cortez turns to Instagram Live (a Facebook property) to break down barriers between government and the people. Even when exhausted, she manages to parse complex policy bills with startling clarity and charisma. Yet this sheer effort and skill pose a risk. A largely unstated but pervasive expectation thrust on her by supporters exceeds the capacities of any human, however remarkable, to meet: that Ocasio-Cortez be perfect at everything she does.

Can AOC—or more to the point, the legions of her fans—resist the lure of optimizing feminism, of the fantasy that she can excel at her job 24/7, save the planet, and look great while doing it all? While feminist billionaires may be less popular, the phenomenon of likability, mastery, and incessant work broadly expected of feminist women today remains. In the widespread enthusiasm for the talent and brilliance of AOC and the Squad, we hazard being so dazzled by their ability to break down traditional barriers between politician and the public and articulate an intersectional feminist position from Capitol Hill that their skill becomes a cage of expectation. While Ocasio-Cortez is one of capitalism's sharpest public critics, she is still forced to navigate the optimizing trap that demands unceasing work and unremitting excellence.

꙳ ꙳

In March 2008 at the Facebook Palo Alto headquarters, CEO Mark Zuckerberg made an important new introduction at the weekly all hands staff meeting. Since first encountering Sheryl Sandberg at a Christmas party three months prior, he had been trying to poach her from Google in a recruiting process her husband and many journalists have likened to dating. Multiple times a week, Zuckerberg and Sandberg convened at a Michelin-starred New American restaurant around the corner from her mansion to discuss his vision for Facebook: a social network that connected the entire world.[10] Though Sandberg easily could have assumed a CEO position in Silicon Valley, she believed in this mission and quickly grasped its explosive profit potential. She was now coming to Facebook as chief operating officer, in charge of earning Facebook's first dollar—the company was swimming in venture capital money but had yet to create its own revenue stream—and of everything not related to engineering. Zuckerberg, while retaining the title of CEO, would devote his energy to product development and new acquisitions, as well as winning the Valley's heated competition for technical sophistication.

"Sheryl and I met at a party and we immediately hit it off," Zuckerberg told his seven hundred employees, speaking with more animation and warmth than was characteristic for the twenty-four-year-old. "I was really impressed by how smart she is," he divulged as Sheryl stood by his side and beamed at her new staff.

"When I met Sheryl the first thing I said was that she had really good skin. And she does," Mark affirmed, turning toward the executive fifteen years his senior.

Sandberg's smile didn't budge.

Accustomed to making imperious commands, Zuckerberg issued an edict to the company: "Everyone should have a crush on Sheryl." Former Facebook employee Katherine Losse, whose memoir recounts this cringe-inducing scene, reports that many engineers responded dutifully, quickly testifying to their crushes in a department-wide email chain.[11]

Perhaps Sandberg instinctively knew what she would broadcast in *Lean In* five years later: research shows that success is a contradiction for women. The more women advance professionally, the less people like them. Our sexist culture, *Lean In* underscores, doesn't trust successful women. Both men and women, Sandberg cites, found the entrepreneur profiled in a Harvard Business School case study to be "appealing" and collegial in one article, but "selfish and not 'the type of person you want to hire or work for'" in the another. Yet only one aspect of the article was changed across the two versions: the name "Howard" was swapped out with "Heidi." To be successful in business negotiations, she advises, women thus need to work hard to make themselves appealing: "women must come across as being nice, concerned about others, and 'appropriately' female."[12] Women, in other words, ought to master the feminine performance of making everyone else comfortable while subordinating their own needs to those of the company at large. Smiling your way through outlandish sexism plays the long game—by not rocking the boat, the boat can become yours.

Sandberg launched *Lean In: Women, Work, and the Will to Lead* in 2013, exactly fifty years after Betty Friedan released *The Feminine Mystique*. Sandberg donned the mantel of white feminism's new leader, come to "speak her truth" as Friedan had spoken hers. Friedan had diagnosed a feminine ideal that debilitates middle-class women and society at large by restricting them to the home; she prescribed professional careers as the antidote to women's wasted potential and atrophied lives. Sandberg, half a century later, insists that while progress has been made, "our revolution has stalled." Though women had flooded the workforce, they had yet to achieve parity in the executive class or as wage earners: 479 of the Fortune 500 CEOs were men; 82 percent of congressional representatives were men; and for every dollar men earned, women on average took home only seventy-seven cents. "A truly equal world," the book proclaims, "would be one where women ran half our countries and companies and men ran half our homes." White feminism had a new goal: install women presidents and CEOs and equality would trickle down. *Atlantic* writer Amanda Mull aptly observed that *Lean In* and the #GirlBoss phenomenon that surfaced in its wake rebranded corporate women's "pursuit of power . . . as a righteous quest for equality." The book dominated the *New York Times* bestseller list for over a year; more than two hundred corporations signed on as supporters of the Lean In platform.[13]

Lean In has been widely critiqued for focusing narrowly on the concerns of heterosexual, married corporate women. But the fundamental problem with *Lean In* is not its failure to be inclusive. Inclusivity within capitalism is a fool's errand. Its core problem is that it presents capitalism as the deliverer of equality, when capitalism is actually a chief engine of social harm. Friedan had argued middle-class women should join those chosen to thrive, outsourcing their household work and joining the professions. Fifty years later, *Lean In* takes feminist biopolitics to its logical conclusion: women should optimize their capacities by taking the reins of corporate America's profit extraction machine. Working-class women similarly fall out of Sandberg's view, as they had in Friedan's, but their behind-the-scenes work cleaning, cooking, and providing childcare frees up the feminist boss to devote herself to maximizing her self, her career, and her mentees.

Lean In, in the form of the book and the tens of thousands of "lean in circles" linked to Sandberg's nonprofit (and presumably tax sheltering) Leanin .org, envisions an empowered woman who does it all. This includes maintaining a self-starter attitude that makes her easy to mentor; understanding gender is socially constructed and that women internalize sexism and so has weaponized the self to root it out; developing an inclusive vision that allegedly supports all women; watching Leanin.org videos to learn how to comport her body and voice in a way that exudes authority; securing a husband with whom she balances fifty-fifty the work of maintaining a house and raising children; and dissolving boundaries between her private needs and the demands of the workplace, making it possible to bring her "whole sel[f] to work."[14] Work becomes the privileged site of self-development, and everything is reframed as work.

Sandberg's turn to the corporate workplace as the site of feminist self-realization is fully in keeping with neoliberalism, the stage of capitalism we've been immersed in since the mid-1970s. At core, neoliberalism is propelled by the harmful fantasy that the marketplace is the best place to solve social problems. The neoliberal agenda aims to remove all regulations on corporate power so that the richest can accumulate the greatest wealth, and do so most rapidly, in part through eroding the public sector and the taxes that pay for schools, healthcare, and infrastructure like roads, bridges, and utilities. These policies have produced the worst wealth inequality in US history.[15] Sandberg, as the chief of staff to Larry Summers when he was treasury secretary during the Clinton administration, played a role in bringing about some of neoliberal capitalism's most disastrous policies: deregulating Wall Street, which led to the 2008 global recession, and divesting federal moneys from public infrastructure and the social safety net.

The runaway corporate profits that characterize neoliberalism and that underpin *Lean In* and GirlBoss success are extracted from the poor, largely in the form of undercompensating workers for the value they produce for their companies. Neoliberal policies create millionaires and billionaires, rapidly shrink the middle class due to falling wages and disappearing union protections, and swell the working class by replacing living wages with retail, service, and other low-paid work. As Alexandria Ocasio-Cortez has said, "wherever there is affluence, there is an underclass. There is a service class." Under the ethos of "personal responsibility," the poor themselves are tasked with solving the problems created by the rapidly shrinking public sphere and the deregulation that has concentrated half of the world's money in 1 percent of the world's population. At no time has this been more brutally apparent than during the first ten months of the COVID-19 pandemic, when essential workers risked their lives for poverty-wage jobs and an estimated one in six Americans went hungry, while US billionaires increased their wealth by nearly 40 percent.[16]

Meanwhile, in search of new markets and new sources of profit, neoliberalism has turned to the body and to the self as relatively untapped sources of revenue. These modern industries encourage the wealthy enough to not only thrive, but optimize. The optimized consume food only of superlative taste, appearance, and nutritional value; they polish their teeth, skin, hair, and muscles until they glow; they surround their bodies with minimalist design and maximum performance in the kitchen, bedroom, and bathroom and broadcast it all on social media. The optimized streamline their productivity by removing inefficiencies like cleaning their own house, making their own lunch, or shopping for their own groceries—or sometimes, even chewing at all. Through the constant pursuit of the best, the individual allegedly reaches her full potential. The optimized self becomes the ultimate source and producer of social value.

Feminism in neoliberal times makes similar moves. In "the postindustrial economy," journalist Susan Faludi has observed of Sandberg's brand of empowerment, "feminism has been retooled as a vehicle for expression of the self, a 'self' as marketable consumer object." White feminism has become a trendy way to develop a brand, a side hustle, or at least a compelling social media feed. And while billionaires are rapidly falling out of favor, the trope of the optimized feminist whose politics are inclusive and whose makeup is flawless remains a powerful lure. As a blatant attempt to join the status quo, white feminism is increasingly suspect, but as a lifestyle ideal, the optimized woman shimmers forth from Barre class, Instagram scrolls, protest marches, and even, in the Trump era, the White House.[17]

The optimized life presents further contradictions for many women, even as white feminism mandates they achieve it. While Silicon Valley men like Dave Asprey of Bulletproof and Jack Dorsey of Twitter biohack their way into three hours of sleep and twenty-one hours of performance mastery per day, even acolytes of the maximized self are highly suspicious of women who appear to do it all. Success, Sandberg emphasized repeatedly, is negatively correlated with likability for women. Sandberg's white feminist genius lies in understanding that when white women optimize, that doesn't mean programming away all imperfections. For white women, bugs are perceived to be a feature.

"[I] speak openly about my own weaknesses" at work, Sandberg tells the reader, ostensibly to open communication channels with her employees and solicit their critical feedback.[18] But there's a larger effect here, too—it dulls her edges, renders her palatable through the narration and display of her short-comings. In order for highly successful women to be likable, Sandberg intuits, they must be visibly flawed, embodied, emotional, and non-autonomous. To optimize while white and female requires deliberate displays of vulnerability and admitting that you can't be superwoman; "The Myth of Doing It All" reads the title of one chapter. Like the animated character purposely drawn askew to avoid the uncanny valley, the optimized white woman performs her fallibility to avoid provoking discomfort, filling her pockets all the while.

And so the Sheryl Sandberg one meets in *Lean In* is a self-made, soon-to-be billionaire who brings her emotions into the office, pukes into a toilet from morning sickness before an important pitch, and inspires other women to join her in the ranks of an elevated life. Above all, she had to be convinced to own her role among the "world's most powerful women" when the title was first bestowed upon her. When Sandberg speaks of rushing out of the office to tuck her kids into bed or hosting monthly women's networking events at her home, the reader hardly imagines the 11,500-square-foot mansion with a home theater, gym complete with steam room and sauna, and multiple laundry rooms that she and her husband called home, or that the dinner parties she hosted included $38,500-a-plate Obama fundraisers.[19] Instead, the optimized woman CEO comes across as the richer girl next door, whose charmingly apparent humanity inspires her to help lift up other women to join her at the top.

While the optimized man runs barefoot to the office with his water bottle filled with activated charcoal, the optimized woman cries in the executive
suite. When shed by the CEO, white women's tears become a commodity, an
asset, and a safeguard—proof that capitalism can have a heart. The emotional,
feminist CEO secures her own likability and cleanses the means of production at the same time, sanctifying runaway profits with the humanity streaming down her face. This "feminism of the 1 percent . . . supplies the perfect alibi
for neoliberalism," the authors of *Feminism for the 99%* observe, for executive
feminism "enables the forces supporting global capital to portray themselves
as 'progressive.'"[20]

One hundred sixty-five years earlier, Elizabeth Cady Stanton had launched
US white feminism as a project that would civilize the nation. Now, its task
was to elevate perfectly imperfect white women leaders to validate the brutally exploitative economic system that underpinned their success. This was
less the future that Stanton had in mind than the result of the specific politics white women adopted. For nearly two centuries, white feminists have
set lifting white women into the nation's structures of power as the ultimate
goal, and they've framed that rise up the hierarchy as the very meaning of
equality—even when it requires, by definition, lifting up some through pushing down many others.

Displays of emotion and vulnerability are not only keys to rendering corporate women likable and masking capitalist brutality, however. Sandberg is
among the executives who figured out how to turn intimate confessions, personal disclosures, and private communications into the economy's newest
frontier. As neoliberal capital penetrates ever deeper into the body and self,
feelings have become bytes of data that leave algorithmic trails. In the data-
mining scheme she built at Facebook that turned her into a billionaire, the intimate details of our relationships and our politics become raw resources ripe
for extraction. The question now is not if we will lean in to Sandberg's vision of
capitalism: it's whether anyone will retain the genuine option to back out.

In August 2008, as Sheryl Sandberg was adjusting to her new role as Facebook
chief operating officer and the US stock market was veering toward an impending meltdown, Alexandria Ocasio-Cortez got up to leave her father's hospital

room. Though forty-eight-year-old Sergio Ocasio was struggling with a rare form of lung cancer, and she was closer to her father than to anyone else she knew, it was soon time to return for her sophomore year at Boston University. She began to intuit that this would be the last time she would see him, and that her father perceived her realization that he was dying. She said her goodbyes sadly and carefully. But as she passed through the doorframe, her father called out, and Ocasio-Cortez turned back toward the hospital bed. "Hey, make me proud," he charged his oldest child.[21]

Sergio Ocasio passed in early September, cutting off a connection to the person who knew her "soul better than anyone on this planet." Ocasio-Cortez felt unmoored and alone. A premed major who hoped to become an ob/gyn, she opted to study abroad in Niger, West Africa, and began working alongside midwives to gain experience from practiced healers. She found the women's strength and the way their lives revolved around the joy and fellowship they sought every evening to throw into relief that, in the United States, "work is the sun that your whole life is organized around." She also witnessed the dire consequences of poverty—the stacked deck that cuts life short, sometimes all the way back to the moment of birth: instead of delivering life, some patients' labor ushered in death. With her father's high hopes for her future ringing in her ears, Ocasio-Cortez began to envision a different path, one that didn't set about healing symptoms on a case-by-case basis. She excelled at science and had placed second in the world's largest high school science fair; her prize included having an asteroid named after her. But a new goal materialized, one more fundamental than treating individual patients: "healing sick systems."[22] The goal was of suitable ambition to relieve her father's high expectations she felt continually pressing on her chest. When she returned to Boston, she changed her majors to economics and international relations and studied in the Black radical tradition to gain the tools to analyze power at the systemic level.

The world then felt full of promise to Ocasio-Cortez—time stretched out luxuriously in front of her generation and those that would follow, opening ample space to radically transform the way humans relate to each other, socially, politically, and economically. From the podium at Boston University's Martin Luther King Jr. Day celebration during her senior year of college in 2011, she told the audience that "the world is young" and thrilling advances were under way. "Five hundred million people are all connected to one virtual social network," she enthused about Facebook's recent user milestone. "This is what the dawn of an era looks like. These are our victories." But she saw profound defeats as well, such as "Bronx children who cannot count by coincidence of their zip code," the result of a stratified class system in which "the ideas of Plato and Jefferson become as [un]attainable as the items in a Park Avenue window." It is up to us individually to make wise choices about how we contribute to the world we live in, she charged. "Every day we must ask ourselves the question, 'Today, how will I be great? Tomorrow, how will I be great? In this very moment, how am I being great?'"[23] Social change, she imparted, requires a tireless commitment to defying the status quo and reaching for a higher plane.

Ocasio-Cortez, however, would soon feel that she was not choosing greatness. After her father's untimely death, her mother Blanca struggled to afford the mortgage on the thousand-square-foot suburban Westchester house the Bronx couple had bought to give their children access to a better school system. To help pay these bills, she helped her mother clean houses when she was on breaks from college. Upon her graduation she refused to join her fellow economics majors in their rush to lucrative paychecks on Wall Street. Instead, she worked as an education director for the National Hispanic Institute teaching storytelling skills to children. But her mother faced an impending foreclosure, despite working two jobs, and Ocasio-Cortez's nonprofit salary was insufficient to help stave it off. She resigned her position and took a job waitressing and bartending at a Mexican restaurant called Flats Fix near Union Square. The pay was higher, but she nonetheless found herself in "agony." Restaurant work was certainly not what her father had in mind. She had broken her promise. Day by day, self-disappointment pierced her. She was failing to climb to the level of greatness; therefore, she was "nothing."[24]

Ocasio-Cortez realized that she needed to make a choice: "I am either going to destroy myself or I am going to be good." And she realized that meant defining good on her own terms, something that would require her to adjust her "understanding of the world." The problem was not that being a waitress was inherently demeaning. The problem was that mapping her life in terms of "stature" and "achievement" was making her miserable.[25]

Ocasio-Cortez began to root out something just as toxic as women's tendency to underestimate their own leadership capacities—the constant self-pressure to become the best possible version of themselves and to achieve career positions to match. She thought back to what her parents had instilled in her: that the question is "not *what* do you want to be, but *how* do you want to be." And *how* was a matter of day-to-day ethics, spirituality, and self-acceptance, not status and standout accomplishments bulleted on a resume. She began to throw off the neoliberal demands for maximum performance she had internalized and then promoted to others from the MLK Day stage. In its place, she embraced the *how*, finding a daily rhythm enabling her to "attempt to lead a moral life." This change pulled her out of depression and launched her into high spirits at Flats Fix. While the "capitalist economy would say, you should want better than that," she relates that during her many years as a waitress and bartender, "I was happiest because my *how* was in harmony with who I wanted to be."[26]

On a personal level, Ocasio-Cortez identified the optimizing logic that was destroying her and replaced it with a philosophy focused on day-to-day morality and joy. From that strong base, she launched her career in politics, ironically soon reaching a higher prominence than likely she had ever dreamed. Her mission, she explains, is "to advance a better world," not to hold on to the congressional seat she needs to defend every two years or to achieve "social acceptance in [the] small class of powerful and wealthy people" to which her colleagues belong.[27] For her, feminist leadership entails being accountable to the social justice movements that powered her win.

In November 2018, two months before they were even sworn in, Ocasio-Cortez and Rashida Tlaib, a fellow Democratic Socialist, trumpeted their calls for systemic change from the Hill. During their orientation as new members of the House of Representatives, they joined the youth activists of the Sunrise Movement calling for a Green New Deal resolution on the floor of the House—Ocasio-Cortez even joined the sit-in in Speaker of the House Nancy Pelosi's office.[28] It was a striking debut that underscored their commitment to alliance-based movement organizing instead of individual success.

Yet while Ocasio-Cortez had released herself from the demands of self-optimizing, that same expectation of a continual grind and continual excellence is baked into the role of the highly visible twenty-first-century feminist. To many of her fans, she is less a leader than an icon. A secular world still needs its goddesses, and that burden falls onto women like AOC. "Feminist prayer candles" are adorned with her face, authors name her one of the "queens of the resistance," and magazines from *Time* to *Vanity Fair* graced their covers with her image less than two years into office. Hers is a precipitous success, driven by collective glee at her apparent ability to be a fierce radical, glamour girl, and astute, snappy communicator all at the same time—and that imposes its own kind of optimizing trap.

Self-optimizing white women secure their likability through maintaining visible flaws that temper their success, but a more cutthroat standard generally applies to women of color. Optimizing even allows room for a certain amount of mediocrity for white women, though it is white men who by far have the widest berth.[29] Whiteness is so overwhelmingly understood to be capacity itself, that mounting evidence of failure and lack of qualifications often don't hinder white men's careers or reputations—instead, they fail upward. Meanwhile, white women can turn their weakness into reassuring assets, defusing the threat they pose to white men.

But for women of color, a different standard applies. To be racialized is to be seen as innately incapable, at best in need of a helping hand, or, at worst, as a threat to the social order. While tears remain a form of white women's authority, for women of color, the expectations are nothing short of perfection. There is no margin for error, much less for ineptness to masquerade as mastery. Flawlessness and nothingness become the binary options, and neither leaves any room for regular old humanity.

Seemingly aware of these impossible demands thrust upon women of color leaders to be infallible, Ocasio-Cortez crafts an approach to visibility she calls "intentional vulnerability." Cooking dinner while explaining congressional procedure on Instagram at 10 p.m., she explained to scholar-activists Cornel West and Tricia Rose on their podcast *The Tight Rope*, she was bound to make mistakes. Broadcasting her imperfections would not only relieve her of the "messiah" expectations thrust upon her—it would indirectly knock all political leaders off their self-imposed pedestals. "I needed to break the mythology of perfection in people who hold power," she reflected, so that Washington politics looks less like an impenetrable edifice and more like "human being[s] making decisions." Her vulnerability and accessibility would both subvert the optimizing demands placed upon her and chip away at the barrier between congressional officials and the people they allegedly serve. The effect has been magnetic. Her 11 p.m., hour-long Instagram speech the night before the House of Representatives voted to impeach President Trump for the second time in January 2021 drew a live audience of over a hundred thousand; by the next morning, the video had more than 1.5 million views.[30]

Intentional vulnerability is a dicey prospect on a mass stage, however. Extending her working hours until late in the night, Ocasio-Cortez's attempt to reveal her humanity and educate her audience simultaneously risks generating further work demands in which she's never truly off the clock. There's a larger structure, too, that is difficult to sidestep despite radical aims. Emotion and vulnerability, especially shared by women, drive the contemporary social media economy. In a form of capitalism that commodifies performing and marketing the self, even late-night vulnerability can become another valuable asset.

$$\sim \sim$$

The day after AOC occupied Pelosi's office with the Sunrise Movement, Sheryl Sandberg woke to a bombshell. The skies above her mansion were full of smoke from the most lethal and destructive wildfire in California history, the Camp Fire, burning 150 miles to the north. But this bombshell hit closer to home. "Sheryl Sandberg was seething," began a story splashed across the front of the *New York Times* that documented the tactics of deflection, denial, and counterattack that she and Mark Zuckerberg wield to protect Facebook's market dominance. The social network launched in 2004 as a way to stay connected to friends, family, and colleagues; its leaders quickly grew it into a massive media empire. Authoritarian governments in the United States and around the world use the platform to spread false information, a practice Facebook refuses to curb. In response, journalists have widely deemed the company's imperative for unchecked growth and penchant for secrecy to be undermining democracy. Facebook had become for many, the *Times* declared, the symbol "of corporate overreach and negligence." The article revealed Sandberg to sit at the helm of an aggressive campaign to lobby powerful decision-makers, discredit Facebook's critics and detractors, and lie when confronted with her own corporate malfeasance. The exposé struck a powerful blow at Sandberg's reputation that reverberated across the media landscape. "The Rise, Lean, and Fall of Facebook's Sheryl Sandberg" read one particularly incisive follow-up.[31]

Journalists such as Kara Swisher claim that Sandberg is just following the rules of Big Tech and that targeting her, instead of Facebook CEO and principal shareholder Mark Zuckerberg, reeks of misogyny.[32] Yet Sandberg isn't just playing the Big Tech game. She is one of its key inventors. Zuckerberg didn't recruit Sandberg for her good skin and crush-worthy smile. He recruited her in 2008 precisely because of her role in developing surveillance capitalism at Google.

"Surveillance capitalism" is scholar Shoshana Zuboff's term for the Big Tech–driven neoliberal economy we live in today. The most potent form of capital—that is, assets that produce value—has become data that capture individual behavior. The year Sandberg became the general manager of Google's business unit, Google executives had finally figured out how the company could make money. Every search on its site produces data in excess of the search itself, such as information about a user's location, how they phrase queries, and where they click. Zuboff reveals that in 2001 the company transformed such information into "behavioral surplus": surplus data that could be used to create predictive products it would sell to advertisers. The AdWords team, led by Sandberg, immediately changed its strategy for selling ads. While in the past Google sold ads based on keywords (e.g., if a user searched for a recipe for a cake that looks like a litter box, ads for litter boxes would populate the margins of the page), now it started selling ads based on individual profiles it assembled and deduced from the entirety of a user's experience on Google and the web at large. Search words were no longer the raw material that powered Google. Instead, users themselves became what Zuboff calls "human natural resources," mined to make bets on what kind of people we are and what we can be convinced to do. While Sandberg did not conceive of these ad-targeting innovations or write the algorithms that made them possible, as the head of online sales she oversaw the company's efforts to turn its engineering acumen into an unprecedented source of capital. In the process, she grew her sales team from four people to four thousand, swelling the parking lot in the process. By 2007, her unit hauled in two-thirds of Google's $17 billion annual revenue.[33]

Zuckerberg hired Sandberg to bring surveillance capitalism to Facebook and turn the company's first profit. No company has a bigger treasure trove of personal experience than Facebook—data that were waiting to be made profitable. The site is built to solicit disclosure of your daily grievances, what you ate for breakfast, what your kids wore on the first day of school, whether or not you voted and whom you voted for, who came to your birthday party, and who was brave enough to touch the kitty litter cake. "We have better information than anyone else," she boasted after her move to the social network. "We know gender, age, location, and it's real data as opposed to the stuff other people infer."[34] Facebook is a network of human natural resources.

But the information that powers surveillance capitalism goes far beyond self-disclosures, and access to these details isn't merely benign, Zuboff argues. Big Tech's information results from ongoing "digital dispossession" in which the daily emotions and texture of our lives, both online and offline, are extracted and transformed into highly valuable data bought and sold on a market in which we have no control or any share of the profit. The data Google and Facebook mine are not used to benefit the public good—they're used to shape our behavior without our knowledge, building the wealth of the 1 percent in the process.[35]

The vulnerability Sandberg shares and the intimacy she cultivates in the Lean In brand are more than humility and a way to make her own outrageous success acceptable. Personal details are also the raw material of the new kind of capitalism she has helped create: they are the resources she mines, in both her feminist agenda and her corporate career. Emotion, connection, sharing, and friendship now power the engines of surveillance capitalism, the logic that has built Google and Facebook into two of the fifteen most profitable companies in the world.[36] And while Sandberg might defend women's rights to a seat at the boardroom table, in practice she uses gender as a key prediction factor to improve the bets Facebook makes on our future behavior. The irony of Sandberg's Lean In platform is that the more successful she becomes as a capitalist, the more ruthless she reveals white feminism itself to be.

Yet while I disagree with the claim that holding Sandberg at fault for the predatory nature of Big Tech is an act of misogyny, the particular anger directed at Sandberg does fit a longer pattern of sexism. Facebook CEO Zuckerberg is generally portrayed as a shrewd, if overly restrained and calculating, boy-genius-turned-businessman who is guided by rationality. It's hard to imagine an alliterative *New York Times* lede trumpeting his emotional state akin to "Sheryl Sandberg was seething." But white women and white feminists, in large part through their own attempts to gain social power via alternately civilizing, cleansing, or optimizing the status quo, often take the fall when public opinion turns against those same unequal systems.

White women have long been assigned the task of stabilizing society, playing housewife to the entire public sphere. Since at least Elizabeth Cady Stanton, white feminists have expanded that role into one of redemption. They gain access to white supremacist capitalist structures in part through promising to rehabilitate the structures of inequality through their presence. When that project inevitably fails, and settler colonialism, corporate capitalism, or electoral politics remains as brutal as ever, it is white women who absorb much of the blame and outrage—and white men who largely escape notice.

Sandberg's corporate brand of white feminism has long helped cover Facebook's exploitative practice, giving it a palatable sheen, just as her story of vomiting into the toilet renders her fallible and thus, in the misogynist logic that influences all of us to one degree or another, more likable. But as the atrocities of neoliberalism become more and more apparent in the hundreds of thousands left to die in the COVID pandemic while billionaires have doubled their wealth; in the rising seas, raging wildfires, and newly incessant hurricanes plaguing our shores; and in the state's reliance on mass incarceration and police brutality to protect private property, more and more people look instead to a feminism that tries to halt capitalism's death march rather than one that empowers careerwomen to claim it for themselves.

On the second hundred-degree day in a row in July 2020, Alexandria Ocasio-Cortez climbed the steps on the east side of the US Capitol. As she ascended toward the building, she crossed paths with two Republican colleagues with whom she'd never spoken, Representative Ted Yoho of Florida and Representative Roger Williams of Texas.

"Do you really believe that people are shooting and killing each other because they're hungry?" Yoho called out at her, wagging his finger toward her face. "You know, you're unbelievable. You're disgusting."[37]

Ocasio-Cortez had recently held a virtual town hall about police brutality where she recontextualized New York's summertime rise in crime as the result of poverty and hunger exacerbated by the pandemic, not planned minor reductions to the NYPD budget in the wake of anti–police brutality protests. Clips of her comments that "crime is a problem of a diseased society, which neglects its marginalized people," spliced in as if in response to a specific question about gun violence, had dominated the conservative news cycle.[38]

Yoho pressed on. "You are out of your freaking mind," he berated the congresswoman.

"You are being rude," she informed him, and the pair kept walking. But Yoho wasn't finished.

"Fucking bitch," Yoho muttered as he and Williams continued down the stairs.[39]

A reporter overheard the entire exchange, driving yet another news cycle revolving around Ocasio-Cortez. Williams's office issued a denial. Two days later Yoho made a brief statement from the House floor apologizing for "the abrupt manner" of his conversation with the congresswoman, while denying that he had hurled insults her way. "Having been married 45 years with two daughters, I'm very cognizant of my language," he insisted.[40] It's a familiar script, when a man accused of misogyny claims his role as patriarch-protector renders his sexism impossible—when the role itself is part and parcel of the power that sexist cultures grant to men.

Incensed by Yoho's and other men's use of "women, wives, and daughters as shields and excuses for poor behavior," Ocasio-Cortez turned the individual attack on her into an opportunity to expose the ubiquity of misogyny. Though her initial response was to ignore the entire incident, the other Squad members insisted that her treatment was unacceptable—that she had the right, and perhaps the responsibility, to fight back. With their encouragement, she requested her own floor time to address their colleagues two days later. Despite the high-pressure context, she took her usual, confident approach to public speaking, scribbling a few notes in advance and making up the speech on the spot. She donned a red blazer and red lipstick, which Ayanna Pressley immediately knew meant Ocasio-Cortez meant business.[41]

"Representative Yoho's comments were not deeply hurtful or piercing to me," Ocasio-Cortez divulged. "Because I have worked a working-class job. I have waited tables in restaurants." She was not shocked by his language, nor was she seeking his personal apology. Instead, she wanted to unmask "the entire structure of power" that accepts "violence and violent language against women."[42]

Philosopher Kate Manne explains that the common understanding of misogyny as a personal hatred of women fails to get at the true effects of male power, which is structural rather than individual. Sexism, Manne clarifies, is an ideology that dictates women owe dominant men attention, affection, and care—and, as Pauli Murray would add, a structure that sequesters power and capital in the hands of men. Misogyny is the behavior that results, and it enforces the structure of sexism by rewarding women who submit and punishing those who don't. Yoho unleashed misogyny by swearing at Ocasio-Cortez on the Capitol steps—and rather than solicit his apology, she determined to expose how his actions reinforced the larger system of sexism. His slur "was not just an incident directed at me," she elucidated, but part of a structure that expects women to submit to men; "what Mr. Yoho did was give permission to other men to do that to his daughters." The C-SPAN video of her speech instantly became the most popular clip from the House floor in the network's history.[43]

Ocasio-Cortez brought intersectional feminist politics to the House of Representatives with the speech, reframing an act of seemingly individual harm as evidence of the broad structure of gendered power, and it drew an audience of millions. Her remarks were quickly touted as evidence of another AOC triumph. "AOC's speech about Ted Yoho's 'apology' was a comeback for the ages," announced a *Washington Post* column, while the *LA Times* TV critic declared her speech "the best TV I've seen in years."[44] Once more, Ocasio-Cortez became an icon and a showpiece for feminists, her vulnerability turned into evidence of her ceaseless prowess.

Ocasio-Cortez, it seems, continues to win the impossible game, articulating structural analyses of power that seek change from the bottom while generating the video views generally reserved for celebrity clips or animal antics. Meanwhile, her coalition approach to progressive politics deflects attention away from her alone, and the alliance with Pressley, Omar, and Tlaib is expanding to include Ferguson activist Cori Bush and former schoolteacher Jamaal Bowman, who, like Ocasio-Cortez, hails from a Bronx-area district. Where the public expects individual, iconic women of color figureheads, these politicians respond instead with a working alliance that foregrounds class, race, climate change, and gender simultaneously.

Yet when the standards have become continual work, continual availability, and all with extraordinary skill, no one can live up to the pressure. There is no way to win the optimizing game, as an individual or as a squad. Success means an ever-increasing grind that rides the razor's edge dividing wild success from vicious backlash. Ocasio-Cortez nailed her rebuttal to Yoho, but it begs the question. What if she had been ill that day, not up to her usual impromptu eloquence? Whether or not those who hold Ocasio-Cortez in the highest esteem allow her the space to be imperfect, to stumble on her words, or to feel too vulnerable to push back against an extraordinary insult remains an open question.

Ocasio-Cortez, for her part, conveys a deeply grounded approach of "non-attachment" to her position that allows her to focus on her policy priorities, not securing her congressional seat or maintaining her reputation.[45] But for many of her fans, who range from liberal wine moms to Democratic Socialists, AOC represents a flawless feminist savior/Goddess. Her supporters expect her to knock it out of the park in each and every speech, even when she's calling out a colleague on the House floor for harassment. Ultimately, it is us, not Ocasio-Cortez, who fall into the optimizing trap, awaiting perfection on the House floor, Twitter, and Instagram Live. Chances are, we likely place a similar demand on ourselves to maintain flawlessness—though perhaps with just the right amount of endearing vulnerability.

The solution to the trap of optimizing feminism may look a lot like the most promising—and also the most difficult—approach to slowing the carbonization of the atmosphere. Trying harder, trying differently, trying to outgame the game will not work, even with a leader as skilled as AOC. Similarly, producing millions of electric cars, filling the sea with wind turbines, or dimming the sun will not change the cycle of extraction and overproduction upon which the capitalist economy is built. If we stay in the terms of the system, we end up merely reproducing that system.

The solution instead may be simply doing less. Producing less, buying less, working less, demanding less of ourselves and our leaders. In a world primed to accept women's public role in society—whether as a white feminist or intersectional feminist—when she comes to redeem it, the most radical thing of all might be to insist on the individual and collective right to rest, joy, and pleasure. Pleasure may sometimes take the form of engaging with social media. But it may also take other forms altogether, solitary or communal, that retreat from the digital stage and from any commodifiable form of value. It may look like a walk in the woods, nine hours of sleep a night, or full weekends off from one's jobs and side hustles and the screen. Tricia Hersey, founder of the Atlanta-based Nap Ministry, advocates for the liberatory potential of sleep and breaks for Black women and for all. "Rest is a spiritual practice, a racial justice issue and a social justice issue," she argues, a cornerstone of the good life long denied to the racialized poor.[46] Rest, tuning out, and logging off are radical demands in an economy in which not one but two jobs are often required to stay afloat, when sleep has become a middle-class luxury.

Even as we face astounding collective political and economic struggles in the 2020s, to reclaim our energies and our spirits we will need to uproot capitalism's most toxic legacy from within ourselves: that our lives and our movements consist of nothing more than work, and that the best way to navigate the unequal structures of power is to outhustle them.

CONCLUSION
TWO FEMINISMS, ONE FUTURE

Our movements can't only be composed of the people who are most disenfranchised. Our movements also have to be composed of people from across the class spectrum and people who also have power. . . . If we want to compete for power, then part of what it means is we have to amass our power as a unit. And it also means we have to take some of theirs.

—Alicia Garza, *How We Get Free*

There is no reasonable excuse that remains for white women to continue to betray women of color. White women have a choice. It is a choice they have always had to some degree, but never before have they been in such a strong position to make the right one.

—Ruby Hamad, *White Tears/Brown Scars*

How many more must die before we internalize the message of our fundamental interdependence—any disease of one is a disease of the collectivity; any alienation from self is alienation from the collectivity?

—M. Jacqui Alexander, *Pedagogies of Crossing*

WHEN I BEGAN WRITING THIS BOOK IN THE SPRING OF 2018, I WAS TEMPORARILY LIVING IN Palo Alto, California, a few miles from Facebook headquarters. Inside, I combed through research I'd been gathering for nearly two decades on the history of racism and sexism in the United States. Outside, yard signs sprung up from the artificial grass and manicured lawns around me advertising a single message: Recall Judge Persky. Persky was the adjudicator of Brock Turner's sexual assault case who famously sentenced the defendant, routinely summarized as a Stanford swimmer and future Olympian, to only six months of a possible fourteen-year prison term. The survivor's riveting courtroom statement on the impact of Turner's assault on her life, vulnerable in its candor and knifelike in its precision, had captivated millions of people around the world. Moved by the statement and outraged at the leniency Judge Persky had granted Turner, a child of privilege, feminist legal scholar Michele Dauber launched a campaign to recall the judge from his post. "We need justice for women now," she argued, and justice looked to her, as it did for many others, like suitably lengthy prison time. While some protested that firing judges for handing out short sentences would backfire, inevitably greasing the racist gears of the world's largest mass incarceration machine, Palo Alto voted overwhelmingly that June to recall Judge Persky.[1] Feminism seemed to demand it.

I was back home in Brooklyn when I began researching the final chapter of this book in June 2020. Inside, I kept the careful quarantine my mobility-limited and immunocompromised body required in COVID-19-ravaged New York. Outside, at least two Black Lives Matter marches a day streamed down the boulevard as part of a national uprising against state violence and its ruthless assault on Black people, marches I could cheer from the open windows and sometimes the sidewalk. The weekend of Brooklyn Pride, fifteen thousand people converged on the block, spilling across the intersections. As police choppers blustered overhead, the massive crowd, all dressed in white, rallied and then marched silently across central Brooklyn carrying one message: Black Trans Lives Matter. It was likely the largest gathering for trans rights in US history and it convened to underscore how gender violence, racist power, and police brutality intersect—and thus are experienced in heightened intensity—in Black trans lives. Organizers emphasized that police kill Black transgender people at the highest rates of all; in 2020, nearly half of the forty-four trans people murdered by civilians or police were Black trans women.

Black trans death is an epidemic of state and individual violence, the deadly juncture of the biopolitics of race, sex, and state power. Fifteen thousand people came together to pinpoint and obliterate the underlying logic that some lives are less valuable than others, that police and prisons deliver justice, and that to be Black and trans is to be disposable. "Let today be the last day that you ever doubt Black trans power!" writer Raquel Willis proclaimed from the steps of the Brooklyn Museum.[2] Justice demanded it.

The distance between the two events is at once calculable—two years and three thousand miles apart—and incalculable. In June 2018, the carceral agenda of white feminism reigned supreme in the successful Recall Judge Persky campaign, without regard for how protesting short prison terms might impact the most vulnerable. But in June 2020, intersectional feminism led the way as a large multiracial coalition of people, trans and cis, queer and straight, assembled to affirm that Black trans people are integral to the fight for racial justice, recognizing that the vantage of the margins leads right into the center of power in all its complexity.

A significant shift is happening across progressive movements, visible in the short time span of just two years. White feminism, and its agenda to optimize white women, appears to be losing some of its power. Empowering individual women to sidestep sexism in pursuit of their own rise to the top increasingly registers as complicity with the white supremacist status quo rather than representing the inspiring trajectory of a heroine. Across the country, a greater number of people took to the streets in the 2020 Black Lives Matter uprising than had ever protested in the history of the United States, and they did so to call attention to racist systems and to advocate abolishing or defunding the police—not just to toss individual bad apples and ask for the slow drip of incremental reform.

A conceptual transformation mirrors this political move leftward. Progressives are beginning to ditch frameworks that posit that racism and sexism result from individual emotional responses such as fear and hate. Instead, more and more people recognize that discrimination originates from deeply rooted structures of injustice that individuals adhere to, wittingly or not, because they seem to serve their own self-interest.

The history we tell of the United States and its social movements is a key element of this political and conceptual shift. Has the United States come to have the greatest race, sex, and wealth inequality in the industrialized world merely by accident, or by design? Increasingly, particularly as researchers and readers alike are less likely to be white men in positions of power, we are uncovering new evidence of the latter. Discrimination does not originate from the unenlightened malice of closed minds. Rather, hierarchies of race and sex arise from centuries of social institutions, cultural practices, and economic structures designed to over-resource white men, and to a lesser degree white women, and under-resource everyone else. In getting the history right, we also open up the chance for a new kind of future.

Yet we still have a long way to go—the death, displacement, and job losses the racialized poor suffered in the COVID pandemic reveal the extent to which our social structures protect some at the expense of others. Tepid approaches to equality that target isolated incidents and individual success, rather than systemic problems, will not disappear on their own: they need to be out-organized. Capitalist imperialism and the white supremacist patriarchy that sustains it produce a paradigm hard to break away from—it is in the water, it saturates the air, it permeates both as individual common sense and as the climate, akin to weather, as Christina Sharpe has written of the afterlife of slavery.[3]

~ ~

The counterhistory of feminism is seemingly becoming the history of feminism. Sheryl Sandberg is no longer celebrated as feminism's most vital voice; the Squad, rather than the Facebook COO, captivates feminist imaginations. People frequently point to Kimberlé Crenshaw's theory of intersectionality as the key feminist insight for the twenty-first century. Younger feminists are as likely to know about Sojourner Truth and her legendary "Ain't I a Woman" speech advocating for Black women's rights as they are to know the name Elizabeth Cady Stanton or perhaps even Susan B. Anthony. In 2016 Sojourner Truth was even set to appear on the $10 bill, before the Trump administration came into power and blocked all plans to diversify the figureheads on US currency.

There's just one problem. Sojourner Truth never said, "Ain't I a Woman." Nor did she deliver any other sentence of the lecture that is now synonymous with her name. The speech is legendary in a literal sense. Truth was born enslaved in upstate New York in the 1790s, and her native language was low-Dutch. After learning English beginning at age nine, she prided herself in her mastery of its standard form. The word *ain't* or any of the other southern dialect that fills the speech would never have fallen from her lips. In the 1990s, Black feminist historian Nell Irvin Painter showed that the text of the now famous talk Truth delivered at the 1851 Women's Convention in Akron, Ohio, doesn't come from the transcription the *Anti-Slavery Bugle* published a few weeks after the event. Instead, the most widely cited and anthologized version of Truth's speech comes from an account the white activist and writer who led the convention, Frances Dana Barker Gage, published twelve years later. Gage crammed the text with *ain'ts,* other southern colloquialisms, and fabrications about Truth's children and experience with the lash as if Truth were her puppet and she the puppet master. "May I say a few words? I want to say a few words about this matter," the original transcription of Truth's speech begins. But Gage ventriloquizes another character altogether, a stereotypical plantation mammie. "Well, chillen, whar dar's so much racket dar must be som'ting out o'kilter," opens her fictitious version.[4]

We remember a mythical, racist rendering of Sojourner Truth that white women found palatable, yet we forget the work of her contemporary, Frances E. W. Harper. How did this fabricated rendering of Sojourner Truth's voice and image become louder than her own and louder than Harper's, despite the numerous novels, speeches, and books of poetry Harper published to wide circulation? The answer is simple: the writers who created the possibility of such a thing as the history of feminism were the same activists who codified white feminist politics. When Stanton and Anthony assembled their *History of Woman Suffrage*, they represented their own priorities and investments as feminism, full stop. They disappeared the counterhistory. Feminism—like all social movements, a kaleidoscope of conflicting goals, strategies, and tactics—ground to a halt under their eye. In place of a moving mosaic, one monochromatic image dropped into place: a feminist is the defender of Woman. Woman was a being suffering only the injustices of sex, and feminism appeared to be the single-minded focus on winning her rights. All other social justice goals fell into darkness, altogether out of sight.

Sojourner Truth is so widely, but incorrectly, remembered today, Nell Irvin Painter proposes, because when Stanton and Anthony compiled their history of the movement, they packaged Truth as "tend[ing] first and last toward women."[5] The *History of Woman Suffrage* included Truth's speech, but it was Gage's words that filled the pages. Truth was transformed into a colorful caricature who promoted the white feminist agenda.

Other white feminists also scripted Truth as a featured star of their own plots. After Truth introduced herself to Harriet Beecher Stowe, Stowe subsequently published an extensive account of their acquaintance in *The Atlantic*. Like Gage, Stowe filled her columns with entirely made-up southern dialect and historical "facts" Truth allegedly shared about her life, such as her passage from Africa.[6] (Again, she was born in upstate New York.)

Now, the counterhistory of feminism is gradually coming into view, largely due to the work of Black feminists who have, for decades, investigated the limitations of white feminism, uncovered another feminist history, and furthered the theory and praxis of justice developed by Black women. Over the decades, a pantheon of feminist activists has emerged who have been suppressed by white feminism's attempt to monopolize the past. These historical figures, along with present-day activists, often still do not have the full recognition as feminist leaders they deserve. Other leaders of intersectional feminism I considered incorporating into this book include journalist Ida B. Wells, socialist Lucy Parsons, labor activist Mother Jones, writer and activist Lorraine Hansberry, activist-philosopher Grace Lee Boggs, organizer Dolores Huerta, scholar-revolutionary Angela Davis, and the women of the Combahee River Collective, including Audre Lorde and Barbara Smith, among many, many others. The counterhistory of feminism far outreaches the limits of these pages.

～ ～

Intersectional feminism is building strength and power, and models to empower Woman are falling out of favor. But, at the same time, white feminism is not going anywhere. Instead, it has renovated to keep up with the times. Though it is challenged, the white feminist paradigm clings to life, reinventing itself into ever-new forms. Conservatives embraced the railroaded Supreme Court confirmation of Amy Coney Barrett as a triumph for feminism, while liberals expand the optimizing trap to ensnare Black women voters as saviors of the republic, placing the fate of democracy on their shoulders. And as white feminism updates itself with a veneer of inclusion and is increasingly embraced by liberals and conservatives alike, it becomes harder and harder to detect.

Liberal white feminism now embraces inclusion as a brand, believing that if Black women like Sojourner Truth and other women of color are stirred into the mix, an altogether new feminism is born. Often these renovated feminisms merely attempt once more to fill Black women's mouths with white women's words. But inclusion doesn't eradicate white feminism—it merely extends its reach. The trouble with white feminism is not that it ignores and leaves out many women. Its harm is far more fundamental than a lack of awareness: white feminism perpetuates a pattern of dispossession.

In today's white feminism, diversity and awareness become tools for optimizing white-dominated organizations. Black, Latinx, and Indigenous women and nonbinary people become prized tokens, valuable assets showcasing the progressive bona fides of organizational boards and social media feeds. Yet often while the employees have changed, the structure stays the same, and it is women of color who pay the biggest price. Black and other employees of color have exposed how white supremacy thrives within leading feminist institutions. "Top feminist organizations are plagued by racism," the *Lily* recently investigated, while NPR broadcast that "NOW [National Organization for Women] president resigns amid allegations of creating toxic work environment."[7] The optimizing trap attempts to ensnare women of color like Alexandria Ocasio-Cortez with the demand for constant work and constant perfection, and to redeem white feminism. It saves its sharpest teeth, however, for Black women. Inclusive white feminisms cast Black women into a new role, ostensibly laudatory but in reality nearly as artificial and stifling as the plantation mammie with colorful, fictional patterns of speech: the Black woman savior/goddess.

Following the 2020 election, white women filled social media with outlandish reverence for Black women's gallant deeds. Stacey Abrams was glorified as a goddess, unnamed activists as saviors, and Black women voters as rescuers of the nation's soul. Black women organizers and voters indeed deserve an enormous amount of credit for swinging Georgia, Michigan, and Pennsylvania, pushing Trump out of the White House and flipping the Senate. The superhuman language, however, is counterproductive. Stacey Abrams

merits far better than to be called a goddess and cast into plaster atop a ped-
estal, her tenacity becoming another optimizing trap. President? Perhaps. But
not idol and deliverer. Insisting that Black Women Will Save Us fails to recognize how the rallying cry itself isolates Black women from the rest of the
nation and even of humanity while saddling them with the burden of doing all
the work. When Black women ride to the rescue, everyone else has tacit permission to carry on undisturbed. It is not Black women's job to optimize their
activism, saving white women or saving America. It is the responsibility of
white women and all Americans, especially non-Black Americans, to change
the structures that wield anti-Black and other racisms as tools for hoarding
economic, political, and social power.

Mental health and nursing expert Cheryl Woods-Giscombé has found
that the role of the "strong Black woman" that romanticizes tough and re-
silient heroines seemingly inured to hardship actually *increases* the negative
impacts of racism and other structural inequalities on Black women. The
"superwoman schema," as she terms it, badgers Black women into a corner
in which their feelings and vulnerabilities must be repressed, while they are
expected to direct care freely and abundantly toward others. Energy flows
only outward, draining the self. The superwoman sacrifices herself to save
others, and chronic stress and associated mental and physical problems are
her rewards.[8]

The caricature of the Black superwoman who rescues America from its own
racism is but an updated version of the ventriloquized Black woman activist.
Both are roles white women and sympathetic white men create for their own
comfort. The details have changed since Gage and Stowe hijacked Truth's
body as a vehicle for their own words, but the structure of service remains.
Today, inclusive white feminists attempt to siphon Black women's intelligence
and energy into their own consciences by scripting roles of Black superwomen
who seemingly can bear the weight of the nation's violence without suffering
a bruise or shedding a tear. These are distinct forms of drain and theft, but the
fundamental act of extraction continues unabated. So, too, does the psychological, physical, and social cost of being cast as an insensible stock character,
bled of the birthright of fully dimensional personhood animated by tender
flesh and even tenderer feelings, persist.

Even when it tries on inclusivity and praises its goddesses, white feminism is inherently an act of dispossession.

~ ~

In these conditions, how do we recognize white feminism when we see it? And how do we grasp the growing countermovement, discerning when a feminist politics is genuinely aiming to challenge the broader structure of power that privileges the few at the expense of the many?

The past provides us with an indispensable guide to identifying and dismantling white feminist politics today. The histories in *The Trouble with White Women* make clear that though white feminism's outward appearance may be changing, its internal structure has remained remarkably consistent over its nearly two hundred years of existence. White feminist politics developed in key stages, from the civilizing agendas of the nineteenth century to the cleansing campaigns of the twentieth and the optimizing imperatives of today. Yet these distinct styles are built on the same underlying supports: first, the theory that sexism is the most significant force of oppression and that the discrimination women face is, therefore, more similar than different—Woman is always on the receiving end of violence, never holding the lash; second, the method of extracting emotion, energy, labor power, and spirit from others, especially Black, Indigenous, Latinx, and Asian women and men and the poor, to benefit this mythical universal Woman; and finally, the promise that Woman's ascension into power will rehabilitate the institutions of racist empire, transforming them into bastions of equality.

We can recognize white feminism at work today wherever we see the elevation of a woman, of any race, to the top of the hierarchy on the grounds that she will allegedly redeem it. "The future is female," an Instagram-friendly slogan proclaims in a sleek sans serif font, heralding in both word and image that progress hinges on the female sex. The phrase sounds new, but it isn't—it was rediscovered via a 1975 photograph of TERF singer Alix Dobkin wearing the phrase on a T-shirt shortly before she was a ringleader of the protest against Olivia Records because of the presence of Sandy Stone.[9] Yet the slogan is also a slicker version of something Margaret Sanger might have said while insisting that the world's progress pivoted on the quality of women's births.

Women's "emotional intelligence is what's going to make this company succeed," New York senator Kirsten Gillibrand declared while campaigning for the 2020 Democratic presidential nomination and earnestly recycled a joke that "if it wasn't Lehman Brothers but Lehman Sisters, we might not have had the [2008] financial collapse." A sentimental capitalism: Harriet Beecher Stowe would have been proud. "Female leaders handled coronavirus better," an international headline touts, seemingly announcing the arrival of this new, improved horizon. The article reports on an economics study revealing that countries led by women experienced fewer COVID-19 cases and deaths than their male-led counterparts. Yet while the study analyzes global lockdown policies and how soon they were implemented, the researchers claim that the crucial factor in health outcomes lies in the head of government's identity—not in the decisions they made. "Being female-led has provided countries with an advantage in the current crisis," the study's coauthor asserts, as if leaders' administrative choices ooze forth from some gendered essence pooling within.[10] Apparently, when a woman is in charge, the arc of the moral universe bends more sharply toward justice, as if outfitting her curves.

The counterhistory of feminism offers an essential rubric for differentiating white feminism in woke masquerade from those truly intersectional efforts to change the structure of power, not only its face. When we listen to Harriet Jacobs's searing indictment of slavery's exploitation of women's fertility or to Dr. Dorothy Ferebee's insistence on folding reproductive and childcare services for the poor into a broader health agenda, we learn feminism's power and potential for structural transformation. Over the past 160 years, three central elements distinguish intersectional feminism's approach to justice: first, the theory that the experiences of Black women and others pinned to the bottom by race, class, and sex best illuminate the extent and effects of power and oppression; second, the method of building alliance and solidarity across social positions, to effectively dismantle—rather than merely reform—the institutions we have inherited from a legacy of genocide, enslavement, and empire; and finally, the goal of fundamentally redistributing resources to create more equitable systems that serve the many, rather than privilege the few.

Above all, intersectional feminism leads us forward because it is a movement to eradicate systemic inequality. While today the phrase "intersectional identities" has become common, it is an empty phrase, evacuated of any relation to Black feminist theory. Scholar and author Keeanga-Yamahtta Taylor clarifies that when the Combahee River Collective coined the term "identity politics," they "saw it as an analysis that would validate Black women's experiences while simultaneously creating an opportunity for them to become politically active to fight for the issues most important to them."[11] The key focus, then, is not on Woman as an individual subjectivity or that politics should be based on identity, but on recognizing that those on the bottom of the power hierarchy are its experts. These feminists approach sexism as a system fully embedded within racism, homophobia, transphobia, empire, wealth accumulation, and more. As made clear by Pauli Murray's insistence that employment protections on the basis of race and sex were necessary, intersectionality interrogates the institutions that engineer the basic chances of life and death.

We can recognize intersectional feminism by its goal to collectively defeat the social systems that allow some people, both women and men, to optimize their own potential by draining the vitality and resources of everyone else. While white feminism leans in to the structures of disposability that give shape to everyday life, intersectional feminism seeks to demolish the entire edifice. Pauli Murray wasn't satisfied chipping away at Jim Crow piecemeal, showing one at a time that a segregated institution wasn't an equivalent of its counterpart for whites—she wanted to invalidate the very premise that separate could ever be equal. Intersectionality aims not for awareness or inclusion but for "revolutionary action," in the words of the Combahee River Collective, to build mass power that can genuinely threaten the status quo.[12]

Dismantling the interlocking systems that result in, for example, a Black woman being 69 percent more likely to die from heart disease than a white woman, requires a breathtaking amount of vision, effort, and persistence.[13] White feminism promotes empowering female figureheads to rise to the top. But today, intersectional feminism takes on goals like organizing for Black lives, raising the minimum wage, expanding universal healthcare, protesting mass incarceration, supporting the reproductive choices of poor women, and ending the Israeli occupation of Palestine, all of which have dramatic consequences for the lives of millions of women, men, and nonbinary people.

And together, the many far outnumber the few. Capitalism is working fine for the 1 percent but not for the 99 percent—and even Sheryl Sandberg suffers

jaw-dropping misogyny in her own workplace. And though the white supremacist patriarchy seems to work for white men, especially if they are rich, it is
itself a gilt cage, often bereft of friendship and care and rife with competition
and violence. As Zitkala-Ša modeled with building the first political organization that united Native tribes across the country and Sandy Stone advocated
by framing trans lives that push beyond the sex binary as part of a larger antiracist, anti-imperialist counterdiscourse, intersectional feminism proceeds
through illuminating overlapping alliances. It mobilizes through building
points of common cause into solidarities that unite across distinct identity
positions. Individuals, however empowered they may be, don't overthrow
centuries-old systems of exploitation. But coalitions do, or at least they have
a fighting chance.

~ ~

Yet intersectionality is not a war, seeking to raze everything to the ground.
An intention to destroy reproduces just that, for it contains no seeds of other
forms of life. The endpoint isn't extermination—it's rebirth and transformation. Intersectional praxis is simultaneously an act of demolition and creation,
an affirmative act of love, faith, and care. It creates practices in which flourishing belongs to the commons, not to the few, and in which those who have
paid the highest prices in the white supremacist patriarchy, especially cis and
trans Black women, are valued for their knowledge and leadership. It works to
topple hierarchies of individuals and build ecologies of care in their place. We
need to uproot racism, sexism, ableism, the sex binary, and more. But we also
need to nurture the hearts and minds that drive us to revolutionary action and
to attend to the energy that courses through us all. Mutual aid, interdepen-
dent networks, reciprocal relationships, the union of mind, body, emotion,
and spirit within our own lives and within our feminism: these are the modes
of social movements that can broadly redistribute the relative chances of life
and death.

     While researching and writing this book, I have been struck by the expan-
siveness of the intersectional vision of the world, how it extends beyond the
material plane altogether and into the realm of the spiritual. In white feminism, power is largely something owned by white men that must be seized.
The worldview of capitalist modernity sets the limits of its vision for justice

until optimizing the self becomes the ultimate horizon. But for Frances E. W. Harper, Zitkala-Ša, Pauli Murray, and Alexandria Ocasio-Cortez, power ultimately does not belong to humans but to the realm of spirit—it is not something to be grabbed but to be shared, with gratitude. The worldview of intersectional feminism is bigger than the individual, bigger than the human institutions that provide or deny rights and opportunities. The horizon instead is the flow of life that connects us all.

Feminists may support equality for women, but our true task is to determine what exactly equality looks like. The feminist movement is the grounds of an ongoing struggle to hash out the theories, methods, and goals that might bring us closer to gender, racial, and economic justice. "The future is female" slogan images an inevitable feminist future without conflict, as if a straightforward, undebatable politics and vision flows forth from the bodies of cis women. But the history of feminism is the history of the fight to define feminism, to determine what it advocates and whom it represents. This internal tension doesn't compromise feminism—it comprises it. Distinct approaches to feminism are the vehicles through which new visions, platforms, and approaches arise. Yet we are not stuck in the history of feminism, doomed to repeat its fault lines. The past teaches us that feminism can become an anti-racist project that is incompatible with white supremacy in any form.

White feminism cannot become truly inclusive of women of color, trans and disabled people, and the poor, for its politics are fundamentally at odds with their survival. The goal, instead, is for intersectional feminism to out-organize the white feminist fantasy of a world civilized and optimized by the empowerment of women. Intersectionality is both a confrontation with power and a praxis of care. Some of our best hopes for abolishing the structures that render people, species, and even the planet disposable—and for constructing habitable worlds in their place—arise from its politics. To know the counter-history of feminism is to have an emerging blueprint for a collective future.

ACKNOWLEDGMENTS

FEMINIST RESEARCH IS ONLY POSSIBLE BECAUSE OF FEMINIST COMMUNITY. I THANK GENERA-tions of scholars and writers who came before me and who are working today for revealing the complexity, tensions, shortcomings, and breakthroughs of the movements for gender justice. Due to limited space, only a small fraction of their efforts is explicitly cited here. Yet this book would not exist if not for their rigor and care in bringing the histories of feminism to light.

For enabling me to join this conversation, I am grateful to my advisers, colleagues, and students, especially Barbara Welke, Shelley Streeby, Lisa Lowe, Nayan Shah, Rosaura Sánchez, Michael Davidson, Ann Fabian, Mary Hawkesworth, Abe Busia, Brittney Cooper, Maya Mikdashi, Ethel Brooks, Jasbir Puar, Marisa Fuentes, Treva Ellison, Sarah Blackwood, Dana Luciano, Kyla Wazana Tompkins, Lauren Klein, Karen Weingarten, and the students of my Feminist Theory: Historical Perspectives class at Rutgers in the momentous term of spring 2020. Three writers, and their classes, showed me how to write compelling prose that invites the reader in: Xeni Fragakis, Brian Gresko, and T Kira Madden. Three people were pivotal in enabling this research to flower into an actual book: journalist Nawal Arjani; my visionary agent Ed Maxwell at Greenburger Associates, who taught me every step of the process; and my research assistant/comrade Leo Lovemore, PhD, whose keen eye and steady hand kept this project growing even when I got lost in the weeds.

At Bold Type Books, editor Katy O'Donnell and publisher Clive Priddle made a more-than-welcoming home for this project. Katy's edits propelled the book into the most vital territory: I am grateful for her exceptional attention to the smallest details and largest stakes of the project. I thank the Bold Type and Hachette team for guiding the book through the many stages between draft and print, including editorial assistant Claire Zuo, editor Remy Cawley, production editor Brynn Warriner, art director Pete Garceau, copyeditor Jennifer Top, fact checker Cecilia Nowell, and marketing director Lindsay Fradkoff.

Working on this manuscript reignited my love of feminist books and grounded me throughout a pandemic. I thank the spaces and writers that provided crucial company: the Writers Studio at the Center for Fiction and then, in the Zoom era, my virtual writing pals Kyla Wazana Tompkins, Dana Luciano, Jordan Alexander Stein, Tavia Nyong'o, Raúl Coronado, and Sarah Blackwood. I am grateful to my sister, Lisanne Dinges, for her enthusiasm for the project and dedication to the nitty gritty of bringing research to life, title by title and page by page. I am happily indebted to those dear friends who lived with the project, too, and generously shared their wisdom even when they probably wished I was talking about something else, especially Ali Howell, Rossi Kirilova, Gus Stadler, Pete Coviello, Eng-Beng Lim, Elizabeth Marcus, Cat Fitzpatrick, Porochista Khakpour, Greta LaFleur, Catherine Zimmer, Ilana Sichel, Kent Bassett, Shuchi Talati, Jacob Hodes, Kelly Pendergrast, Diana Cage, Maxe Crandall, Elizabeth Steeby, and Jules Gill-Peterson.

I extend my gratitude to the healers who have helped pluck me out of the grips of the tick-borne illness that has defined my last decade: Lilia Gorodinsky, Yuka Lawrence, and Kevin Weiss.

May we all live lives marked by less suffering and more mutual care.

NOTES

INTRODUCTION: FEMINIST FAULT LINES

1. While exit polls reported 52 percent of white women voted for Trump, later analyses put the figure at 47 percent. "An Examination of the 2016 Electorate, Based on Validated Voters," Pew Research Center, August 9, 2018, www.pewresearch.org/politics/2018/08/09/an-examination-of-the-2016-electorate-based-on-validated-voters/; Amanda Barroso, "61% of U.S. Women Say 'Feminist' Describes Them Well; Many See Feminism as Empowering, Polarizing," Pew Research Center, July 7, 2020, www.pewresearch.org/fact-tank/2020/07/07/61-of-u-s-women-say-feminist-describes-them-well-many-see-feminism-as-empowering-polarizing/; James Gillespie, "Dad's a Feminist, Says Ivanka Trump," *The Times*, July 3, 2016, www.thetimes.co.uk/article/dads-a-feminist-says-ivanka-3bz9krjp0.

2. Jessie Daniels, "The Trouble with 'Leaning In' to (White) Corporate Feminism," *Racism Review*, March 18, 2014, www.racismreview.com/blog/2014/03/18/white-corporate-feminism/.

3. Paula Gunn Allen, "Who Is Your Mother? Red Roots of White Feminism," *Sinister Wisdom* 25 (1984): 41; Kimberlé Crenshaw, "Demarginalizing the Intersection of Race and Sex: A Black Feminist Critique of Antidiscrimination Doctrine, Feminist Theory and Antiracist Politics," *University of Chicago Legal Forum* 1989, no. 1 (1989): 143–144; Patricia Hill Collins, *Black Feminist Thought: Knowledge, Consciousness, and the Politics of Empowerment* (New York: Routledge, 1990), 5; bell hooks, *Feminist Theory: From Margin to Center* (Boston: South End Press, 1984), 1–2; bell hooks, *Ain't I a Woman: Black Women and Feminism* (Boston: South End Press, 1981), 1–2.

4. "White Feminism," *Dictionary.com*, 2020, www.dictionary.com/e/gender-sexuality/white-feminism/.

5. Ruby Hamad, "We Shouldn't Be Surprised by White Women's Complicity," *Medium*, December 9, 2020, https://gen.medium.com/we-shouldnt-be-surprised-by-white-women-s-complicity-7d9e66b0bd4b; Audre Lorde, "The Master's Tools Will Never Dismantle the Master's House," in *Sister Outsider: Essays and Speeches*, ed. Audre Lorde (Berkeley, CA: Crossing Press, 2007), 110.

6. Crenshaw, "Demarginalizing the Intersection," 145; Collins, *Black Feminist Thought*, 18.

7. Brittney Cooper, "Feminist Digital Pedagogies Conference: Post-Intersectionality," Institute for Women's Leadership, Rutgers University, April 30, 2014, www.youtube.com/watch?v=2wrIlDA1s_M.

8. Rachel Elizabeth Cargle, "When Feminism Is White Supremacy in Heels," *Harper's Bazaar*, August 16, 2018, www.harpersbazaar.com/culture/politics/a22717725/what-is-toxic-white-feminism/.

9. Elizabeth Cady Stanton, Theodore Stanton, and Harriot Stanton Blatch, *Elizabeth Cady Stanton as Revealed in Her Letters, Diary and Reminiscences*, vol. 1 (New York: Harper and Brothers, 1922), 253.

10. Brent Scher, "Gillibrand: If Lehman Brothers Were Lehman Sisters, We Would Have Avoided Financial Collapse," *Washington Free Beacon*, May 15, 2018, https://freebeacon.com/politics/gillibrand-lehman-brothers-lehman-sisters-avoided-financial-collapse/.

11. Frances Ellen Watkins Harper, "We Are All Bound Up Together," in *Proceedings of the Eleventh Women's Rights Convention, May 10, 1866* (New York: Robert J. Johnston, 1866), 46.

12. Audre Lorde, "An Open Letter to Mary Daly," in *This Bridge Called My Back: Writings by Radical Women of Color*, 4th ed., ed. Cherríe Moraga and Gloria Anzaldúa (Albany: SUNY Press, 2015), 90.

CHAPTER ONE: WOMAN'S RIGHTS ARE WHITE RIGHTS?

1. Laura Curtis Bullard, "Elizabeth Cady Stanton," in *Our Famous Women: Comprising the Lives and Deeds of American Women Who Have Distinguished Themselves* (Hartford, CT: A. D. Worthington, 1884), 613.

2. Judith Wellman, *The Road to Seneca Falls: Elizabeth Cady Stanton and the First Woman's Rights Convention* (Urbana: University of Illinois Press, 2004), 193, 277n30. This was not Stanton's first-ever public speech, despite what she liked to claim. See Lori Ginzberg, *Elizabeth Cady Stanton: An American Life* (New York: Hill and Wang, 2010), 57.

3. Alice S. Rossi, ed., "Selections from the *History of Woman Suffrage*: Seneca Falls Convention," in *The Feminist Papers: From Adams to Beauvoir* (Boston: Northeastern University Press, 1988), 419–420; Ginzberg, *Elizabeth Cady Stanton*, 59–63.

4. Sally Gregory McMillen, *Seneca Falls and the Origins of the Women's Movement* (New York: Oxford University Press, 2009), 93–94.

5. Elizabeth Cady Stanton, "Preface," in *Eighty Years and More: Reminiscences 1815–1897* (London: T. Fisher Unwin, 1898); Frederick Douglass, *The Life and Times of Frederick Douglass* (Mineola, NY: Dover Publications, 2003), 345.

6. Elizabeth Cady Stanton, Susan B. Anthony, and Matilda Joslyn Gage, eds., *History of Woman Suffrage, Volume 2 (1861–1876)* (Rochester, NY: Susan B. Anthony, 1881), 354–355; Elizabeth Cady Stanton, "Address to Anniversary of American Equal Rights Association, May 12, 1869, New York City," in *Elizabeth Cady Stanton, Feminist as Thinker*, ed. Ellen Carol DuBois (New York: NYU Press, 2007), 191.

7. Stanton, Anthony, and Gage, *History of Woman Suffrage*, 382.

8. Elisabeth Griffith, *In Her Own Right: The Life of Elizabeth Cady Stanton* (New York: Oxford University Press, 1985), 137. Anthony declares this in 1866. See Ida Husted Harper, *The Life and Work of Susan B. Anthony*, vol. 1 (Indianapolis: Bowen-Merrill, 1899), 261.

9. "Annual Meeting of the American Equal Rights Association: Second Day's Proceedings," *Revolution* 3, no. 21 (May 27, 1869): 321, quotes slightly paraphrased for grammatical continuity, and the original source paraphrases Harper's words. As it was, Chinese immigrants were not granted the right to vote until 1943.

10. Ibid., 322. The original source paraphrases Harper's words.

11. Stephanie E. Jones-Rogers, *They Were Her Property: White Women as Slave Owners in the American South* (New Haven, CT: Yale University Press, 2019).

12. "Annual Meeting of the American Equal Rights Association: Second Day's Proceedings," 322.

13. Brittney Cooper also argues that Anna Julia Cooper may in fact be the first Black feminist theorist. Brittney Cooper, *Beyond Respectability: The Intellectual Thought of Race Women* (Champaign: University of Illinois Press, 2017), 2.

14. Ellen Carol Dubois, "Introduction," in *The Elizabeth Cady Stanton–Susan B. Anthony Reader: Correspondence, Writings, Speeches*, ed. Ellen Carol Dubois (New York: Schocken Books, 1981), 9; Stanton, *Eighty Years*, 2, 20.

15. Stanton, *Eighty Years*, 23; Ginzberg, *Elizabeth Cady Stanton*, 22.

16. Melba Joyce Boyd, *Discarded Legacy: Politics and Poetics in the Life of Frances E. W. Harper, 1825–1911* (Detroit: Wayne State University Press, 1994), 36–37.

17. William Still, *The Underground Railroad* (Philadelphia: Porter and Coates Publishers, 1872), 756; W. Somerset Maugham, "'Pride and Prejudice', *Atlantic*, 181, 5, May 1948," in *Jane Austen: Critical Assessments*, vol. 1, ed. Ian Littlewood (Lake Dallas, TX: Helm Information, 1998), 460.

18. "120 Years of Literacy: 1870," National Center for Educational Statistics, https://nces .ed.gov/naal/lit_history.asp. For more on African American literacy rates in this period see Elizabeth McHenry, *Forgotten Readers: Recovering the Lost History of African American Literary Societies* (Durham, NC: Duke University Press, 2002), 4–5.

19. McHenry, *Forgotten Readers*, 79; Stanton, *Eighty Years*, 81, 79; Ginzberg, *Elizabeth Cady Stanton*, 36–38.

20. An exception to the restriction against owning property was that courts often determined white women in the South were able to own slaves in their own right as married women. See Jones-Rogers, *They Were Her Property*, xi–xv.

21. The phrase "white women's rights" is Louise Michelle Newman's. See Louise Michelle Newman, *White Women's Rights: The Racial Origins of Feminism in the United States* (New York: Oxford University Press, 1999).

22. Elizabeth Cady Stanton, "Address Delivered at Seneca Falls, July 19, 1848," in *The Elizabeth Cady Stanton–Susan B. Anthony Reader: Correspondence, Writings, Speeches*, ed. Ellen Carol Dubois (New York: Schocken Books, 1981), 35.

23. Stanton, *Eighty Years*, 187.

24. Elizabeth Cady Stanton, "Address to the Legislature of New York on Women's Rights, February 14, 1854," in *The Elizabeth Cady Stanton–Susan B. Anthony Reader: Correspondence, Writings, Speeches*, ed. Ellen Carol Dubois (New York: Schocken Books, 1981), 45; Sally Roesch Wagner, "Is Equality Indigenous? The Untold Iroquois Influence on Early Radical Feminists," *On the Issues* 5, no. 1 (1996): 21.

25. Gloria T. Hull, Patricia Bell Scott, and Barbara Smith, eds., *But Some of Us Are Brave: All the Women Are White, All the Blacks Are Men* (New York: The Feminist Press, 1993).

26. Stanton, *Eighty Years*, 237–238, 192.

27. Ginzberg, *Elizabeth Cady Stanton*, 47, 108, 20; "When Did Slavery End in New York?," New York Historical Society Museum and Library, January 12, 2012, www.nyhistory.org /community/slavery-end-new-york; Stanton, *Eighty Years*, 4.

28. Still, *Underground Railroad*, 756–757; "The Fugitive Slave Law of 1850," *Bill of Rights in Action* 34, no. 2 (Winter 2019), www.crf-usa.org/images/pdf/Fugitive-Slave-Law-1850.pdf.

29. Still, *Underground Railroad*, 757.

30. Ibid., 757–758.

31. Ibid., 758–759, 761; Boyd, *Discarded Legacy*, 42; Frances Smith Foster, "Introduction," in *A Brighter Coming Day: A Frances Ellen Watkins Harper Reader*, ed. Frances Smith Foster (New York: The Feminist Press, 1990), 13.

32. Still, *Underground Railroad*, 758.

33. Frances E. W. Harper, "The Slave Mother," in *A Brighter Coming Day: A Frances Ellen Watkins Harper Reader*, ed. Frances Smith Foster (New York: The Feminist Press, 1990), 84.

34. Harper, "We Are All Bound Up Together," 217.

35. Frances E. W. Harper, "Our Greatest Want," in *A Brighter Coming Day: A Frances Ellen Watkins Harper Reader*, ed. Frances Smith Foster (New York: The Feminist Press, 1990), 103.

36. Frances E. W. Harper, "Free Labor," in *A Brighter Coming Day: A Frances Ellen Watkins Harper Reader*, ed. Frances Smith Foster (New York: The Feminist Press, 1990), 81.

37. Elizabeth Cady Stanton, "Address of Elizabeth Cady Stanton," in *Proceedings of the Eleventh National Woman's Rights Convention, Held at the Church of the Puritans, New York, May 10, 1866* (New York: Robert J. Johnston, 1866), 52.

38. Harper, "We Are All Bound Up Together," 217; Still, *Underground Railroad*, 778.

39. Harper, "We Are All Bound Up Together," 217.

40. Ibid., 218.

41. Ibid.

42. Ibid., 217.

43. Boyd, *Discarded Legacy*, 119–120; Still, *Underground Railroad*, 767–767, 772–773.

44. Still, *Underground Railroad*, 768, 772, 775.

45. Ibid., 770.

46. Ibid., 775; William J. Collins and Robert A. Margo, "Race and Home Ownership from the End of the Civil War to the Present," *American Economic Review* 101, no. 3 (2011): 356; Pete Daniel, *Dispossession: Discrimination Against African American Farmers in the Age of Civil Rights* (Chapel Hill: University of North Carolina Press, 2013).

47. Still, *Underground Railroad*, 775–776.

48. Elizabeth Cady Stanton, "Address to the First Anniversary of the American Equal Rights Association, May 9, 1867," in *Proceedings of the First Anniversary of the American Equal Rights Association, Held at the Church of the Puritans, New York, May 9 and 10, 1867* (New York: Robert J. Johnson, 1867), 14.

49. Faye E. Dudden, *Fighting Chance: The Struggle over Woman Suffrage and Black Suffrage in Reconstruction America* (New York: Oxford University Press, 2011), 8–10; Christine Stansell, *The Feminist Promise: 1792 to the Present* (New York: Modern Library, 2011), 89; Rosalyn Terborg-Penn, *African American Women in the Struggle for the Vote, 1850–1920* (Indianapolis: Indiana University Press, 1998), 31; Angela Davis, *Women, Race, and Class* (New York: Vintage, 1983), 81.

50. Geoffrey C. Ward and Kenneth Burns, *Not for Ourselves Alone: The Story of Elizabeth Cady Stanton and Susan B. Anthony* (New York: Knopf, 1999), 131. The word comes from Stowe's sister-in-law Isabella Hooker Beecher, whose participation Stanton and Anthony also sought. Joan D. Hedrick, *Harriet Beecher Stowe: A Life* (New York: Oxford University Press, 1994), 358.

51. Ginzberg, *Elizabeth Cady Stanton*, 122; "Mrs. Stanton Before the District Committee," *Revolution*, February 11, 1869, 88; "Which Shall It Be—a Negro or a Woman?," *Revolution*,

September 15, 1870, 169; "White Woman's Suffrage Association," *Revolution*, June 4, 1868, 337.

52. Griffith, *In Her Own Right*, 126–127; Ellen Carol Dubois, *Woman Suffrage and Women's Rights* (New York: NYU Press, 1998), 100.

53. Elizabeth Cady Stanton, "The Solitude of Self," in *The Elizabeth Cady Stanton–Susan B. Anthony Reader: Correspondence, Writings, Speeches*, ed. Ellen Carol Dubois (New York: Schocken Books, 1981), 251, 254, 247.

54. Ibid., 252.

55. Griffith, *In Her Own Right*, xvi.

56. Boyd, *Discarded Legacy*, 119.

57. Frances E. W. Harper, "Woman's Political Future—Address by Frances E. W. Harper of Virginia," in *The World's Congress of Representative Women: A Historical Résumé for Popular Circulation of the World's Congress of Representative Women*, ed. May Wright Sewall (Chicago: Rand McNally, 1894), 435.

58. Foster, "Introduction," 25.

59. See for example Hazel Carby, *Reconstructing Womanhood: The Emergence of the Afro-American Woman Novelist* (New York: Oxford University Press, 1989), 80. Feminist critics, in general, see her sentimentalism as a strategic cover for injecting radical politics into everyday life.

60. Frances E. W. Harper, *Iola Leroy* (Boston: Beacon Press, 1987), 219.

61. Geoffrey Sanborn, "Mother's Milk: Frances Harper and the Circulation of Blood," *ELH* 73, no. 3 (2005), 691–715.

62. Harper, "Woman's Political Future," 435, 436.

63. Quoted in DuBois, *Elizabeth Cady Stanton Reader*, 296–297; Elizabeth Cady Stanton, "Our Proper Attitude Toward Immigration," in *Elizabeth Cady Stanton, Feminist as Thinker*, ed. Ellen Carol DuBois (New York: NYU Press, 2007), 296–297.

64. Catt, *Woman Suffrage by Constitutional Amendment*, 76.

CHAPTER TWO: WHITE SYMPATHY VERSUS BLACK SELF-DETERMINATION

1. Harriet Jacobs, *Incidents in the Life of a Slave Girl* (New York: Open Road, 2016), 82.

2. Ibid., 93.

3. Jacobs refers to Mark Ramsey as "Uncle Phillip" in *Incidents*. Jean Fagan Yellin, *Harriet Jacobs: A Life* (New York: Basic Books, 2004), 212.

4. Jacobs, *Incidents*, 99–100.

5. Ibid., 98.

6. Yellin, *Harriet Jacobs*, 101–103.

7. Jacobs, *Incidents*, 50.

8. Harriet Beecher Stowe, *Household Papers and Stories* (Boston: Ticknor and Fields, 1868), 382.

9. James Baldwin, *Notes of a Native Son* (Boston: Beacon Press, 1983), 14.

10. Luvvie Ajayi, "About the Weary Weaponizing of White Women Tears," *AwesomelyLuvvie.com*, April 17, 2018, https://awesomelyluvvie.com/2018/04/weaponizing-white-women-tears.html; Brittney Cooper, *Eloquent Rage: A Black Feminist Discovers Her Superpower* (New York: Picador, 2018), 171–200; Robin DiAngelo, *White Fragility: Why It's So Hard for White People to Talk About Racism* (Boston: Beacon Press, 2018), 131.

11. Charles Edward Stowe, *The Life of Harriet Beecher Stowe: Compiled from Her Letters and Journals* (Boston: Houghton Mifflin, 1890), 145.

12. Joan D. Hedrick, *Harriet Beecher Stowe: A Life* (New York: Oxford University Press, 1995), 192–193, 207–208.

13. Ibid., 208.

14. Ibid., 209.

15. Stowe, *The Life of Harriet Beecher Stowe*, 201–202.

16. Hedrick, *Harriet Beecher Stowe*, 209, 219, italics in original.

17. Stowe, *The Life of Harriet Beecher Stowe*, 149–153.

18. Harriet Beecher Stowe, *Uncle Tom's Cabin* (New York: Open Road, 2014), 269, 453.

19. Ibid., 378, 62.

20. Ibid., 509, 533.

21. Ibid., 441, 438, 552.

22. Lauren Berlant, *The Female Complaint* (Durham, NC: Duke University Press, 2008), 35.

23. Jacobs, *Incidents*, 159; Yellin, *Harriet Jacobs*, 245.

24. Jacobs, *Incidents*, 162.

25. Ibid., 164.

26. "Harriet Jacobs to Amy Kirby Post, Cornwall, Orange Co., NY, 1852(?)," in *The Harriet Jacobs Family Papers*, vol. 1, ed. Jean Yellin (Chapel Hill: University of North Carolina Press, 2008), 191.

27. Ibid.

28. Yellin, *Harriet Jacobs*, 119–120; "Harriet Jacobs to Amy Kirby Post, February 14, 1853," in *The Harriet Jacobs Family Papers*, vol. 1, ed. Jean Yellin (Chapel Hill: University of North Carolina Press, 2008), 193–194.

29. While the letter no longer exists, Jacobs's recounting of its contents to Amy Post survives. "Harriet Jacobs to Amy Kirby Post, February 14, 1853," 94. See Yellin, *Harriet Jacobs*, 119–121.

30. "Harriet Jacobs to Amy Kirby Post, April 4, 1853," in *The Harriet Jacobs Family Papers*, vol. 1, ed. Jean Yellin (Chapel Hill: University of North Carolina Press, 2008), 195.

31. Yellin, *Harriet Jacobs*, 121.

32. Hedrick, *Harriet Beecher Stowe*, 249.

33. Harry Stone, "Charles Dickens and Harriet Beecher Stowe," *Nineteenth-Century Fiction* 12, no. 3 (1957): 188; Katherine Kane, "The Most Famous American in the World," ConnecticutHistory.org, https://connecticuthistory.org/the-most-famous-american-in-the-world/; Stowe, *The Life of Harriet Beecher Stowe*, 191–192.

34. Hedrick, *Harriet Beecher Stowe*, 237.

35. Ibid., 223.

36. Ibid., 240.

37. Ibid., 235–237, 248.

38. Ibid., 236; "Stowe's Global Impact," Harriet Beecher Stowe Center, www.harrietbeecherstowecenter.org/harriet-beecher-stowe/her-global-impact/; "*Uncle Tom's Cabin* by Harriet Beecher Stowe," First Amendment Museum, September 27, 2020, https://firstamendmentmuseum.org/banned/; Frederick Douglass, "First Meeting with Stowe, 1853," in *Stowe in Her Own Time*, ed. Susan Belasco (Iowa City: University of Iowa Press, 2009), 86. The exact wording of this apocryphal quote varies. See Daniel R. Vollaro, "Lincoln, Stowe, and the

'Little Woman/Great War' Story: The Making, and Breaking, of a Great American Anecdote," *Journal of the Abraham Lincoln Association* 30, no. 1 (2009): 18–34.

39. Robert S. Levine, ed., "Delany and Douglass on *Uncle Tom's Cabin*," in *Martin R. Delany: A Documentary Reader* (Chapel Hill: University of North Carolina Press, 2003), 234, 235; Frederick Douglass, "Mrs. Stowe's Position," in *Frederick Douglass' Paper*, May 6, 1853, http://utc.iath.virginia.edu/africam/afar03rt.html.

40. Hedrick, *Harriet Beecher Stowe*, 247.

41. Ibid., 245; Stowe, *The Life of Harriet Beecher Stowe*, 234. For an image of the bracelet, see Kane, "The Most Famous American in the World."

42. "Harriet Jacobs to Amy Kirby Post, May 1853," in *The Harriet Jacobs Family Papers*, vol. 1 (Chapel Hill: University of North Carolina Press, 2008), 195–196.

43. "Mrs. Ex-President Tyler's Address to the Women of England," *Daily South Carolinian*, March 8, 1853, https://link.gale.com/apps/doc/GT3005440026/NCNP?u=new67449&sid=NCNP&xid=48292960; Wendy F. Hamand, "'No Voice from England': Mrs. Stowe, Mr. Lincoln, and the British in the Civil War," *New England Quarterly* 61, no. 1 (1988): 5.

44. Yellin, *The Harriet Jacobs Family Papers*, vol. 1, 197–201; Yellin, *Harriet Jacobs*, 122.

45. Yellin, *Harriet Jacobs*, 129.

46. Linton Weeks, "How Black Abolitionists Changed a Nation," NPR, February 26, 2015, www.npr.org/sections/npr-history-dept/2015/02/26/388993874/how-black-abolitionists-changed-a-nation; Jacobs, *Incidents*, 69, 143.

47. Marianne Noble, "The Ecstasies of Sentimental Wounding in *Uncle Tom's Cabin*," *Yale Journal of Criticism* 10, no. 2 (1997): 295–296.

48. Jacobs, *Incidents*, 52.

49. Angela Davis, *Women, Race, and Class* (New York: Vintage, 1981), 31; Franny Nudelman, "Harriet Jacobs and the Sentimental Politics of Female Suffering," *ELH* 59, no. 4 (1992): 939–940.

50. Yellin, *Harriet Jacobs*, 137–138.

51. "Child to J.G. Whittier," *The Harriet Jacobs Family Papers*, vol. 1, 343.

52. "Jacobs to Amy Kirby Post," *The Harriet Jacobs Family Papers*, vol. 1, 282; "Child to Lucy Searle Jacobs," *The Harriet Jacobs Family Papers*, vol. 1, 296; Yellin, *Harriet Jacobs*, 140–141.

53. Christy Pottroff, "Harriet Jacobs, Publisher and Activist," *Avidly, Los Angeles Review of Books*, November 18, 2019, http://avidly.lareviewofbooks.org/2019/11/18/harriet-jacobs-publisher-and-activist/.

54. Yellin, *Harriet Jacobs*, 143, 147.

55. Thanks to Sarah Blackwood for sharing this story. The Library of Congress changed its designation of the book's author from Lydia Maria Child to Harriet Jacobs in 1987. Lisa W. Foderaro, "Slave Narrative Gets Postscript," *New York Times*, February 13, 2005, www.nytimes.com/2005/02/13/nyregion/books/slave-narrative-gets-postscript.html.

56. Yellin, *Harriet Jacobs*, 158.

57. Ibid., 176.

58. Ibid., 177, 161.

59. Frances E. W. Harper, "We Are All Bound Up Together," in *A Brighter Coming Day: A Frances Ellen Watkins Harper Reader*, ed. Frances Smith Foster (New York: The Feminist Press, 1990), 217.

60. Yellin, *Harriet Jacobs*, 202–209.

61. Michele Currie Navakas, *Liquid Landscape: Geography and Settlement at the Edge of Early America* (Philadelphia: University of Pennsylvania Press, 2017), 142; Hedrick, *Harriet Beecher Stowe*, 335, 307.

62. Stowe, *The Life of Harriet Beecher Stowe*, 400.

63. Louise Michele Newman, *White Women's Rights: The Racial Origins of Feminism in the United States* (New York: Oxford University Press, 1999), 26; Peggy Pascoe, *Relations of Rescue: The Search for Female Moral Authority in the American West, 1874–1939* (New York: Oxford University Press, 1993). See also Judith Ann Giesberg, *Civil War Sisterhood: The U.S. Sanitary Commission and Women's Politics in Transition* (Boston: Northeastern University Press, 2006).

64. Harriet Beecher Stowe, *Palmetto-Leaves* (Boston: James R. Osgood, 1873), 301.

65. Ibid., 306.

66. Harriet Beecher Stowe and Catharine Beecher, *The New Housekeepers' Manual* (New York: J. B. Ford, 1873), 327, 330, 318; John T. Foster Jr. and Sarah Witmer Foster, eds., *Calling Yankees to Florida: Harriet Beecher Stowe's Forgotten Tourist Articles* (Cocoa, FL: Florida Historical Society Press, 2011), 116; "The New Housekeepers Manual," Andrews McMeel Publishing, https://publishing.andrewsmcmeel.com/book/the-new-housekeepers-manual-catharine-beecher/.

67. Stowe calls her Minnah in *Palmetto-Leaves* and Winnah in "Our Florida Plantation." Stowe, *Palmetto-Leaves*, 308–314.

68. Harriet Beecher Stowe, "Our Florida Plantation," *The Atlantic*, May 1879, www.theatlantic.com/magazine/archive/1879/05/our-florida-plantation/538932/.

69. Navakas, *Liquid Landscape*, 137; Hedrick, *Harriet Beecher Stowe*, 330; Foster and Foster, *Calling Yankees*, 116.

70. Stowe, *Palmetto-Leaves*, 272, 283, 317.

71. Shana Klein, "Those Golden Balls Down Yonder Tree: Oranges and the Politics of Reconstruction in Harriet Beecher Stowe's Florida," *Southern Cultures* 23, no. 3 (2017): 30.

72. Yellin, *Harriet Jacobs*, 221, 161, 220; Jean Yellin, ed., *The Harriet Jacobs Family Papers*, vol. 2 (Chapel Hill: University of North Carolina Press, 2008), 746.

73. Hedrick, *Harriet Beecher Stowe*, 245.

CHAPTER THREE: SETTLER MOTHERS AND NATIVE ORPHANS

1. Zitkala-Ša, *American Indian Stories* (Washington, DC: Hayworth Publishing, 1922), 22, 8.

2. "Yankton Sioux Treaty Monument," National Parks Service, April 10, 2015, www.nps.gov/mnrr/learn/historyculture/yankton-sioux-treaty-monument.htm.

3. Ša, *American Indian Stories*, 41–42.

4. Ibid., 66; Wolfgang Mieder, "'The Only Good Indian Is a Dead Indian': History and Meaning of a Proverbial Stereotype," *Journal of American Folklore* 106, no. 419 (1993): 38; Richard Henry Pratt, "The Advantages of Mingling Indians with Whites," in *Americanizing the American Indians: Writings by the "Friends of the Indian," 1880–1900* (Cambridge, MA: Harvard University Press, 1973), 261.

5. Statistics as of October 2020. Anna Flagg and Andrew R. Calderón, "500,000 Kids, 30 Million Hours: Trump's Vast Expansion of Child Detention," The Marshall Project, October 30, 2020, www.themarshallproject.org/2020/10/30/500-000-kids-30-million-hours-trump-s-vast-expansion-of-child-detention.

6. Joan T. Mark, *A Stranger in Her Native Land: Alice Fletcher and the American Indians* (Lincoln: University of Nebraska Press, 1989), 19–20; Association for the Advancement of Women, *Souvenir Nineteenth Annual Congress of the Association for the Advancement of Women Invited and Entertained by the Ladies' Literary Club* (Washington, DC: Todd Brothers, 1877), 123.

7. Mark, *A Stranger in Her Native Land*, 19, 28.

8. Alice Fletcher, "Standing Bear," *Southern Workman* 38 (1909): 78.

9. Mark, *A Stranger in Her Native Land*, 124, 197. Fletcher's biographical entry in the Library of Congress notes that she worked extensively with the Omaha tribe, as well as the Pawnee, Sioux, Arapaho, Cheyenne, Chippewa, Oto, Osage, Nez Perce, Ponca, and Winnebago tribes; "Alice Cunningham Fletcher (1838–1923)," Library of Congress, www.loc.gov /item/ihas.200196222/. Margaret D. Jacobs, *White Mother to a Dark Race: Settler Colonialism, Maternalism, and the Removal of Indigenous Children in the American West and Australia, 1880–1940* (Lincoln: University of Nebraska Press, 2009).

10. Other scholars who have suggested this term include Jennifer Henderson and Maile Arvin. See Jennifer Henderson, *Settler Feminism and Race Making in Canada* (Toronto: University of Toronto Press, 2003); Maile Arvin, "Indigenous Feminist Notes on Embodying Alliance Against Settler Colonialism," *Meridians* 18, no. 2 (2019): 335–357.

11. The US government usually ascribed this victory to Red Cloud alone, due in part to a refusal to acknowledge the communal structure of Lakota culture and politics. See Catherine Price, *The Oglala People, 1841–1879: A Political History* (Lincoln: University of Nebraska Press, 1996); "Invisible Nation: Mapping Sioux Treaty Boundaries," *Northlandia* blog, February 18, 2017, https://northlandia.wordpress.com/2017/02/18/invisible -nation-mapping-sioux-treaty-boundaries/.

12. Little Bighorn is known as the Battle of Greasy Grass among the Lakota. O. C. Marsh, *A Statement of Affairs at Red Cloud Agency, Made to the President of the United States* (New Haven, CT: O. C. Marsh, 1875), 4–5.

13. Nick Estes, *Our History Is the Future: Standing Rock Versus the Dakota Access Pipeline, and the Long Tradition of Indigenous Resistance* (New York: Verso, 2019), 78, 110; Alice C. Fletcher, *Life Among the Indians: First Fieldwork Among the Sioux and Omahas*, ed. Joanna C. Scherer and Raymond J. DeMallie (Lincoln: University of Nebraska Press, 2013), 207.

14. Alice Fletcher, "The Indian Woman and Her Problems," *Woman's Journal* 32, no. 44 (1900): 354. Fletcher's article paraphrases Sitting Bull's words.

15. Mark, *A Stranger in Her Native Land*, 61–62; Fletcher, "The Indian Woman and Her Problems," 354.

16. Fletcher, "The Indian Woman and Her Problems," 354. Fletcher's transcription of this scene, published in 1900, was a considerable embellishment of her 1882 account "Among the Omahas." See Alice Fletcher, "Among the Omahas," *Woman's Journal* 13, no. 6 (February 11, 1882): 46–47.

17. Joy Rohde, "'From the Sense of Justice and Human Sympathy': Alice Fletcher, Native Americans, and the Gendering of Victorian Anthropology," *History of Anthropology Newsletter* 27, no. 1 (2000): 10.

18. Ibid.

19. Fletcher, *Life Among the Indians*, 122.

20. Peggy Pascoe, *Relations of Rescue: The Search for Female Moral Authority in the American West, 1874–1939* (New York: Oxford University Press, 1993), 58.

21. Fletcher, *Life Among the Indians*, 163–164. See also Russell Means, "Patriarchy: The Ultimate Conspiracy; Matriarchy: The Ultimate Solution: History—or His-Story," *Griffith Law Review* 20, no. 3 (2011): 520–521; J. Owen Dorsey, "Omaha Sociology," *Third Annual Report of the Bureau of Ethnology* (Washington, DC: Government Printing Office, 1884), 267; Robert A. Williams Jr., "Gendered Checks and Balances: Understanding the Legacy of White Patriarchy in an American Indian Cultural Context," *Georgia Law Review* 24, no. 4 (1990): 1019–1044.

22. Mark, *A Stranger in Her Native Land*, 108.

23. Ibid., 117; Louise Michele Newman, *White Women's Rights: The Racial Origins of Feminism in the United States* (New York: Oxford University Press, 1999), 119.

24. Newman, *White Women's Rights*, 119.

25. Ša, *American Indian Stories*, 50.

26. Ibid., 52–54.

27. Ibid., 57, 54, 56.

28. Ibid., 66; Ruth Spack, "Dis/engagement: Zitkala-Ša's Letters to Carlos Montezuma, 1901–1902," *MELUS* 26, no. 1 (2001): 182; Tadeusz Lewandowski, *Red Bird, Red Power: The Life and Legacy of Zitkala-Ša* (Norman: University of Oklahoma Press, 2016), 11.

29. Ša, *American Indian Stories*, 60–61.

30. Richard Henry Pratt, *Battlefield and Classroom: Four Decades with the American Indian, 1867–1904*, ed. Robert M. Utley (New Haven: Yale University Press, 1964), 312; Pratt, "Advantages of Mingling," 263, 269.

31. Pratt, *Battlefield and Classroom*, 220, 223; "Address to a Weekly Meeting of Protestant Ministers in Baltimore, 1891," Richard Henry Pratt Papers, Yale Collection of Western Americana, Beinecke Rare Book and Manuscript Library.

32. Amy E. Kaplan, "Manifest Domesticity," *American Literature* 70, no. 3 (1998): 581–606; Margaret D. Jacobs, "The Great White Mother: Maternalism and American Indian Child Removal in the American West, 1880–1940," in *One Step over the Line: Toward a History of Women in the North American Wests*, ed. Elizabeth Jameson and Sheila McManus (Edmonton: University of Alberta Press, 2008), 197.

33. Ibid.

34. Paula Gunn Allen, "Who Is Your Mother? Red Roots of White Feminism," *Sinister Wisdom* 25 (1984).

35. Luther Standing Bear, *Land of Spotted Eagle* (Lincoln, NE: Bison Books, 2006), 232; Spack, "Dis/engagement," 186.

36. Pratt, *Battlefield and Classroom*; George Hyde, *A Sioux Chronicle* (Norman: University of Oklahoma Press, 1956), 57.

37. Mark, *A Stranger in Her Native Land*, 79, 84–85; Jacobs, "A Great White Mother," 197.

38. Alice Fletcher, "The Sun Dance of the Ogallala Sioux," *Proceedings for the American Association for the Advancement of Science* 31 (1883): 580; Kyla Schuller, "The Fossil and the Photograph: Red Cloud, Prehistoric Media, and Dispossession in Perpetuity," *Configurations* 24, no. 2 (2016): 259; Mark, *A Stranger in Her Native Land*, 81.

39. Mark, *A Stranger in Her Native Land*, 80; Alice C. Fletcher and Francis La Flesche, *The Omaha Tribe*, vol. 2 (Lincoln: University of Nebraska Press, 1992), 455.

40. Mark, *A Stranger in Her Native Land*, 95; Adrienne Mayor, *Fossil Legends of the First Americans* (Princeton, NJ: Princeton University Press, 2007), 301.

41. Mark, *A Stranger in Her Native Land*, 85; Mark Rifkin, "Romancing Kinship: A Queer Reading of Indian Education and Zitkala-Ša's American Indian Stories," *GLQ: A Journal of Lesbian and Gay Studies* 12, no. 1 (2006): 31.

42. Rifkin, "Romancing Kinship," 69, 72–73.

43. Lewandowski, *Red Bird*, 21.

44. Zitkala-Ša, "Side by Side (March 1896)," in *American Indian Stories, Legends, and Other Writings*, ed. Cathy N. Davidson and Ada Norris (New York: Penguin Books, 2005), 221–226.

45. Ša, *American Indian Stories*, 79.

46. Spack, "Dis/engagement," 175; Ša, *American Indian Stories*, 83.

47. Ibid., 82–83.

48. Ibid., 85.

49. Ibid., 95, 99.

50. Ibid., 96; Zitkala-Ša, *Dreams and Thunder: Stories, Poems, and the Sun Dance Opera*, ed. P. Jane Hafen (Lincoln, NE: Bison Books, 2005), 125.

51. Dexter Fisher, "Foreword," in *American Indian Stories*, by Zitkala-Ša (Lincoln, NE: Bison Books, 1985); Cathy Davidson and Ada Norris, eds., "Introduction," in *American Indian Stories, Legends, and Other Writings*, by Zitkala-Ša (New York: Penguin Books, 2005), xviii, xiii; Jacqueline Emery, ed., *Recovering Native American Writings in the Boarding School Press* (Lincoln: University of Nebraska Press, 2017), 254; Lewandowski, *Red Bird*, 46.

52. Emery, *Recovering Native American Writings*, 258.

53. Ša, *American Indian Stories*, 96, 14.

54. Lakota scholar Nick Estes stresses her commitment to Native cultural renewal. See Estes, *Our History Is the Future*, 208; Lewandowski, *Red Bird*, 51.

55. Ša, *American Indian Stories*, 101–103.

56. Lewandowski, *Red Bird*, 56; Rifkin, "Romancing Kinship," 35; Ruth Spack, "Translation Moves: Zitkala-Ša's Bilingual Indian Legends," *Studies in American Indian Literatures* 18, no. 4 (2006): 43.

57. Estes, *Our History Is the Future*, 71.

58. Mark, *A Stranger in Her Native Land*, 87–88.

59. Alice C. Fletcher, "Our Duty Toward Dependent Races," in *Transactions of the National Council of Women of the United States, Washington D.C., February 22, 1891*, ed. Rachel Foster Avery (Philadelphia: J. B. Lippincott Company, 1891), 84.

60. Mark, *A Stranger in Her Native Land*, 118.

61. Rifkin, "Romancing Kinship," 28.

62. Mark, *A Stranger in Her Native Land*, 88–89.

63. Ibid., 93.

64. Fletcher and La Flesche, *The Omaha Tribe*, vol. 2, 326.

65. Pascoe, *Relations of Rescue*, 58; Alice C. Fletcher, "On Indian Education and Self Support," *Century Magazine* 4 (1883): 314.

66. Mark, *A Stranger in Her Native Land*, 106.

67. Ibid., 106–107; Newman, *White Women's Rights*, 126.

68. Newman, *White Women's Rights*, 121.

69. Mark, *A Stranger in Her Native Land*, 117–120.

70. Ibid., 200.

71. Rifkin, "Romancing Kinship," 28. On "female moral authority" see Pascoe, *Relations of Rescue*, xvi. On "Boston marriages" see Lillian Faderman, *Odd Girls and Twilight Lovers: A*

History of Lesbian Life in Twentieth-Century America (New York: Columbia University Press, 1991), 15, 18. Jasbir K. Puar, *Terrorist Assemblages: Homonationalism in Queer Times* (Durham, NC: Duke University Press, 2007), 2.

72. Mark, *A Stranger in Her Native Land*, 253, 207, 152.

73. Ibid., 294.

74. Ibid., 203–204, 206.

75. Fletcher, "Our Duty Toward Dependent Races," 81.

76. Ibid., 81–82.

77. Frances E. W. Harper, "Duty to Dependent Races," in *Transactions of the National Council of Women of the United States, Assembled in Washington, D.C., February 22 to 25, 1891*, ed. Rachel Foster Avery (Philadelphia: J. B. Lippincott, 1891), 86.

78. Ibid., 88, 91.

79. Mark, *A Stranger in Her Native Land*, 203–256, 137; "Changing the Face of Medicine: Dr. Susan La Flesche Picotte," National Library of Medicine, National Institute of Health, June 3, 2015, https://cfmedicine.nlm.nih.gov/physicians/biography_253.html; June Helm, ed., *Pioneers of American Anthropology: The Uses of Biography* (Seattle: University of Washington Press, 1966), 50; Margaret Mead, *The Changing Culture of an Indian Tribe* (New York: Columbia University Press, 1932).

80. "Land Tenure Issues," Indian Land Tenure Foundation, https://iltf.org/land-issues/issues/.

81. Brenda Child, *Boarding School Seasons: American Indian Families 1900–1940* (Lincoln: University of Nebraska Press, 1998), 2–4.

82. Lewandowski, *Red Bird*, 60–61; Spack, "Dis/engagement," 191, 181.

83. Lewandowski, *Red Bird*, 82–83; Allen, "Who Is Your Mother?"

84. Estes, *Our History Is the Future*, 211, 214; Zitkala-Ša, "Editorial Comment: July–September 1918," in *American Indian Stories, Legends, and Other Writings*, ed. Cathy N. Davidson and Ada Norris (New York: Penguin Books, 2005), 182–183; Lewandowski, *Red Bird*, 164.

85. Lewandowski, *Red Bird*, 176, 178–179, 182; Davidson and Norris, "Introduction," xxviii.

86. Lewandowski, *Red Bird*, 181; Estes, *Our History Is the Future*, 221.

87. "Mrs. R. T. Bonnin, an Indian Leader," *New York Times*, January 27, 1938, 21; Lewandowski, *Red Bird*, 187.

CHAPTER FOUR: BIRTHING A BETTER NATION

1. Madeline Gray, *Margaret Sanger: A Biography of the Champion of Birth Control* (New York: Richard Marek Publishers, 1979), 55.

2. Margaret Sanger, *My Fight for Birth Control* (London: Faber and Faber Limited, 1932), 53.

3. Ibid.

4. Margaret Sanger, *An Autobiography* (New York: W. W. Norton, 1938), 91.

5. Ibid., 92.

6. Ibid.; Sanger, *My Fight for Birth Control*, 57.

7. Sanger, *An Autobiography*, 86–87.

8. Margaret Sanger, "The Eugenic Value of Birth Control Propaganda," *Birth Control Review* (October 1921): 5; Margaret Sanger, *Woman and the New Race* (New York: W. W. Norton,

1920), 229; Angela Franks, *Margaret Sanger's Eugenic Legacy: The Control of Female Fertility* (Jefferson, NC: McFarland, 2005), 13.

9. Margaret Sanger, *The Pivot of Civilization* (New York: Brentano's, 1922), 25.

10. Sanger, "The Eugenic Value of Birth Control Propaganda," 5.

11. Jacqueline Trescott, "Making a Practice of Persistence: Dorothy Ferebee, the Elegant Doctor with a Social Conscience," *Washington Post*, May 5, 1978, B4.

12. "Dorothy Ferebee. Transcript," in *Black Women Oral History Project, 1976–1981*, Schlesinger Library, Radcliffe Institute, Harvard University. Punctuation slightly modified for emphasis.

13. Diane Kiesel, *She Can Bring Us Home: Dr. Dorothy Boulding Ferebee, Civil Rights Pioneer* (Sterling, VA: Potomac Books, 2015), 18.

14. Ibid., 31; "Ferebee," Black Women Oral History Project.

15. Vanessa Northington Gamble, "'Outstanding Services to Negro Health': Dr. Dorothy Boulding Ferebee, Dr. Virginia M. Alexander, and Black Women Physicians' Public Health Activism," *American Journal of Public Health* 106, no. 8 (2016): 1399.

16. For a concise history of the reproductive justice movement in the United States, see Loretta Ross and Rickie Sollinger, *Reproductive Justice: An Introduction* (Oakland: University of California Press, 2017), 9–57.

17. "New York Urbanized Area: Population and Density from 1800 (Provisional)," *Demographia*, http://demographia.com/db-nyuza1800.htm; Jacob A. Riis, *How the Other Half Lives: Studies Among the Tenements of New York* (New York: Charles Scribner and Sons, 1890), 62.

18. Franks, *Margaret Sanger's Eugenic Legacy*, 13.

19. "The 'Feeble-Minded' and the 'Fit': What Sanger Meant When She Talked About Dysgenics," *Margaret Sanger Papers Project*, December 13, 2016, https://sangerpapers.wordpress.com/2016/12/13/the-feeble-minded-and-the-fit-what-sanger-meant-when-she-talked-about-dysgenics/.

20. In Sanger's time, it was known as Hotel Plaza. Jean M. Baker, *Margaret Sanger: A Life of Passion* (New York: Hill and Wang, 2012), 183; Ellen Chesler, *Woman of Valor: Margaret Sanger and the Birth Control Movement in America* (New York: Simon and Schuster, 2007), 202, 200.

21. American Birth Control Conference, *Birth Control: What It Is, How It Works, What It Will Do: The Proceedings of the First American Birth Control Conference* (New York: Graphic Press, 1921), 16.

22. Ibid., 15.

23. Sanger, *The Pivot of Civilization*, 280–281.

24. Jill Grimaldi, "The First American Birth Control Conference," *Margaret Sanger Papers Project*, November 12, 2010, https://sangerpapers.wordpress.com/2010/11/12/the-first-american-birth-control-conference/.

25. Quoted in Isabel Wilkerson, *Caste: The Origins of Our Discontents* (New York: Random House, 2020), 80.

26. Sanger, *Pivot of Civilization*, 101, 99, 98; Loretta Ross, "Trust Black Women: Reproductive Justice and Eugenics," in *Radical Reproductive Justice: Foundation, Theory, Practice, Critique*, ed. Loretta Ross, Lynn Roberts, Erika Derkas, Whitney Peoples, and Pamela Bridgewater (New York: The Feminist Press, 2017), 65; Baker, *Margaret Sanger*, 281–282.

27. Margaret Sanger, "Birth Control and Racial Betterment," *Birth Control Review* (February 1919): 11–12; Franks, *Margaret Sanger's Eugenic Legacy*, 47.

28. Edward A. Ross, "The Causes of Race Superiority," *Annals of the Institute for Political Science* 18 (1901): 67–89; Laura L. Lovett, "Fitter Families for Future Firesides: Florence Sherborn and Popular Eugenics," *Public Historian* 29, no. 3 (Summer 2007): 73.

29. Sanger, "The Eugenic Value of Birth Control Propaganda," 5; Sanger, *Pivot of Civilization*, 175, 104.

30. Susanne Klausen and Alison Bashford, "Fertility Control," in *The Oxford Handbook of the History of Eugenics*, ed. Alison Bashford and Philippa Levine (New York: Oxford University Press, 2010), 111; Sanger, *Pivot of Civilization*, 12, 229, 270.

31. "Jan. 2, 1923 First Legal Birth Control Clinic Opens in U.S.," *Margaret Sanger Papers Project*, February 12, 2014, https://sangerpapers.wordpress.com/2014/02/12/jan-2-1923-first-legal-birth-control-clinic-opens-in-u-s/; Gray, *Margaret Sanger*, 200–201.

32. "Jan. 2, 1923 First Legal Birth Control Clinic"; Sanger, *An Autobiography*, 368, 449.

33. Wangui Muigai, "Looking Uptown: Margaret Sanger and the Harlem Branch Birth Control Clinic," *Margaret Sanger Papers Project*, Newsletter no. 54 (Spring 2010); see also Carole R. McCann, *Birth Control Politics in the United States, 1916–1945* (Ithaca, NY: Cornell University Press, 1994), 139, 141.

34. McCann, *Birth Control Politics*, 139–160.

35. Kiesel, *She Can Bring Us Home*, 28, 164–166.

36. Jess Whatcott, "Sexual Deviance and 'Mental Defectiveness' in Eugenics Era California," *Notches: (Re)Marks on the History of Sexuality*, March 14, 2017, https://notchesblog.com/2017/03/14/sexual-deviance-and-mental-defectiveness-in-eugenics-era-california/.

37. Kiesel, *She Can Bring Us Home*, 29; Michele Mitchell, *Righteous Propagation: African Americans and the Politics of Racial Destiny After Reconstruction* (Chapel Hill: University of North Carolina Press, 2004), 77–78, 106; Michael Gregory Dorr and Angela Logan, "'Quality, Not Mere Quantity, Counts': Black Eugenics and the NAACP Baby Contests," in *A Century of Eugenics in America: From the Indiana Experiment to the Human Genome Era*, ed. Paul A. Lombardo (Bloomington: Indiana University Press, 2011), 86, 88; Kyla Schuller, *The Biopolitics of Feeling: Race, Sex, and Science in the Nineteenth Century* (Durham, NC: Duke University Press, 2018), 197.

38. Gamble, "'Outstanding Services to Negro Health,'" 1398–1399.

39. Kiesel, *She Can Bring Us Home*, 64–65.

40. "Ferebee," Black Women Oral History Project; Susan L. Smith, *Sick and Tired of Being Sick and Tired: Black Women's Health Activism in America, 1890–1950* (Philadelphia: University of Pennsylvania Press, 1995), 150.

41. "Ferebee," Black Women Oral History Project; Gamble, "'Outstanding Services to Negro Health,'" 1399.

42. Smith, *Sick and Tired*, 124–125; Kiesel, *She Can Bring Us Home*, 55.

43. "Ferebee," Black Women Oral History Project; Gamble, "'Outstanding Services to Negro Health,'" 1400; Kiesel, *She Can Bring Us Home*, xviii.

44. Kiesel, *She Can Bring Us Home*, 68; Smith, *Sick and Tired*, 160; Gamble, "'Outstanding Services to Negro Health,'" 1400.

45. Joyce Follet, "Making Democracy Real: African American Women, Birth Control, and Social Justice, 1910–1960," *Meridians* 18, no. 1 (2019): 123, 132; Smith, *Sick and Tired*, 167, 157.

46. Kiesel, *She Can Bring Us Home*, xix; Dorothy Boulding Ferebee, "Speech by Dorothy Boulding Ferebee, M.D. Entitled 'Planned Parenthood as a Public Health Measure for the Negro Race,' January 29th, 1942," Florence Rose Papers, Sophia Smith Collective, Smith College, Northampton, MA, https://libex.smith.edu/omeka/items/show/447 (this collection is hereafter cited as Rose, Smith).

47. Follet, "Making Democracy Real," 123.

48. Sanger, *An Autobiography*, 492; Chesler, *Woman of Valor*, 253, 385; "Margaret Sanger: The Arizona Years," *Margaret Sanger Papers Project*, Newsletter no. 9 (Winter 1994/1995).

49. Chesler, *Woman of Valor*, 374.

50. Ibid., 367, 381; "Letter from Margaret Sanger to Dr. C. J. Gamble, December 10, 1939," Margaret Sanger Papers, Sophia Smith Collection, Smith College, Northampton, MA (this collection is hereafter cited as Sanger, Smith); "Special Negro Project, Under the Direction of the Birth Control Federation of America, Inc.," organizational spreadsheet, Rose, Smith; "Better Health for 13,000,000," Planned Parenthood Federation of America Report, 1943, Rose, Smith, 5; Ferebee, "Speech by Dorothy Boulding Ferebee, 1942," 2.

51. "Letter from Margaret Sanger to Dr. C. J. Gamble," Sanger, Smith.

52. Ibid.; "Letter from Margaret Sanger to Cele" (Mrs. Damon), November 24, 1939," Sanger, Smith.

53. "Letter from Margaret Sanger to Mary Rheinhardt, February 4, 1940," Rose, Smith.

54. "Letter from Margaret Sanger to Cele" (Mrs. Damon), November 24, 1939," Sanger, Smith; Follet, "Making Democracy Real," 106.

55. Brittney Cooper, *Beyond Respectability: The Intellectual Thought of Race Women* (Champaign: University of Illinois Press, 2017), 67; "Letter from Dr. C. J. Gamble to Margaret Sanger, December 2, 1939," Rose, Smith.

56. "Letter from Florence Rose to Mrs. Lasker, March 22, 1941," Rose, Smith.

57. "Minutes of National Advisory Council Meeting, Friday, December 11, 1942," Rose, Smith.

58. Ferebee, "Speech by Dorothy Boulding Ferebee, 1942."

59. "Letter from Florence Rose to W. E. B. Du Bois, July 22, 1941," Sanger, Smith; W. E. B. Du Bois, "Black Folk and Birth Control," *Birth Control Review* 16, no. 6 (June 1932): 167.

60. "Letter from Unknown to Dr. Joseph H. Willits, November 16, 1939," Rose, Smith.

61. McCann, *Birth Control Politics*, 164; "Memo, Jan. 1944," Rose, Smith.

62. "Better Health for 13,000,000," Rose, Smith, 7–8.

63. "Birth Control or Race Control? Sanger and the Negro Project," *Margaret Sanger Papers Project*, Newsletter no. 28 (Fall 2001); "Highlights of 1944–1945 Program," Rose, Smith.

64. Dana Seitler, "Unnatural Selection: Mothers, Eugenic Feminism, and Charlotte Perkins Gilman's Regeneration Narratives," *American Quarterly* 55, no. 1 (2003): 66.

65. Follet, "Making Democracy Real," 113; Ferebee, "Speech by Dorothy Ferebee, 1942"; Kiesel, *She Can Bring Us Home*, 128.

66. Loretta Ross, Lynn Roberts, Erika Derkas, Whitney Peoples, and Pamela Bridgewater, eds., "Introduction," in *Radical Reproductive Justice: Foundation, Theory, Practice, Critique* (New York: The Feminist Press, 2017), 4–15.

CHAPTER FIVE: TAKING FEMINISM TO THE STREETS

1. Pauli Murray, "Letter to the Editor," *Washington Post*, August 23, 1963.

2. Carol Giardina, "MOW to NOW: Black Feminism Resets the Chronology of the Founding of Modern Feminism," *Feminist Studies* 44, no. 3 (2018): 747; "History of the National Press Club," National Press Club, www.press.org/npc-history-facts.

3. Giardina, "MOW to NOW," 747–748.

4. DC Historic Preservation Office, "Civil Rights Tour: Political Empowerment—National Council of Negro Women," *DC Historic Sites*, https://historicsites.dcpreservation.org/items/show/955; Dorothy Height, *Open Wide the Freedom Gates* (New York: PublicAffairs, 2003), 146; Giardina, "MOW to NOW," 740.

5. Giardina, "MOW to NOW," 736–737; Height, *Open Wide*, 145; M. Rivka Polatnik, "Diversity in Women's Liberation Ideology: How a Black and a White Group of the 1960s Viewed Motherhood," *Signs* 21, no. 3 (1996): 679, 743: together, "they transformed a series of high-stakes confrontations with male leaders into a sustained and far-reaching movement for women's equality."

6. Pauli Murray, "Jim Crow and Jane Crow," in *Black Women in White America: A Documentary History*, ed. Gerda Lerner (New York: Vintage Books, 1972), 596; Dorothy Height, "We Wanted the Voice of a Woman to Be Heard," in *Sisters in the Struggle: African American Women in the Civil Rights–Black Power Movement*, ed. Bettye Collier-Thomas and V. P. Franklin (New York: New York University Press, 2001), 90, 86.

7. Pauli Murray, "Why Negro Girls Stay Single," *Negro Digest* 5, no. 9 (July 1947): 5; Brittney Cooper, *Beyond Respectability: The Intellectual Thought of Race Women* (Champaign: University of Illinois Press, 2017), 88, 100.

8. An important exception: Giardina, "MOW to NOW." The phrase is Muriel Fox's, one of the founders of NOW. Betty Friedan, "Up from the Kitchen Floor: Kitchen Floor Woman Power," *New York Times*, March 4, 1973, 8.

9. Betty Friedan, *Life so Far* (New York: Simon and Schuster, 2000), 45, 48.

10. Ibid., 61–62; Daniel Horowitz, *Betty Friedan and the Making of 'The Feminine Mystique': The American Left, the Cold War, and Modern Feminism* (Amherst: University of Massachusetts Press, 1997), 94–101.

11. Friedan, *Life so Far*, 97.

12. Betty Friedan, *The Feminine Mystique* (New York: W. W. Norton, 1963), 15.

13. Pauli Murray, *Song in a Weary Throat: An American Pilgrimage* (New York: Harper and Row, 1987), 36.

14. Ibid., 37–39.

15. Ibid., 47.

16. Ibid., 55–56; Ruth Wilson Gilmore, *Golden Gulag: Prisons, Surplus, Crisis, and Opposition in Globalizing California* (Berkeley: University of California Press, 2007), 28.

17. Ruha Benjamin, *Race After Technology: Abolitionist Tools for the New Jim Code* (New York: Polity Press, 2019), 42.

18. Jamie Ducharme and Elijah Wolfson, "Your ZIP Code Might Determine How Long You Live—and the Difference Could Be Decades," *Time*, June 17, 2019, https://time.com/5608268/zip-code-health/.

19. Kenneth W. Mack, *Representing the Race: The Creation of the Civil Rights Lawyer* (Cambridge, MA: Harvard University Press, 2012), 212.

20. Murray, *Song in a Weary Throat*, 67, 106–107.

21. Ibid., 138–140, 115.

22. Ibid., 125, 118. It would be another fourteen years, in 1951, before the university admitted a Black student.

23. Ibid., 183.

24. Rosalind Rosenberg, *Jane Crow: The Life of Pauli Murray* (New York: Oxford University Press, 2017), 70.

25. Murray, *Song in a Weary Throat*, 109, 221.

26. Ibid., 221–222.

27. Ibid., 239.

28. Ibid., 104, 241.

29. Troy Saxby, *Pauli Murray: A Personal and Political Life* (Chapel Hill: University of North Carolina Press, 2020), 129.

30. Both Simon D. Elin Fisher and Doreen Drury argue this letter was written by the couple, Murray and McBean. Simon D. Elin Fisher, "Challenging Dissemblance in Pauli Murray Historiography, Sketching a History of the Trans New Negro," *Journal of African American History* 104, no. 2 (2019): 181; Doreen M. Drury, "'Experimentation on the Male Side': Race, Class, Gender, and Sexuality in Pauli Murray's Quest for Love and Identity, 1910–1960" (PhD diss., Boston College, 2000), 201; Doreen M. Drury, "Boy-Girl, Imp, Priest: Pauli Murray and the Limits of Identity," *Journal of Feminist Studies in Religion* 29, no. 1 (Spring 2013): 147; Simon D. Elin Fisher, "Pauli Murray's Peter Panic Perspectives from the Margins of Gender and Race in Jim Crow America," *Transgender Studies Quarterly* 3, no. 1–2 (2016): 98; Rosenberg, *Jane Crow*, 58, 59.

31. Fisher, "Challenging Dissemblance," 177, 199.

32. Drury, "Boy-Girl," 144; Cooper, *Beyond Respectability*, 106.

33. Cooper, *Beyond Respectability*, 179; "Betty Friedan and *The Feminine Mystique*," *The First Measured Century*, PBS, 2000, www.pbs.org/fmc/segments/progseg11.htm.

34. Friedan, *The Feminine Mystique*, 314, 365, 322, 348.

35. bell hooks, *Feminist Theory: From Margin to Center* (Boston: South End Press, 1984), 1–2; bell hooks, *Ain't I a Woman: Black Women and Feminism* (Boston: South End Press, 1982), 188.

36. Friedan, *The Feminine Mystique*, 377, 350; hooks, *Feminist Theory*, 1.

37. Friedan, *The Feminine Mystique*, 366, 364, 377, 199, 276, 297, 309, 378; Friedan, *Life so Far*, 132.

38. See Friedan, *Life so Far*, 141, for Friedan's media tour innovations; also 57–58.

39. Betty Friedan, *It Changed My Life: Writings on the Women's Movement* (Cambridge, MA: Harvard University Press, 1998), 309; Friedan, *Life so Far*, 131.

40. Rosenberg, *Jane Crow*, 187.

41. Horowitz, *Betty Friedan*, 212; Rosenberg, *Jane Crow*, 204. Friedan and Murray shared a literary agent, Marie Rodell, but likely never met in this period.

42. Murray, *Song in a Weary Throat*, 262.

43. Ibid., 255; "Transcript of *Brown v. Board of Education* (1954)," US National Archives and Records Administration, www.ourdocuments.gov/doc.php?flash=false&doc=87&page=transcript.

44. Murray, *Song in a Weary Throat*, 255.

45. Serena Mayeri, "Pauli Murray and the Twentieth-Century Quest for Legal and Social Equality," *Indiana Journal of Law and Social Equality* 2, no. 1 (2014): 83; Rosenberg, *Jane Crow*, 275; Murray, *Song in a Weary Throat*, 355–356.

46. Pauli Murray and Mary Eastwood, "Jane Crow and the Law: Sex Discrimination and Title VII," *George Washington Law Review* 34, no. 2 (December 1965): 237; Caroline Chiapetti, "Winning the Battle but Losing the War: The Birth and Death of Intersecting Notions of Race and Sex Discrimination in *White v. Crook*," *Harvard Civil Rights–Civil Liberties Law Review* 52 (2017): 470–471.

47. Murray, *Song in a Weary Throat*, 367; Murray and Eastwood, "Jane Crow," 233n10.

48. Murray and Eastwood, "Jane Crow," 256, 239–240.

49. Chiapetti, "Winning the Battle," 470.

50. Brittney Cooper, "Black, Queer, Feminist, Erased from History: Meet the Most Important Legal Scholar You've Likely Never Heard Of," *Salon*, February 18, 2015, www.salon.com/test/2015/02/18/black_queer_feminist_erased_from_history_meet_the_most_important_legal_scholar_youve_likely_never_heard_of/.

51. Murray's "reasoning from race," in legal scholar Serena Mayeri's analysis, does not depend on "simple parallels or assertions of equivalence" in experience. Instead, she uses analogies to expose "interconnections" between forms of structural power. Serena Mayeri, *Reasoning from Race: Feminism, Law, and the Civil Rights Revolution* (Cambridge, MA: Harvard University Press, 2011), 5, 33; Friedan, *Life so Far*, 179; Saxby, *Pauli Murray*, 246.

52. Kimberlé Crenshaw, "Demarginalizing the Intersection of Race and Sex: A Black Feminist Critique of Antidiscrimination Doctrine," *University of Chicago Legal Forum* 1 (1989): 166n77. Brittney Cooper argues that Murray's work is the most direct predecessor to the feminist theories of intersectionality that law professor Kimberlé Crenshaw and sociologist Patricia Hill Collins elaborated in the late 1980s and 1990s. Cooper, *Beyond Respectability*, 88.

53. Combahee River Collective, "The Combahee River Collective Statement," in *How We Get Free: Black Feminism and the Combahee River Collective*, ed. Keeanga-Yamahatta Taylor (Chicago: Haymarket Books, 2017), 22–23.

54. Murray, *Song in a Weary Throat*, 361.

55. Ibid., 361–362.

56. Ibid., 365.

57. Ibid.

58. Horowitz, *Betty Friedan*, 243.

59. Friedan, *Life so Far*, 163.

60. Key to this "network" was Pauli Murray's introducing Friedan to Catherine East. Friedan, *It Changed My Life*, 96.

61. John Herbers, "Help Wanted: Picking the Sex for the Job," *New York Times*, September 28, 1965; Frances M. Beal, "Black Women's Manifesto, Double Jeopardy: To Be Black and Female," pamphlet (New York: Third World Women's Alliance, 1969), www.hartford-hwp.com/archives/45a/196.html.

62. Friedan, *Life so Far*, 174.

63. Rosenberg, *Jane Crow*, 300.

64. Ibid., 308–309.

65. Ibid.

66. Friedan, *Life so Far*, 186; Louis Harris and Associates, *Harris 1972 American Women's Opinion Poll: A Survey of the Attitudes of Women on Their Roles in Politics and the Economy* (Ann

Arbor, MI: Inter-university Consortium for Political and Social Research [distributor], 1992), 4, https://doi.org/10.3886/ICPSR07326.v1.

67. Friedan coined the phrase in 1969, and it was first attributed to her in print by Susan Brownmiller in 1970. Susan Brownmiller, "Sisterhood Is Powerful," *New York Times*, March 15, 1970, 230; Horowitz, *Betty Friedan*, 123–124; Friedan, *Life so Far*, 224, 222.

68. Carolyn Bronstein, *Battling Pornography: The American Feminist Anti-Pornography Movement, 1976–1986* (New York: Cambridge University Press, 2011), 54.

69. Radicalesbians, "The Woman Identified Woman," 1970, 1.

70. Brown recounts this scene in Mary Dore's 2014 documentary *She's Beautiful When She's Angry*, 00:42:40; Friedan, *Life so Far*, 224, 223.

71. Friedan, "Up from the Kitchen Floor," 30; Friedan, *Life so Far*, 211. (This phrase is the whole title of chapter 9.)

72. Judith Hennessee, *Betty Friedan: Her Life* (New York: Random House, 1999), 135; Faderman, *Odd Girls*, 212; Paula Giddings, *When and Where I Enter: The Impact of Black Women on Race and Sex in America* (New York: William Morrow, 1984), 346.

73. Caroline Kitchener, "'How Many Women of Color Have to Cry?': Top Feminist Organizations Are Plagued by Racism, 20 Former Staffers Say," *The Lily*, July 13, 2020, www.thelily.com/how-many-women-of-color-have-to-cry-top-feminist-organizations-are-plagued-by-racism-20-former-staffers-say/.

74. Friedan, "Up from the Kitchen Floor," 31; Pauli Murray, "Letter to the Editor," *New York Times*, March 25, 1973, 2; Saxby, *Pauli Murray*, 260.

75. Betty Friedan, *The Second Stage* (Cambridge, MA: Harvard University Press, 1998), 308.

76. Rosenberg, *Jane Crow*, 333, 375; Patricia Bell-Scott, *The Firebrand and the First Lady: Portrait of a Friendship: Pauli Murray, Eleanor Roosevelt, and the Struggle for Social Justice* (New York: Alfred A. Knopf, 2017), 346.

77. Murray, *Song in a Weary Throat*, 419; Cooper, *Beyond Respectability*, 106, 110.

78. Suzanne Braun Levine and Mary Thom, eds., *Bella Abzug: How One Tough Broad from the Bronx Fought Jim Crow and Joe McCarthy, Pissed Off Jimmy Carter, Battled for the Rights of Women and Workers, Rallied Against War and for the Planet, and Shook Up Politics Along the Way* (New York: Farrar, Straus and Giroux, 2008), 212.

79. Bell-Scott, *The Firebrand and the First Lady*, 338; Cooper, *Beyond Respectability*, 128, 129.

80. Saxby, *Pauli Murray*, 254–255, 278; Rosenberg, *Jane Crow*, 354, 357, 373.

81. "Besser Interview for *Ms. Magazine*, January 29, 1977," Papers of Pauli Murray, Schlesinger Library, Radcliffe Institute, Harvard University, https://hollisarchives.lib.harvard.edu/repositories/8/archival_objects/1406463.

82. Saxby, *Pauli Murray*, 279.

CHAPTER SIX: TERF GATEKEEPING AND TRANS FEMINIST HORIZONS

1. Barbara McLean, "Diary of a Mad Organizer," *Lesbian Tide*, June 30, 1973, 36.

2. Finn Enke, "Collective Memory and the Transfeminist 1970s: Toward a Less Plausible History," *Transgender Studies Quarterly* 5, no. 1 (2018): 14; Beth Elliott, "Ballad of the Oklahoma Women's Liberation Front," *Buried Treasure* [album], 2005, www.youtube.com/watch?v=XnDr-VVGjQQ.

3. Emma Heaney, "Women-Identified Women: Trans Women in 1970s Lesbian Feminist Organizing," *Transgender Studies Quarterly* 3, no. 1–2 (2016): 139; McLean, "Diary," 36.

4. Ibid.; Cristan Williams, "Sex Essentialist Violence and Radical Inclusion: An Interview with Robin Tyler, Jan Osborn, and Michele Kammerer," *TCP Blog*, The Conversations Project, February 1, 2016, http://radfem.transadvocate.com/sex-essentialist-violence-and-radical-inclusion-an-interview-with-robin-tyler-jan-osborn-and-michele-kammerer/.

5. Enke, "Collective Memory," 18–19.

6. McLean, "Diary," 36.

7. Robin Morgan, *Going Too Far: The Personal Chronicle of a Feminist* (New York: Random House, 1977), 171; Robin Morgan, "Keynote Address: Lesbianism and Feminism: Synonyms or Contradictions?," *Lesbian Tide* 2, no. 10–11 (May–June 1973): 30.

8. Morgan, "Keynote Address," 31, 30.

9. Ibid., 32.

10. Ibid.; McLean, "Diary," 37.

11. Susan Stryker and Talia Bettcher, "Introduction: Trans/Feminisms," *Transgender Studies Quarterly* 3, no. 1–2 (2016): 10; Cristan Williams, "Radical Inclusion: Recounting the Trans Inclusive History of Radical Feminism," *Transgender Studies Quarterly* 3, no. 1–2 (2016): 254; Heaney, "Women-Identified Women," 138.

12. Zackary Drucker, "Sandy Stone on Living Among Lesbian Separatists as a Trans Woman in the 70s," *Vice*, December 19, 2018, www.vice.com/en/article/zmd5k5/sandy-stone-biography-transgender-history.

13. Ibid.

14. Susan Stryker, "Another Dream of Common Language: An Interview with Sandy Stone," *Transgender Studies Quarterly* 3, no. 1–2 (2016): 296.

15. Ibid.

16. Ibid., 297; Davine Anne Gabriel, "Interview with the Transsexual Vampire: Sandy Stone's Dark Gift," *TransSisters: Journal of Transsexual Feminism* 8 (Spring 1995): 16.

17. Gabriel, "Interview," 17; Drucker, "Sandy Stone."

18. "Cris Williamson," Goldenrod Music, www.goldenrod.com/product-category/womensmusic/cris-williamson/.

19. Stryker, "Another Dream," 299.

20. Drucker, "Sandy Stone"; Stryker, "Another Dream," 300; Cristan Williams, "TERF Hate and Sandy Stone," *TransAdvocate*, August 16, 2014, www.transadvocate.com/terf-violence-and-sandy-stone_n_14360.htm; Gabriel, "Interview," 18.

21. Comment by Henry Ohana on "Teresa Trull—Woman-Loving Women (1977)," YouTube, www.youtube.com/watch?v=yAP5T5GDMTs&list=PLiD_igaPoeqcI51WW2WbbYm0WXH8wnHdD&index=9.

22. Chloé Lula, "12 Essential Songs from the Lesbian Label Olivia Records," *New York Times*, June 23, 2020, www.nytimes.com/2020/06/23/arts/music/olivia-records-lesbian-playlist.html.

23. Williams, "TERF Hate."

24. Ibid.

25. Ibid.

26. Ibid.

27. Drucker, "Sandy Stone."

28. Ibid.

29. Williams, "TERF Hate"; Janice Raymond, *The Transsexual Empire: The Making of the She-Male* (New York: Teachers College Press, 1994), 103; "Responses to 'Open Letter to Olivia Records,'" *Lesbian Connection* 3, no. 7 (February 1978): 17.

30. Williams, "TERF Hate."

31. Comment by Beth Elliott on Marti Abernathey, "Transphobic Radical Hate Didn't Start with Brennan: The Sandy Stone–Olivia Records Controversy," *TransAdvocate*, August 24, 2011, www.transadvocate.com/transphobic-radical-hate-didnt-start-with-brennan-the -sandy-stone-olivia-records-controversy_n_4112.htm.

32. Susanna J. Sturgis and Jan Raymond, "Interview: An Interview with Jan Raymond," *Off Our Backs* 9, no. 9 (1979): 15; Thomas S. Szasz, "Male and Female Created He Them," *New York Times*, June 10, 1979. Steinem's article in *Ms.* was reprinted in Gloria Steinem, *Outrageous Acts and Everyday Rebellions* (New York: Holt, Rinehart, and Winston, 1983), 208–209.

33. Raymond, *Transsexual Empire*, 183 (italics in original), xvi, xxi, 119, 91, 104; Sturgis and Raymond, "Interview," 15.

34. Raymond, *Transsexual Empire*, 101–102, 108.

35. Ibid., 112.

36. Ibid., 119, 117.

37. Combahee River Collective, "The Combahee River Collective Statement," in *How We Get Free: Black Feminism and the Combahee River Collective*, ed. Keeanga-Yamahatta Taylor (Chicago: Haymarket Books, 2017), 15, 21.

38. Raymond, *Transsexual Empire*, 118.

39. Audre Lorde, "An Open Letter to Mary Daly," in *This Bridge Called My Back: Writings by Radical Women of Color*, ed. Cherríe L. Moraga and Gloria E. Anzaldúa (Berkeley, CA: Third Woman Press, 2002), 104.

40. Raymond, *Transsexual Empire*, dedication page.

41. Thomas Buckley, "Johns Hopkins Doing Sex-Changing Surgery," *New York Times*, November 21, 1966.

42. Raymond, *Transsexual Empire*, 178.

43. "TERFs and Trans Healthcare," TheTerfs.com, http://theterfs.com/terfs-trans-health care/; Cristan Williams, "Fact Checking the NCHCT Report," *TransAdvocate*, September 18, 2014, www.transadvocate.com/fact-checking-janice-raymond-the-nchct-report_n_14554 .htm; Janice G. Raymond, "Technology on the Social and Ethical Aspects of Transsexual Surgery," National Center for Health Care Technology, June 1980, www.susans.org/wiki /Technology_on_the_Social_and_Ethical_Aspects_of_Transsexual_Surgery. See also Raymond's rebuttal, "Fictions and Facts About the Transsexual Empire," JaniceRaymond .com, https://janiceraymond.com/fictions-and-facts-about-the-transsexual-empire.

44. The policy change didn't go into effect until 1989. For a critical dissection of Raymond's report and its influence see Williams, "Fact Checking"; Abigail Coursolle, "California Pride: Medi-Cal Coverage of Gender-Affirming Care Has Come a Long Way," National Health Law Program, June 22, 2018, https://healthlaw.org /california-pride-medi-cal-coverage-of-gender-affirming-care-has-come-a-long-way/.

45. Carol Riddell, "Divided Sisterhood: A Critical Review of Janice Raymond's *The Transsexual Empire*," in *The Transgender Studies Reader*, ed. Susan Stryker and Stephen Whittle (New York: Routledge, 2006), 151.

46. "Trans and Non-Binary History," Queer Santa Cruz, https://virtual.santacruzmah .org/queersc/sections/Trans.html; Gabriel, "Interview," 47.

47. Dawn Levy, "Two Transsexuals Reflect on University's Pioneering Gender Dysphoria Program," *Stanford Report*, May 3, 2000.

48. Gabriel, "Interview," 16.

49. Levy, "Two Transsexuals."

50. Donna J. Haraway, *Simians, Cyborgs, and Women: The Reinvention of Nature* (New York: Routledge, 1991), 180, 155.

51. Sandy Stone, "The *Empire* Strikes Back: A Posttranssexual Manifesto," *Camera Obscura* 10, no. 2 (1992): 157.

52. Ibid., 159. I thank Cat Fitzpatrick for pointing out to me the effects of Stone's conciliatory position.

53. Ibid., 164.

54. Ibid.; Gabriel, "Interview," 24.

55. Stone, "The *Empire* Strikes Back," 164, 167–168. "Imagine if Raymond had written 'all blacks rape women's bodies,'" Stone remarked (p. 167), guilty of a Black/trans analogy of her own.

56. Sylvia Rivera, "Y'all Better Calm Down," in *Loud and Proud: LGBTQ+ Speeches That Empower and Inspire*, ed. Tea Uglow (London: White Lion, 2020), 31; Susan Stryker, *Transgender History* (New York: Seal Press, 2009), 86–87; Leslie Feinberg, "Street Transvestite Action Revolutionaries: Lavender and Red, Part 73," *Worker's World*, September 24, 2006; STAR, "Transvestite-Transsexual Action Organization and Fems Against Sexism" (1970), in *The Verso Book of Feminism: Revolutionary Words from Four Millennia of Rebellion*, ed. Jessie Kindig (New York: Verso Books, 2020), 212.

57. Elizabeth Bernstein, "Carceral Politics as Gender Justice? The 'Traffic in Women' and Neoliberal Circuits of Crime, Sex, and Rights," *Theory and Society* 41, no. 3 (2012): 252; Elizabeth Bernstein, "Militarized Humanitarianism Meets Carceral Feminism: The Politics of Sex, Rights, and Freedom in Contemporary Antitrafficking Campaigns," *Signs* 36, no. 1 (2010): 50.

58. Bernstein, "Militarized Humanitarianism," 57.

59. Julia O'Connell Davidson, "'Sleeping with the Enemy'? Some Problems with Feminist Abolitionist Calls to Penalise Those Who Buy Commercial Sex," *Social Policy and Society* 2, no. 1 (2003): 55; Janice Raymond, "Radical Feminist Activism in the 21st Century," *Labrys*, June 2015, www.labrys.net.br/labrys27/radical/janice.htm; Bernstein, "Militarized Humanitarianism," 57.

60. Elizabeth Bernstein, "The Sexual Politics of the 'New Abolitionism,'" *differences* 18, no. 5 (2007): 143; Victoria Law, "Against Carceral Feminism," *Jacobin*, October 17, 2014, www.jacobinmag.com/2014/10/against-carceral-feminism/.

61. Bernstein, "Carceral Politics as Gender Justice?," 253; Anne E. Fehrenbacher, Ju Nyeong Park, Katherine H.A. Footer, Bradley E. Silberzahn, Sean T. Allen, and Susan G. Sherman, "Exposure to Police and Client Violence Among Incarcerated Female Sex Workers in Baltimore City, Maryland," *American Journal of Public Health* 110 (2020): S152–S153; "Women in Prison: An Overview," *Words from Prison*, American Civil Liberties Union; Monica N. Modi, Sheallah Palmer, and Alicia Armstrong, "The Role of Violence Against Women Act in Addressing Intimate Partner Violence: A Public Health Issue," *Journal of Women's Health* 23, no. 3 (2014): 253.

62. Gabriel, "Interview," 26.

63. Sheila Jeffries, *Gender Hurts: A Feminist Analysis of the Politics of Transgenderism* (New York: Routledge, 2014), 61.

64. Wyatt Ronan, "Breaking: 2021 Becomes Record Year for Anti-Transgender Legislation," Human Rights Campaign, March 13, 2021, www.hrc.org/press-releases/breaking -2021-becomes-record-year-for-anti-transgender-legislation/.

65. Sandy Stone, "Sandy's FAQ—Transgender," SandyStone.com, https://sandystone .com/faq.shtml; Sandy Stone, "Bloomington: Post-Posttranssexual: Transgender Studies and Feminism," SandyStone.com, https://sandystone.com/.

CHAPTER SEVEN: LEANING IN OR SQUADDING UP

1. Sheryl Sandberg, *Lean In: Women, Work, and the Will to Lead* (New York: Knopf, 2013), 4.

2. Ibid., 26.

3. Ken Auletta, "A Woman's Place," *New Yorker*, July 4, 2011, www.newyorker.com/magazine /2011/07/11/a-womans-place-ken-auletta; Sandberg, *Lean In*, 9; bell hooks, "Dig Deep: Beyond Lean In," *Feminist Wire*, October 28, 2013, https://thefeministwire.com /2013/10/17973/.

4. Jia Tolentino, *Trick Mirror: Reflections on Self-Delusion* (New York: Random House, 2019), 84.

5. Charlotte Alter, "Alexandria Ocasio-Cortez's Facebook Videos of Her Trip to Standing Rock Reveal Her Political Awakening," *Time*, February 19, 2020, https://time.com/5786180 /alexandria-ocasio-cortez-standing-rock/.

6. Gabriella Paiella, "The 28-Year-Old at the Center of One of This Year's Most Exciting Primaries," *The Cut*, June 25, 2018, www.thecut.com/2018/06/alexandria-ocasio-cortez -interview.html; Brenda Jones and Krishan Trotman, *Queens of the Resistance: Alexandria Ocasio-Cortez* (New York: Plume, 2020), 56; Alter, "Alexandria Ocasio-Cortez's Facebook Videos."

7. Julia Conley, "If Democrats Want to Honor Legacy of Dr. King, Says Ocasio-Cortez, 'We Have to Be Dangerous Too,'" *Portside*, February 1, 2020, https://portside.org/2020-02-01 /if-democrats-want-honor-legacy-dr-king-says-ocasio-cortez-we-have-be-dangerous-too; Alexandria Ocasio-Cortez [@AOC], Twitter, July 3, 2018, https://twitter.com/aoc/status/1014 172302777507847?lang=en; Paiella, "The 28-Year-Old at the Center."

8. John Wagner, "'No Person in America Should Be Too Poor to Live': Ocasio-Cortez Explains Democratic Socialism to Colbert," *Washington Post*, June 29, 2018, www .washingtonpost.com/politics/no-person-in-america-should-be-too-poor-to-live-ocasio -cortez-explains-democratic-socialism-to-colbert/2018/06/29/d6752050-7b8d-11e8-aeee -4d04c8ac6158_story.html.

9. Zoe Ruffner, "Congresswoman Alexandria Ocasio-Cortez on Self-Love, Fighting the Power, and Her Signature Red Lip," *Vogue*, August 21, 2020, www.vogue.com/article /alexandria-ocasio-cortez-beauty-secrets.

10. Oprah Winfrey, "Sheryl Sandberg Tells Oprah About Her 'Date' with Mark Zuckerberg, Her Marriage and Feeling Like a Fraud," *HuffPost*, June 6, 2013, www.huffpost.com /entry/sheryl-sandberg-interview_n_3367204.

11. Katherine Losse, *The Boy Kings: A Journey into the Heart of the Social Network* (New York: Free Press, 2012), 168.

12. Sandberg, *Lean In*, 40, 39, 47.

13. Ibid., 5–7; data about the gender pay gap for Black women are highlighted on the Lean In website, https://leanin.org/data-about-the-gender-pay-gap-for-black-women; Amanda

Mull, "The Girl Boss Has Left the Building," *The Atlantic*, June 25, 2020, www.theatlantic
.com/health/archive/2020/06/girlbosses-what-comes-next/613519; Susan Faludi, "Facebook Feminism, Like It or Not," *The Baffler* 23 (2013), https://thebaffler.com/salvos
/facebook-feminism-like-it-or-not.

14. Sandberg, *Lean In*, 89.

15. Gina Heeb, "US Income Inequality Jumps to Highest Level Ever Recorded," *Business Insider*, September 27, 2019, https://markets.businessinsider.com/news/stocks
/income-inequality-reached-highest-level-ever-recorded-in-2018-2019-9-1028559996.

16. Catherine Thorbecke, "Nearly Half of the World's Entire Wealth Is in the Hands of
Millionaires," ABC News, October 22, 2019, https://abcnews.go.com/Business/half-worlds
-entire-wealth-hands-millionaires/story?id=66440320; Nina Strochlic, "One in Six Americans Could Go Hungry in 2020 as Pandemic Persists," *National Geographic*, November 24,
2020, www.nationalgeographic.com/history/article/one-in-six-could-go-hungry-2020
-as-covid-19-persists; Matt Egan, "America's Billionaires Have Grown $1.1 Trillion Richer
During the Pandemic," CNN, January 26, 2021, www.cnn.com/2021/01/26/business
/billionaire-wealth-inequality-poverty/index.html.

17. Faludi, "Facebook Feminism." Tolentino's account of Barre class as a key site of optimizing culture is indispensable. Tolentino, *Trick Mirror*, 75–77.

18. Sandberg, *Lean In*, 85.

19. Ibid., 37; Erin Carlyle, "Facebook COO Sheryl Sandberg Sells Atherton Home for
$9.25 Million," *Forbes*, October 14, 2014, www.forbes.com/sites/erincarlyle/2014/10/14
/facebook-coo-sheryl-sandberg-sells-atherton-home-for-9-25-million/#5574a78d3968.

20. Cinzia Arruzza, Tithi Bhattacharya, and Nancy Fraser, *Feminism for the 99%: A Manifesto* (New York: Verso, 2019), 5, 12.

21. Jones and Trotman, *Queens of the Resistance*, 42.

22. Cornel West and Tricia Rose, "Alexandria Ocasio-Cortez Is Not Understood
for Who She Really Is," *The Tight Rope*, July 23, 2020, www.youtube.com/watch?v
=24MSsYWa8j4&ab_channel=TheTightRope.

23. Alexandria Ocasio-Cortez, "Alexandria Ocasio-Cortez Remarks at 2011 Boston University Martin Luther King Jr., Celebration" [video], Boston University, 2011, www.bu.edu
/buniverse/view/?v=osDd30.

24. Jones and Trotman, *Queens of the Resistance*, 49; West and Rose, "Alexandria Ocasio-
Cortez Is Not Understood"; Michelle Ruiz, "AOC's Next Four Years," *Vanity Fair*, October 28,
2020, www.vanityfair.com/news/2020/10/becoming-aoc-cover-story-2020.

25. West and Rose, "Alexandria Ocasio-Cortez Is Not Understood."

26. Ibid.

27. Ibid.

28. Ryan Grim and Briahna Gray, "Alexandria Ocasio-Cortez Joins Environmental
Activists in Protest at Democratic Leader Nancy Pelosi's Office," *The Intercept*, November 13, 2018, https://theintercept.com/2018/11/13/alexandria-ocasio-cortez-sunrise
-activists-nancy-pelosi/.

29. Ijeoma Oluo, *Mediocre: The Dangerous Legacy of White Male America* (New York: Seal
Press, 2020).

30. West and Rose, "Alexandria Ocasio-Cortez Is Not Understood"; Bianca Betancourt,
"Alexandria Ocasio-Cortez Shares Her Harrowing Experience Surviving the Capitol Riots,"
Harper's Bazaar, January 13, 2021, www.harpersbazaar.com/culture/politics/a35201831

/alexandria-ocasio-cortez-capitol-riots-recap/; Stuart Emmrich, "Alexandria Ocasio-Cortez on the Capitol Mob Attack: 'I Thought I Was Going to Die,'" *Vogue*, January 13, 2021, www .vogue.com/article/alexandria-ocasio-cortez-video-on-the-capitol-mob-attack.

31. Sheera Frankel, Nicholas Confessore, Cecilia Kang, Matthew Rosenberg, and Jack Nicas, "Delay, Deny and Deflect: How Facebook's Leaders Fought Through Crisis," *New York Times*, November 14, 2018, www.nytimes.com/2018/11/14/technology/facebook-data -russia-election-racism.html; Nicholas Confessore and Matthew Rosenberg, "Damage Control at Facebook: 6 Takeaways from the *Times*'s Investigation," *New York Times*, November 14, 2018, www.nytimes.com/2018/11/14/technology/facebook-crisis-mark-zuckerberg -sheryl-sandberg.html; Anne Helen Petersen, "The Rise, Lean, and Fall of Facebook's Sheryl Sandberg," *BuzzFeed News*, December 14, 2018, www.buzzfeednews.com/article /annehelenpetersen/sheryl-sandberg-facebook-lean-in-superwoman-supervillain.

32. Kara Swisher, "Lean Out," *New York Times*, November 24, 2018, www.nytimes .com/2018/11/24/opinion/sheryl-sandberg-mark-zuckerberg-facebook.html.

33. Shoshana Zuboff, *The Age of Surveillance Capitalism: The Fight for a Human Future at the New Frontier of Power* (New York: PublicAffairs, 2019), 7, 74, 100; "Sheryl Sandberg," *Enhancv*, https://enhancv.com/resume-examples/famous/sheryl-sandberg/#famous-resume.

34. Zuboff, *The Age of Surveillance Capitalism*, 92.

35. Ibid., 99–100.

36. Lean In Circles, "About Circles," July 27, 2017, https://cdn-media.leanin.org /pagedata/2017-07-27/1501192899793/circles_guide_english_webfinal.pdf; Jeff Desjardins, "The World's 20 Most Profitable Companies," *Visual Capitalist*, October 21, 2019, www .visualcapitalist.com/the-worlds-20-most-profitable-companies/.

37. Manu Raju, "Ocasio-Cortez Reveals New Details About Viral Incident with Rep. Ted Yoho," CNN, July 24, 2020, www.cnn.com/2020/07/24/politics/aoc-ted-yoho-latest /index.html.

38. Mike Lillis, "Ocasio-Cortez Accosted by GOP Lawmaker over Remarks: 'That Kind of Confrontation Hasn't Ever Happened to Me,'" *The Hill*, July 21, 2020, https:// thehill.com/homenews/house/508259-ocaasio-cortez-accosted-by-gop-lawmaker-over -remarks-that-kind-of.

39. Ibid.

40. Melissa Quinn, "GOP Lawmaker Apologizes for 'Abrupt Manner' of Heated Exchange with Alexandria Ocasio-Cortez," CBS News, July 22, 2020, www.cbsnews.com/news /alexandria-ocasio-cortez-aoc-ted-yoho-confrontation/.

41. "Rep. Alexandria Ocasio-Cortez (D-NY) Responds to Rep. Ted Yoho (R-FL)," C-SPAN, July 23, 2020, youtube.com/watch?v=LI4ueUtkRQ0&ab_channel=C-SPAN; Alexandria Ocasio-Cortez [@AOC], "I want to thank everyone . . . ," Instagram, July 28, 2020, www.instagram.com/p/CDMrZIzAI1B; Ruiz, "AOC's Next Four Years."

42. "Rep. Alexandria Ocasio-Cortez (D-NY) Responds to Rep. Ted Yoho (R-FL)."

43. Kate Manne, *Down Girl: The Logic of Misogyny* (New York: Oxford University Press, 2018), 79–80; "Rep. Alexandria Ocasio-Cortez (D-NY) Responds to Rep. Ted Yoho (R-FL)"; Chris Cillizza, "The Absolutely Remarkable Social Media Power of Alexandria Ocasio-Cortez," CNN, July 24, 2020, www.cnn.com/2020/07/24/politics/aoc-ted-yoho-cspan /index.html.

44. Monica Hesse, "AOC's Speech About Ted Yoho's 'Apology' Was a Comeback for the Ages," *Washington Post*, July 23, 2020, www.washingtonpost.com/lifestyle/style/aocs

-speech-about-ted-yohos-apology-was-a-comeback-for-the-ages/2020/07/23/524e689a
-cb90-11ea-91f1-28aca4d833a0_story.html; Mary McNamara, "Column: Alexandria
Ocasio-Cortez's Tear-Down of Ted Yoho Is the Best TV I've Seen in Years," *Los Angeles Times*, July 24, 2020, www.latimes.com/entertainment-arts/story/2020-07-24
/alexandria-ocasio-cortez-speech-tom-yoho-great-tv.

45. West and Rose, "Alexandria Ocasio-Cortez Is Not Understood."

46. "Our Work Has a Framework," *The Nap Ministry*, January 11, 2021, http://thenap
ministry.wordpress.com/.

CONCLUSION: TWO FEMINISMS, ONE FUTURE

1. Richard Gonzales and Camila Domonoske, "Voters Recall Aaron Persky, Judge
Who Sentenced Brock Turner," NPR, June 5, 2018, www.npr.org/sections/thetwo
-way/2018/06/05/617071359/voters-are-deciding-whether-to-recall-aaron-persky-judge
-who-sentenced-brock-tur.

2. Andrew Nguyen, "15,000 Marched in Brooklyn for Black Trans Lives," *The Cut*,
June 15, 2020, www.thecut.com/2020/06/fifteen-thousand-marched-in-brooklyn-for
-black-trans-lives.html; "Fatal Violence Against the Transgender and Gender Non-
Conforming Community in 2020," Human Rights Campaign, www.hrc.org/resources
/violence-against-the-trans-and-gender-non-conforming-community-in-2020; Anushka Pa-
til, "How a March for Black Trans Lives Became a Huge Event," *New York Times*, June 15,
2020, www.nytimes.com/2020/06/15/nyregion/brooklyn-black-trans-parade.html.

3. Christina Sharpe, *In the Wake: On Blackness and Being* (Durham, NC: Duke University
Press, 2016).

4. Elizabeth Cady Stanton, Susan Brownell Anthony, and Matilda Joslyn Gage, eds., *History of Woman Suffrage*, Volume I (Rochester, NY: Susan B. Anthony, 1881),116.

5. Quoted in Jen McDaneld, "Harper, Historiography, and the Race/Gender Opposition in
Feminism," *Signs* 40, no. 2 (2015): 395.

6. Harriet Beecher Stowe, "Sojourner Truth, the Libyan Sibyl," *The Atlantic*, April 1863,
www.theatlantic.com/magazine/archive/1863/04/sojourner-truth-the-libyan-sibyl/308775/.

7. Caroline Kitchener, "'How Many Women of Color Have to Cry?': Top Feminist Organizations Are Plagued by Racism, 20 Former Staffers Say," *The Lily*, July 13, 2020, www
.thelily.com/how-many-women-of-color-have-to-cry-top-feminist-organizations-are
-plagued-by-racism-20-former-staffers-say/; Scott Neuman, "NOW President Resigns
amid Allegations of Creating Toxic Work Environment," NPR, August 18, 2020, www
.npr.org/sections/live-updates-protests-for-racial-justice/2020/08/18/903254443
/now-president-resigns-amid-allegations-of-creating-toxic-work-environment.

8. Cheryl Woods-Giscombé, "Superwoman Schema: African American Women's Views
on Stress, Strength, and Health," *Qualitative Health Research* 20, no. 5 (2010), www.ncbi.nlm
.nih.gov/pmc/articles/PMC3072704/.

9. Marisa Meltzer, "A Feminist T-Shirt Resurfaces from the '70s," *New York Times*, November 18, 2015, www.nytimes.com/2015/11/19/fashion/a-feminist-t-shirt-resurfaces-from-the
-70s.html.

10. Emma Roller, "More Female Bankers Won't Solve Capitalism," *Splinter*, May 15,
2018, https://splinternews.com/more-female-bankers-wont-solve-capitalism-1826049564.
The joke was initially former IMF chair Christine Lagarde's. Jon Henley, "Female-Led
Countries Handled Coronavirus Better, Study Suggests," *The Guardian*, August 18, 2020,

www.theguardian.com/world/2020/aug/18/female-led-countries-handled-coronavirus
-better-study-jacinda-ardern-angela-merkel.

11. Keeanga-Yamahtta Taylor, "Introduction," in *How We Get Free: Black Feminism and the Combahee River Collective*, ed. Keeanga-Yamahtta Taylor (Chicago: Haymarket Books, 2017), 11.

12. Combahee River Collective, "Combahee River Collective Statement," in *How We Get Free: Black Feminism and the Combahee River Collective*, ed. Keeanga-Yamahtta Taylor (Chicago: Haymarket Books, 2017), 22.

13. Richard Allen Williams, "Cardiovascular Disease in African American Women: A Health Care Disparities Issue," *Journal of the National Medical Association* 101, no. 6 (2009), https://pubmed.ncbi.nlm.nih.gov/19585921/.

Kyla Schuller is an award-winning scholar and recipient of fellowships from the Stanford Humanities Center and American Council of Learned Societies who lectures across North America and Europe. Her research has been featured in *The Nation*, and her writing has appeared in outlets including *The Rumpus*, *Los Angeles Review of Books*, and *Avidly*. She is associate professor of Women's, Gender, and Sexuality Studies at Rutgers University–New Brunswick and the author of *The Biopolitics of Feeling: Race, Sex, and Science in the Nineteenth Century* (Duke University Press, 2018).